Personal Financial Planning Cases and Applications Student Textbook

SIXTH EDITION

At press time, this edition contains the most complete and accurate information currently available. Due to the nature of advanced designation examinations, however, information may have been added recently to the actual test that does not appear in this edition. Please contact the publisher to verify that you have the most current edition.

This publication is designed to provide accurate and authoritative information in regard to the subject matter covered. It is sold with the understanding that the publisher is not engaged in rendering legal, accounting, or other professional services. If legal advice or other expert assistance is required, the services of a competent professional should be sought.

We value your input and suggestions. If you found imperfections in this product, please let us know by reporting it to Updates/Errata at www.schweser.com.

PERSONAL FINANCIAL PLANNING CASES AND APPLICATIONS
STUDENT TEXTBOOK, 6TH EDITION
©2009 Kaplan, Inc. All rights reserved.

CLU®, ChFC®, Registered Health Underwriter®, RHU®, REBC® Chartered Life Underwriter®, Chartered Financial Consultant®, Registered Employee Benefits Consultant®, Chartered Advisor for Senior Living™, and CASL™ are registered trademarks of The American College.

CPCU®, ARM®, and AIC® are registered trademarks of the American Institute for CPCU and the Insurance Institute of America.

CFP®, CERTIFIED FINANCIAL PLANNER™, and CFP® are certification marks or registered certification marks of Certified Financial Planner Board of Standards, Inc.

FINRA is a trademark of the Financial Industry Regulatory Authority, Inc.

NASD® is a registered trademark of the National Association of Securities Dealers, Inc.

Published by Kaplan Schweser

Printed in the United States of America.

ISBN: 978-1-42778-003-4

PPN: 5309-0202

09	10	10	09	08	07	06	05	04	03	02	01
J	**F**	M	A	M	J	J	A	S	O	N	D

■ ADDITIONAL PRODUCTS AND SERVICES

Kaplan Schweser Products

Personal Financial Planning Series:

- *Personal Financial Planning Theory and Practice, 5th Edition*
  Original authors: Michael A. Dalton, James F. Dalton, Scott A. Wasserman, Randall S. Guttery, and Randal R. Cangelosi

- *Understanding Your Financial Calculator, 4th Edition*
  Author: James F. Dalton

Schweser Review for the CFP® Certification Examination Series:

- *Live and Web-Delivered Instructional Reviews*

- *Volumes 1–6: CFP® Exam Topics, Schweser Review for the CFP® Exam, July 2009–March 2010 Exams* (Available Spring 2009)

- *Volume 7: Case Book, Schweser Review for the CFP® Exam, July 2009–March 2010 Exams* (Available Spring 2009)

- *Volume 8: Online Mock Exam and Solutions, Schweser Review for the CFP® Exam, July 2009–March 2010 Exams* (Available Spring 2009)

- *Schweser Flashcards for the CFP® Exam, July 2009–March 2010 Exams* (Available Spring 2009)

- *SchweserPro Exam Prep Review Qbank for the CFP® Exam, July 2009–March 2010 Exams* (Available Spring 2009)

- *Online Assessment Exam, July 2009–March 2010 Exams* (Available Spring 2009)

- *SchweserPro Education Qbank for the CFP® Certification Examination, July 2009–March 2010 Exams* (Available Spring 2009)

- *Audio Reviews for the CFP® Exam, July 2009–March 2010 Exams* (Available Spring 2009)

- *InstructorLink™*
    Exam-tips Blog
    Instructor-led Office Hours
    Searchable Frequently Asked Questions
    Online Study Calendar
    Instructor Email Access
    Schweser Video Library

CFP Board-Registered Programs:

- Accelerated Certificate in Financial Planning:
    - Traditional Classroom Program
    - Virtual Classroom Program
- University Programs Executive Certificate in Financial Planning
- Qualified Financial Advisor Online Program

For more information on any Kaplan Schweser product, please call Customer Service at (608) 779-8303.

Contents

Foreword

INTRODUCTION

Personal Financial Planning Cases and Applications is primarily intended for use in a case capstone course for a financial planning curriculum. It can also be used in a specific course such as Investments as the questions in each case are identifiable by major topics (e.g., Insurance, Investments, etc.). This textbook includes fourteen comprehensive financial planning cases. The cases are designed to help the student integrate the six major areas of personal financial planning:

- Fundamentals of Financial Planning
- Insurance Planning
- Investments
- Income Tax Planning
- Retirement Planning
- Estate Planning

CASES

Each case includes a complete family scenario that represents the information the financial planner obtained from the client. Generally, each case scenario includes information obtained from the client as follows:

- Personal Background Information
- Personal and Financial Goals
- Economic Information
- Insurance Information
- Investment Information
- Income Tax Information
- Retirement Information
- Gifts, Estates, Trusts, and Will Information
- Statement of Cash Flows

- Statement of Financial Position
- Information Regarding Assets and Liabilities
- Exhibits

Each case contains between 33 and 64 questions covering the major areas of financial planning with over 600 questions total in the book. Note that the assumptions made in each case (e.g., interest rates) may or may not reflect the current economic environment. Assumptions should be used as given to master the applications of important financial planning topics.

The first six cases focus *individually* on the six major areas of personal financial planning.

Case	Topic
Redding	Fundamentals of Financial Planning
Clement	Insurance Planning
Peyton	Investments
Morrish	Income Tax Planning
Williams	Retirement Planning
Franklin	Estate Planning

The next six cases focus *cumulatively* on the six major areas of personal financial planning.

Case	Topic
Silver	Fundamentals of Financial Planning
Garrett	Fundamentals of Financial Planning, Insurance Planning
Jones	Fundamentals of Financial Planning, Insurance Planning, Investments
Duke	Fundamentals of Financial Planning, Insurance Planning, Investments, Income Tax Planning
Monroe	Fundamentals of Financial Planning, Insurance Planning, Investments, Income Tax Planning, Retirement Planning
Ross	Fundamentals of Financial Planning, Insurance Planning, Investments, Income Tax Planning, Retirement Planning, Estate Planning

The last two cases, *Morgan* and *Trenticosta*, focus on all of the six major areas of personal financial planning.

▌ EXHIBITS

Many of the cases have exhibits to add a sense of reality to the case. The exhibits include actual wills, trusts, SSA 7004, investment statements, etc. Most of the cases have one or more documents designed to familiarize the student with an actual example of such documents. The exhibits in each case provide the student with information within the textbook to answer many of the questions asked without referring back to another textbook or source.

▌ APPENDIX

The textbook contains an extensive appendix that should greatly assist the student in answering the questions and analyzing the cases. Exhibits on the following topics are included:

Major Financial Planning Area	Exhibit #	Brief Description of Selected Exhibits
Fundamentals	1–6	■ Financial planning process
		■ Personal financial statements
		■ House costs and debt repayment
		■ Annual savings
		■ Progress to retirement
		■ Strengths and weaknesses
Insurance	7–13	■ Ratings of companies
		■ Life insurance policy replacement
		■ Homeowners policy summary
		■ Covered perils
		■ Eight general exclusions
		■ Wage replacement and Social Security benefits
		■ Group Term Life Insurance—Cost of $1,000 protection
Investments	14–25	■ Total, systematic, and unsystematic risks
		■ Risk pyramid
		■ Area under the curve
		■ Rates of return
		■ Call and put options
		■ Standard deviation
		■ Performance measurements
		■ Formulas

COMPANION WEBSITE

Available in 2009, our companion website at **www.schweser.com** includes several tools to enhance students' understanding of the case materials. Students should check the site frequently, as new materials will be added. Current features include:

- Answers to the questions at the end of each case. These answers are provided to allow students to check their completed work or assist them in answering questions and solving problems.

- Income tax, estate tax, and retirement information that is adjusted annually; this will allow students to keep current with these changes.

CHANGES FOR THE 6TH EDITION

The 6th Edition of Personal Financial Planning Cases and Applications has gone through a complete redesign. New questions were added to some of the cases. A few questions from previous editions were deleted. This edition reflects changes brought about by 2008 and 2009 tax updates and legislative changes.

If you have used this textbook in the past, you may want to identify the similarities of cases in this edition with cases in previous editions. Exhibit 1 identifies the cases in this edition with previous cases.

Exhibit 1: Case Comparison

Previous Editions	6th Edition
White	Redding
Sumrall	Clement
Smith	Peyton
Ditka	Morrish
Taramina	Williams
Remington	Franklin
Brady	Silver
Yandle	Garrett
Martin	Jones
Becker	Duke
Albrite	Monroe
Sleigh	Ross
Melancon	Morgan
Gillis	Trenticosta

The Case Method

The objective of Personal Financial Planning Cases and Applications is to prepare competent financial planners through the simulated practice of answering comprehensive questions.

Personal financial planning case analysis is the process used to formulate financial recommendations for clients given the clients' current situation, expectations, and goals. Case analysis provides students with practice in bringing experience, theory, and common sense to bear in the formulation of plans and recommendations in realistic situations.

The case method class structure differs from the traditional lecture class structure in that the students must take a more active role in the learning process. The student must determine the problem, select the appropriate tools, and formulate a plan, all in the absence of full and complete information. Additionally, the student will be faced with the fact that often there is not one best plan of action. These complications are indicative of what a personal financial planner faces in the "real world."

While each student is unique and each case is different, students should develop a basic approach to analyzing cases. In reviewing the case scenario, the student will find it useful to briefly read the case scenario to get a feel for the clients and the overall case. Then, the student should reread the case in detail, making written notes to assure an in-depth comprehension of the case situation. The student may wish to subdivide the issues into the six major areas of personal financial planning:

- Fundamentals of Financial Planning

- Insurance Planning

- Investments

- Income Tax Planning

- Retirement Planning

- Estate Planning

The student should begin by identifying the strengths and weaknesses of the financial situation presented by the client in each area. It is important not to confuse symptoms with problems or to make premature evaluations. The student will often find that a problem in one area is related to and complicated by a problem in another area.

Once the student has a thorough understanding of the case situation and has begun to identify areas of concern, the student should then focus on answering the specific questions presented at the end of the case. With practice, the student should become more proficient in identifying the issues presented in the questions before reading the questions. A thorough understanding of the case information will help direct the student to both questions and answers.

Many of the questions direct the student to review the current or proposed situation and evaluate the appropriateness, effectiveness, soundness, or validity of such a situation. In the evaluation process, the student will need to understand the consequences of each decision and be able to suggest possible alternatives taking into consideration known and even unknown information. It is always important to keep in mind that it is the function of the personal financial planner to help clients optimize their situation in order to plan for both present and future needs, as well as their objectives.

The student should keep two important things in mind. The information presented here for each case is probably more complete and better organized than information which the client in practice presents to the professional financial planner. Furthermore, while ratios are intended to generate questions and to focus attention, they are not a perfect tool. By utilizing a variety of ratio measures, the student should get a pretty good idea of debt management, savings rate, financial security, and progress towards financial security in retirement.

Acknowledgements and Special Thanks

We appreciate the tremendous support and encouragement we have received from everyone throughout the development of this project. We are extremely grateful to the users of our texts who provided us with valuable comments concerning all of our previous editions.

This casebook would not have been possible without the extraordinary efforts and dedication of the following:

- Edward W. Clark, ChFC, CASL, CFP®, Joyce Schnur, MBA, CFP®, and Chris White, CFP®, who reviewed the case scenarios, questions, and answers for technical accuracy.

- Marguerite Merritt, who reviewed case scenarios, questions, and answers for grammatical accuracy and format.

We have received so much help from so many people it is possible that we inadvertently overlooked thanking someone. If so, it is our shortcoming, and we apologize in advance. Please let us know if you are that someone and we will correct it in our next printing.

About the Authors

Michael A. Dalton, Ph.D., JD, CPA, CLU, ChFC, CFP®

- Former Chair of the Board of Dalton Publications, L.L.C.

- Former Senior Vice President, Education at BISYS Group.

- Personal financial planning instructor at Georgetown University's Executive Certificate in Financial Planning Program.

- Provider of litigation support for NASD securities arbitration and serves as expert in securities litigation.

- Associate professor of Accounting and Taxation at Loyola University in New Orleans, Louisiana.

- Ph.D. in Accounting from Georgia State University.

- Juris Doctorate from Louisiana State University in Baton Rouge, Louisiana.

- MBA and BBA in Management and Accounting from Georgia State University.

- Former board member of the CFP Board's Board of Examiners, Board of Standards, and Board of Governors.

- Former member (and chair) of the CFP Board's Board of Examiners.

- Member of the Financial Planning Association.

- Member of the *Journal of Financial Planning* Editorial Advisory Board.

- Member of the *Journal of Financial Planning* Editorial Review Board.

- Member of the LSU Law School Board of Trustees (2000–Present).

- Author of *Dalton Review for the CFP® Certification Examination: Volume I—Outlines and Study Guides, Volume II—Problems and Solutions, Volume III—Case Exam Book, Mock Exams A-1 and A-2 (1st–8th Editions).*

- Author of *Estate Planning for Financial Planners (1st–4th Editions).*

- Author of *Retirement Planning and Employee Benefits for Financial Planners (1st–5th Editions).*

- Co-author of *Dalton CFA® Study Notes Volumes I and II (1st–2nd Editions).*

- Co-author of *Personal Financial Planning: Theory and Practice (1st–3rd Editions).*

- Co-author of *Personal Financial Planning: Cases and Applications (1st–4th Editions)*.

- Co-author of *Cost Accounting: Traditions and Innovations* published by West Publishing Company.

- Co-author of *The ABCs of Managing Your Money* published by National Endowment for Financial Education.

- Co-author of *Income Tax Planning for Financial Planners (1st–2nd Editions)*

James F. Dalton, MBA, CPA/PFS, CFA, CFP®

- Senior Vice President of Kaplan Schweser.

- Former Senior Manager of an international accounting firm, concentrating in Personal Financial Planning, investment planning, and litigation services.

- MBA from Loyola University New Orleans.

- Masters of Accounting in Taxation from the University of New Orleans.

- BS in accounting from Florida State University in Tallahassee, Florida.

- Member of the CFP Board of Standards July 1996, Comprehensive CFP® Exam Pass Score Committee.

- Member of the AICPA and the Louisiana Society of CPAs.

- Member of the Financial Planning Association.

- Member of the *Journal of Financial Planning* Editorial Review Board.

- Member of the New Orleans Estate Planning Council.

- Author of Kaplan Financial's *Personal Financial Planning–Understanding Your Financial Calculator*.

- Co-author of Kaplan Financial's *Personal Financial Planning–Cases and Applications*.

- Co-author of *Kaplan Financial Review for the CFP® Certification Examination: Volume I—Outlines and Study Guides, Volume II—Problems and Solutions, Volume III—Case Exam Book, Mock Exams A-1 and A-2 (1st–8th Editions)*.

CONTRIBUTING AUTHORS

Kathy L. Berlin

- Senior Content Specialist, Kaplan Schweser.
- Successfully passed November 2004 CFP® Certification Examination.
- Certified Public Accountant (Inactive).
- BA from Loyola University of New Orleans, Louisiana.
- Former CFO of a large nonprofit organization.
- Co-author of Kaplan Schweser's *Personal Financial Planning Cases and Applications, 5th and 6th Editions* textbook and instructor manual.
- Co-author of Kaplan Financial's *Personal Financial Planning Theory and Practice, 4th and 5th Editions* textbook and instructor manual.
- Co-author of the *Schweser Review for the CFP© Certification Examination, 9th, 10th, 11th, and 12th Editions.*

Kathy Faulkner Hartin, MBA, CPA, CFP®*

- Principal of Faulkner Financial.
- Academic Program Director for Rice University's classroom based CFP® Certification Education Program.
- Board Member of the Pearland Economic Development Corporation.
- Former Vice President and Chief Financial Officer of Kanaly Trust Company.
- MBA and BS in Finance from the University of New Orleans.
- Previously taught the comprehensive Case Analysis course in the University of Houston's CFP® Education Program.
- Co-author of *Personal Financial Planning—Cases and Applications, 1st, 2nd, and 3rd Editions* textbook and instructor manual.
- Edited practice questions and answers contained in *Dalton CFA® Review, Volumes I and II Study Notes* and is a contributing author to the *Dalton CFA® Review Test Bank.*

  * Licensed, not practicing.

Jo Lynne Koehn, Ph.D., CPA, CFP®

- Professor of accounting at University of Central Missouri in Warrensburg, Missouri.

- Ph.D. in Accounting from University of Wisconsin, Madison.

- BS in Accounting and Management from Kansas State University in Manhattan, Kansas.

- Instructor of auditing, financial accounting, and the advanced financial planning course offered as part of the certified financial planning program at University of Central Missouri.

- Co-author of *Personal Financial Planning—Cases and Applications* textbook and instructor manual.

- Contributing author to *Financial Accounting Principles*, Larson, Wild, and Chiappetta, 15th and 16th Editions (Published by Irwin McGraw-Hill).

- Author of articles related to accounting and taxes in a variety of journals, including *The CPA Journal, Issues in Accounting Education, Accounting Enquiries, Taxes,* and *The Tax Adviser.*

Michael Long, CLU, ChFC, CFP®

- Senior Content Specialist, Kaplan Schweser.

- Over 25 years' experience in insurance and securities as a sales manager, classroom instructor, product manager, and advanced underwriting consultant.

- BS in business administration, Indiana State University.

- Co-author of Kaplan Schweser's *Personal Financial Planning Cases and Applications, 6th Edition* textbook and instructor manual.

James Maher, CLU, ChFC, CFP®

- Senior Content Specialist, Kaplan Schweser.

- Former securities and insurance instructor, Kaplan Financial.

- Former General Securities Representative.

- BBA from Florida International University.

- Co-author of Kaplan Schweser's *Personal Financial Planning Cases and Applications, 6th Edition* textbook and instructor manual.

- Co-author of Kaplan Financial's *Personal Financial Planning Theory and Practice, 5th Edition* textbook and instructor manual.

- Co-author of the *Schweser Review for the CFP© Certification Examination, 12th Edition.*

Nancy P. Penton, CFP®

- Senior Content Specialist, Kaplan Schweser.

- Owner and President of Penton Financial Services.

- Co-founder and former president of the Gulf Coast Society of the Institute of Certified Financial Planners.

- Co-founder and past president of the Gulf Coast Society of the Institute of Certified Financial Planners.

- Former manager of Product Development, Advanced Designations, for national financial education firm.

- Former vice president, Private Financial Services, for major banking institution.

- BS program University of New Orleans.

- Co-author of Kaplan Schweser's *Personal Financial Planning Cases and Applications, 6th Edition* textbook and instructor manual.

- Co-author of Kaplan Financial's *Personal Financial Planning Theory and Practice, 5th Edition* textbook and instructor manual.

- Co-author of the *Schweser Review for the CFP© Certification Examination, 12th Edition*.

Cindy Hart Riecke, CLU, ChFC, CFP®

- Senior Director, Kaplan Schweser.

- BS in Business Administration from Louisiana State University in Baton Rouge, Louisiana.

- Member of the Financial Planning Association.

- Former Director of Marketing Development for an international insurance and financial services company.

- Co-author of Kaplan Schweser's *Personal Financial Planning Cases and Applications, 5th and 6th Editions* textbook and instructor manual.

- Co-author of Kaplan Financial's *Personal Financial Planning Theory and Practice, 4th and 5th Editions* textbook and instructor manual.

- Co-author of the *Schweser Review for the CFP© Certification Examination, 9th, 10th, 11th, and 12th Editions*.

Robert Showers, CPA, CFP®

- Adjunct Instructor in Accounting and Finance and the Manager of Investments at University of Central Missouri in Warrensburg, Missouri.

- MBA from the University of South Dakota in Vermillion, South Dakota.

- BS from Morningside College in Sioux City, Iowa.

- Teaches managerial accounting and personal finance at University of Central Missouri.

- Manages a private practice in Warrensburg, Missouri, offering investment and financial planning services to his clients.

- Co-author of *Personal Financial Planning—Cases and Applications* textbook and instructor manual.

Stephan E. Wolter, JD, MBA, ChFC

- Senior Content Specialist, Kaplan Schweser.

- Successfully passed July 2008 CFP® Certification Examination.

- JD from Indiana University, Indianapolis.

- MBA from University of Colorado at Colorado Springs.

- Co-author of Kaplan Schweser's *Personal Financial Planning Cases and Applications, 6th Edition* textbook and instructor manual.

Answer Key available!

Visit **www.schweser.com** to see answers available to students for problems in the student textbook.

Benjamin and Sarah Redding

Benjamin and Sarah Redding have great aspirations for their future. They have only recently realized that they are not as financially well-off as they had thought. They have come to you for advice on how to solve their current cash flow problems and to help them plan to achieve future goals. Today is January 1, 2009.

Personal Background and Information

Benjamin Redding (Age 30)

Benjamin Redding graduated from a state university seven years ago with a bachelor of science degree in accounting. He has been employed for almost seven years at Moore & Moore, a small accounting firm (50 employees).

Benjamin has been married to Sarah Steiner Redding for six years.

Sarah Steiner Redding (Age 29)

Sarah Steiner Redding grew up in a wealthy family and expects to live her married life the same way. While in college, she was crowned Miss State. She graduated from a private university with a bachelor of science degree in elementary education. She is employed as a fourth grade teacher at a private school, Woodridge Preparatory School, and has been for the past five years. To further enrich her students (and for additional income), Sarah tutors three students per week. She incurs no expenses to provide this tutoring.

Children

Benjamin and Sarah have three children: Scott, age 4, and twin girls, Janice and Carly, age 1.

Delores Vidalia

The Reddings employ a young student, Delores Vidalia, to care for their children. Delores, 21 years old, is a part-time night student at a local community college. She cares for the children and cleans the house in exchange for room, board, and a $100 stipend per week. The Reddings pay Delores in cash. Neither the Reddings nor Dolores report this money to the IRS. Delores works 48 weeks per year.

Benjamin's Family

George Redding married Julie Elizabeth Grant Redding in 1969. They had two children, George Jr., and Benjamin. George Jr., died at six months of age of sudden infant death syndrome.

Benjamin's father, George Sr., died of a heart attack six years ago at age 50. He had ample insurance to cover all medical and funeral expenses.

His mother, Julie, a chain-smoker for 37 years, is 53 years old. She was diagnosed with lung cancer three years ago. Because of her rapidly deteriorating condition, her doctor has predicted that she probably will not live beyond five to seven years. She is receiving monthly chemotherapy treatments at a medical center ($200 out-of-pocket per visit).

Her doctor has recommended that she be placed in a home with 24-hour attention as soon as possible. The cost of this care, including room and board, is about $175 per day, or approximately $5,323 per month. Because of her increased medical expenses and need for constant attention, Julie has decided to sell her home. She has contacted Gertrude Gardner, a real estate agent, who has listed her home for $140,000. Julie is adamant that she will accept no less than $135,000.

Benjamin and Sarah have been giving Julie $200 per month to help ease her financial burden. They will be forced to incur most of her future expenses. They realize that the sale of the home will provide some assistance; however, the real estate market is soft, and they have had no offers on the house. Julie owns a paid-up life insurance policy (non-MEC) on her own life with a face amount of $500,000 and a cash value of $75,000.

Benjamin's great-aunt Mabel plans to give Benjamin and Sarah $10,000 each at the beginning of 2009. Benjamin has always looked out for Aunt Mabel, and she wants to show him her gratitude through this gift.

Sarah's Family

Harry Steiner III, married Alice Rose Steiner in 1969. After years of unsuccessful attempts to have a child, they were pleasantly surprised to find out that Alice was pregnant. Sarah is an only child and the Steiners' pride and joy.

Harry Steiner is a highly respected State Supreme Court justice. He has worked in the city for more than 30 years and is considered an extremely influential figure in the community. Harry and Alice's adjusted gross income (AGI) exceeds $275,000.

Alice Steiner was born into an excessively wealthy family. Before they were married, she and Harry decided that she would not work. She is, however, very active in the community through her volunteer work four days a week.

The Steiners were happy to welcome Benjamin into their family. In fact, Harry was so excited that he presented Benjamin with a speedboat in hopes that he would get to spend time getting to know his future son-in-law. As a wedding gift, the Steiners gave Sarah and Benjamin $20,000 toward the purchase of a new home.

In addition, the Steiners set up a $100,000 trust fund to assist their grandchildren with college education expenses. Sarah, the beneficiary of the trust fund, receives the monthly interest from the principal until the trust is dissolved, with first Benjamin and then Children's Hospital as successor beneficiaries in the event of her death. Upon Scott's enrollment in college, he will be given his third of the trust fund, $33,333. Sarah will continue to receive the interest on the remaining $66,666 until Janice and

Carly begin college. If a child should die or decide not to go to college by age 22, that child's share would be donated to Children's Hospital.

Benjamin was previously married to Carol, and together they had one child, Stephen. Benjamin pays Carol $200 each month for child support. Carol's parents have agreed to pay 100% of Stephen's college tuition and expenses.

Personal and Financial Objectives

In reviewing a listing of general financial objectives, the Reddings list the following financial objectives in direct order of importance to their family (i.e., the item numbered 1 has the highest priority and the item numbered 8 has the lowest).

1. They want to provide private education for all three children at Woodridge Preparatory School for grades K–12.

2. They want to provide each child with up to $15,000 per year for college education for up to four years in addition to the trust fund.

3. They want to assist Julie with living and medical expenses until her death.

4. They want to purchase a home for $300,000 in eight years with 20% down. (By that time, Benjamin should be a partner of the firm.) Housing costs are expected to increase with inflation. At that time, they will not sell the current house but will rent it to tenants.

5. They want to be free of mortgage indebtedness by the time Benjamin is 55 years old.

6. They want to prepare a proper retirement plan allowing them a no worry retirement. They feel that income of $75,000 in today's dollars per year will allow them to keep their standard of living.

7. They want to rebuild their savings account/emergency fund back to a minimum of $25,000.

8. They want to save for the twins' future weddings (estimated costs $15,000 each).

Economic Information

- They expect inflation to average 4%.

- They expect Sarah's salary to increase by 5%.

- They expect Benjamin's salary to increase by 5%.

- Mortgage rates are 5.5% for a 15-year fixed and 6.0% for a 30-year fixed. Any refinancing will incur 3% of mortgage as a closing cost.

Insurance Information

Health Insurance

Health insurance is provided for the entire family by Moore & Moore. The Reddings are covered by an HMO. Doctor visits are $10 per visit, while prescriptions are $5 for generic brands and $10 for other brands. There is no copayment for hospitalization in semiprivate accommodations. Private rooms are provided when medically necessary. For emergency treatment, a $50 copayment is required.

Life Insurance

Benjamin has a $110,000 group term insurance policy through Moore & Moore. Highly compensated employees of Moore & Moore receive group term coverage in the amount of five times their salaries. Sarah has a $27,000 group term policy through Woodridge Preparatory School. The owners of the policies are Benjamin and Sarah, respectively, with each other as the respective beneficiary.

Disability Insurance

Benjamin has disability insurance through Moore & Moore. Short-term disability benefits begin for any absence due to accident or illness more than six days and will continue for up to six months at 80% of his salary. Long-term disability benefits are available if disability continues more than six months. If Benjamin is unable to perform the duties of his current occupation, the benefits provide him with 60% of his salary while disabled until recovery, death, retirement, or age 65 (whichever occurs first). All disability premiums are paid by Moore & Moore.

Sarah currently has no disability insurance.

Professional Liability Insurance

Moore & Moore has professional liability insurance covering all employees.

Homeowners Insurance

The Reddings currently have an HO-3 policy endorsed to provide loss settlement on a replacement cost basis for personal property. Dwelling coverage is provided on an open-peril basis and personal property coverage is provided on a named-peril basis. The policy covers all risk and replacement value. The deductible is $500 with a premium of $750 per year.

Automobile Insurance

Benjamin and Sarah have the following coverage on both cars, including:

- $100,000 bodily injury per person;
- $300,000 bodily injury aggregate;
- $50,000 property damage;
- $100,000 uninsured motorist per person; and
- $300,000 uninsured motorist aggregate.

Deductibles are:

- $500 comprehensive (no deductible for glass); and
- $1,000 collision.

This insurance includes medical payments, car rentals, and towing. The cost of the auto insurance is $3,260.50 per year because of two at-fault accidents Sarah has caused in the past three years.

Investment Information (Prospective)

	Expected Return	Beta
Aggressive stocks	13%	1.6
Growth stocks	10%	1.1
S&P 500	9%	1.0
Bonds	7%	0.5
Money market (bank)	2%	0.3

The Reddings consider themselves to be moderate investors.

Income Tax Information

The Reddings are in the 25% marginal tax bracket. Their combined marginal tax bracket (federal and state) is 31%.

Retirement Information

Benjamin and Sarah would both like to retire when they are 65 and 64, respectively, and they expect to be in retirement for 30 years. They would hope to have $75,000 per year of pre-tax income in today's dollars during retirement. They do not want to rely on Social Security benefits for their retirement planning. Any money received from Social Security will be considered extra income.

Benjamin does not participate in a 401(k) plan available through Moore & Moore. In the plan, the firm matches $.50 for every dollar contributed, up to 6% of his contribution (if he contributes 6% of his salary the company contributes 3%). Benjamin may defer a maximum of 16% of his salary.

Sarah is currently enrolled in a defined contribution plan in which the school contributes 7% of her salary and she contributes 3%. The plan provides several options for the investment of her controllable funds: bond funds, mutual stock funds, or money market accounts. She has chosen to invest this contribution in fixed instruments (bond fund). The plan has a 2- to 6-year graduated vesting schedule, and she has been a participant for four years. The total balance of her account fund is $16,500. Although she has not participated, she also has available a 403(b) supplemental retirement plan to which she may contribute up to 13% of her salary.

Gifts, Estates, Trusts, and Will Information

Presently, neither Benjamin nor Sarah have wills; however, both realize the importance of having a will. They would like to create wills leaving everything to each other and the children, while minimizing as much estate and gift tax as possible.

STATEMENT OF CASH FLOWS
Benjamin and Sarah Redding
2008
(Expected to be the same for 2009)

CASH INFLOWS

Salary—Benjamin	$55,000.00	
Salary—Sarah	27,000.00	
Tutoring—Sarah[1]	3,600.00	
Interest—trust	3,000.00	
Savings account withdrawal[2]	5,569.80	
Total inflows		$94,169.80

CASH OUTFLOWS

Defined contribution plan savings—Sarah	$ 810.00	
Mortgage payment (principal and interest)	12,798.24	
Property taxes (residence)	1,250.00	
FICA	6,273.00	
Federal withholding	11,078.20	
State withholding	903.95	
Utilities	5,400.00	
Homeowners insurance	750.00	
Auto note	6,374.16	
Auto expense/maintenance	3,490.00	
Auto insurance	3,260.50	
Child care/House care[3]	4,800.00	
Education loans[4]	2,892.60	
Credit card interest and payments[5]	2,170.08	
Bank loans[6]	7,251.25	
Dry cleaning	900.00	
New clothing	3,550.00	
Food	6,000.00	
Dining out/entertainment	3,600.00	
Miscellaneous	3,600.00	
Support payment to Carol	6,000.00	
Total Outflows		$93,151.98
Discretionary Cash Flow		$ 1,017.82

Notes to Financial Statements
[1]Sarah does not report this money to the IRS.
[2]$366 is earned interest.
[3]The Reddings pay the maid in cash and do not report it to the IRS.
[4]$1,643 is interest, the balance is principal.
[5]The Reddings pay the minimum monthly interest charge on credit cards.
[6]$4,350 is interest, the balance is principal.

STATEMENT OF FINANCIAL POSITION
Benjamin and Sarah Redding
January 1, 2009

ASSETS[1]

Checking account	$ 10,000	
Savings account	13,500	
Trust fund[2]	100,000	
Automobile—Sarah (1999 BMW 328i)	12,575	
Automobile—Benjamin (2007 Nissan Maxima)	16,375	
Boat	12,000	
Home (appraised 7/1/07)	149,000	
Pension—Sarah	16,500	
Total assets		$329,950

LIABILITIES[3,4]

Credit card—Benjamin (18%)	$ 4,750	
Credit card—Sarah (23%)	4,920	
Credit card—joint (16%)	1,200	
Car Note—Benjamin (10%)	18,383	
School loans (6%)	17,919	
Bank loans (12%)	9,909	
Home mortgage balance (7.5%)	148,944	
Total liabilities		$206,025
Net worth		$123,925
Total liabilities and net worth		$329,950

Notes to Financial Statements
[1]All assets are stated at fair market value.
[2]The trust fund is for the children's education; however, Sarah receives the interest on the balance of the trust fund until all children reach age of majority. The trust assets are invested in a CD yielding 3% per year.
[3]Liabilities are stated at principal only.
[4]Percentages shown (%) are interest rates on respective indebtedness.

Information Regarding Assets and Liabilities

Employment

Benjamin is currently employed as a senior accountant at Moore & Moore, earning an annual salary of $55,000. He expects to be promoted to manager within two years. Benjamin hopes to be a partner in eight years.

Sarah earns $27,000 a year teaching at Woodridge Preparatory School. Annual increases range 3–5%. She also earns approximately $3,600 annually tutoring. This money is received in cash. (Although they should, she and Benjamin do not report her tutoring earnings on their tax returns.) In addition, Sarah receives $5,000 a year, before taxes, on the interest earned from the children's trust fund.

Benjamin and Sarah earn approximately 2% interest on their savings account. This is automatically credited on a quarterly basis to the account; however, this amount is so low that they do not consider it income. This savings account/emergency fund began with an account balance of $25,000 when they were first married. In 2008, they withdrew $366 in interest income and $5,203.80 from the savings account to pay bills.

Home

Benjamin and Sarah purchased a four-bedroom house for $170,000 in a nice family neighborhood. They were among the first families to purchase a home in this new subdivision. The money from Sarah's parents was used for the down payment. The mortgage payment is $1,066.52 per month. The interest rate is 7.5%. The original mortgage was $152,531.47, and they have made 29 payments. Utilities range from $400–500 a month.

Although the original value of the house was $170,000, a recent appraisal valued the house at $149,000. The decrease in value did not leave enough equity for the Reddings to be approved for a home equity loan. The appraiser explained that the decrease in value was because of the increase of drug traffic in the subdivision. If the Reddings wanted to refinance (80% of the fair market value of the home), the 3% closing costs would have to be paid at closing and not financed.

Automobiles

In 2007, Benjamin purchased a new Nissan Maxima for $25,000. The current value of the car is $16,375, but his loan balance is $18,383.47. His loan was originally for 60 months at 10% interest. He has made 19 monthly payments of $531.18.

Sarah's prize for winning a state pageant was a new 1999 BMW 328i. Its current value is $5,750.

Boat

The current value of Benjamin's 18-foot Boston Whaler Center Console with a 150 HP Mercury is $12,000. Though Benjamin and Sarah consider this a luxury item, they know that the sale of the boat would only further erode their relationship with Sarah's parents.

Student Loans

Benjamin put himself through school with part-time jobs and student loans. He originally borrowed money to pay for his education through a student loan program. He recently consolidated all of his student loans into one. The loan is for 10 years, and Benjamin is in his second year of payments. The current payment is $241.05 per month.

Credit Cards

Before marriage, Benjamin and Sarah each had their own credit cards almost charged to the limits. After marriage, they applied for a joint credit card and planned to use it for emergency use only. The current interest rates, balances, limits, and annual fees on these cards are as follows.

	Interest	Balance	Limit	Annual Fees
Benjamin	18%	$4,750	$5,000	$50
Sarah	23%	$4,920	$5,000	$50
Joint	16%	$1,200	$5,000	$50

Bank Loans

During the past several years, Benjamin and Sarah have taken out loans to pay for vacations. The current payment is $604.27 per month. The balance of these loans is $9,908.98 (rounded on the Statement of Financial Position to $9,909).

Entertainment

Because of Benjamin and Sarah's hectic work schedules and the three children, they rarely get to spend time alone together. Every Friday night, they go to a moderately priced restaurant for dinner. Sometimes they are joined by some of Benjamin's colleagues, and he uses this time to network. The approximate cost of dinner each Friday for Benjamin and Sarah is $50 including tip.

Friday nights are also a night out for the children. Delores brings the children to The Burger Barn for dinner. The approximate cost is $19 for all three children and Delores.

Education

Because of the quality of the schools in their state, Benjamin and Sarah want Scott, Janice, and Carly to go to private schools, but they are concerned about the cost. To assist in defraying the cost of educating the children, it is expected that all three children will attend Woodridge Preparatory School for K–12th grade. Sarah's position allows for tuition discounts for teachers as follows:

- 50% discount on tuition for students in K–8th grades; and

- 75% discount on tuition for students in 9–12th grades.

Current tuition is $3,665 per student. There is no additional multifamily discount. Tuition is expected to increase at 5% per year. Each child will begin kindergarten at age 5.

Benjamin and Sarah would also like to provide financial assistance to their children while they attend college. They have decided to offer each child up to $15,000 (in today's dollars) per year for tuition, room, and board. Any additional funding will be provided by the trust, student loans, or part-time employment by the children. Today, tuition, fees, and so forth average $25,000 for a public university and are expected to increase at a rate of 5% per year. Each child is expected to begin college immediately after graduation from high school at age 18 and attend for four years.

QUESTIONS

1. List the Reddings' financial strengths and weaknesses.

2. After reading the case, what additional information would you request from the Reddings to complete your data-gathering phase?

3. Calculate the following financial ratios for the Reddings.

$$\frac{\text{Liquid Assets}}{\text{Monthly Expenses}}$$

$$\frac{\text{Net Worth}}{\text{Total Assets}}$$

$$\frac{\text{Total Debt}}{\text{Total Assets}}$$

$$\frac{\text{Total Debt}}{\text{Annual Total Income*}}$$

$$\frac{\text{Annual Housing and Debt Payments}}{\text{Annual Gross Income}}$$

$$\frac{\text{Annual Housing Costs}}{\text{Annual Gross Income}}$$

$$\frac{\text{Investment Assets}}{\text{Annual Gross Income}}$$

$$\frac{\text{Annual Savings}}{\text{Annual Gross Income}}$$

*Annual Total Income is the same as Annual Gross Income.

4. Comment on any of the above ratios that you think are important.

5. Briefly evaluate the Reddings' use of debt.

6. Assuming an earnings rate of 8%, calculate the amount needed today to fund the children's college education.

7. Assuming an earnings rate of 8%, calculate the amount they need to save each month to fund the children's college education. Assume that savings will begin at the end of this month and continue until the youngest children begin college.

8. Assuming an earnings rate of 8%, calculate the monthly savings needed for education assuming that savings will continue until the children's college education is completed.

9. Determine whether the Reddings will currently qualify to refinance their home. Is the house eligible for refinancing by a lender requiring a maximum loan-to-value ratio of 80%? How much cash would the Reddings need if they refinance?

10. (For purposes of this question, ignore whether the Reddings qualify to refinance their home, but maintain the lender's loan-to-value requirement.) Assuming that the Reddings decide to use their savings account to pay down the mortgage to be able to refinance their current mortgage, calculate the monthly payment for each of the following.
    a. 15-year loan
    b. 30-year loan paid over 30 years
    c. 30-year loan paid over the remaining life of their current mortgage

11. Calculate the total savings expected from the refinancing for each of the three loans mentioned in Question 10.

12. Do they qualify for any of the loans in Question 10 if the bank requires a total housing cost ratio less than 28% and a total debt-to-payments income ratio of 36%?

13. If they do not qualify for any of the loans in Question 10 because the lender counts only $82,000 of income, what actions should they consider in order to qualify?

14. Calculate the total amount of money needed today to meet Julie's medical needs. Assume that she lives seven years and that the Reddings invest in bonds.

15. How much do the Reddings need to save on a monthly basis beginning at the end of this month toward a down payment in order to purchase their future home for $300,000? Assume they invest at an interest rate equal to the expected return on the S&P 500 and pay all associated taxes out of their current budget.

16. Does the trust fund of $100,000 belong in the Reddings' Statement of Financial Position?

17. What are the deficiencies in the presentation of the Statement of Financial Position?

18. The Steiners recently decided to provide additional financial assistance to help with their grandchildren's college education expenses. They plan to elect gift-splitting for any gifts they make, and they want to give as much as they can without incurring any gift tax. What is the maximum amount they can contribute this year and meet these objectives using Coverdell Education Savings Accounts (ESAs) and Section 529 plans?

ADDITIONAL QUESTIONS

1. What are the tax consequences of the current treatment of the tutoring income?

2. What, if any, are the tax consequences to the Reddings of the tuition discount the first year that all three children are in school?

3. What are the tax consequences that may result from the current treatment of the employment of Delores?

4. What are the Reddings' present insurance needs?

5. Discuss the Reddings' projected estate problems.

6. What estate planning recommendations would you make to the Reddings?

7. What tax planning recommendations would you make to the Reddings?

8. Estimate the adjusted gross income less itemized deductions for federal income tax for the Reddings for the past year.

9. Would it be beneficial for the Reddings to obtain a signed release from Delores indicating that she does not want withholdings from payments made to her for child care services rendered?

10. Discuss the trust fund set up for the grandchildren by the Steiners. Did the initial funding of this trust create a generation-skipping transfer by the Steiners?

11. If Sarah left Woodridge Preparatory School today, what would be her vested retirement balance?

12. How would Sarah's benefits be affected if her retirement plan was considered top heavy?

13. If Sarah left Woodridge Preparatory School today, what are her options regarding the balance in her retirement plan?

14. If the Reddings had a portfolio with the following asset allocation for retirement, what would be their expected return?

Aggressive stocks	10%
Growth stocks	10%
S&P 500	40%
Bonds	30%
Money market	10%
	100%

15. What is the weighted beta of the above portfolio?

16. Does the above asset allocation match the Reddings' financial objectives and risk tolerance?

17. On the basis of the above portfolio, how much, in today's dollars, would the Reddings need to fund their retirement?

18. What is the approximate amount of life insurance that Benjamin needs to replace all of his income and raises during his work life expectancy assuming an investment rate of return equal to the rate of return associated with growth stocks?

19. Can the Reddings deduct the interest on the student loan for 2009 federal income tax purposes?

20. Discuss ways that Julie might use her life insurance policy to help meet the expenses associated with her terminal illness. Is a viatical agreement appropriate for her situation?

21. What is the maximum tax-deductible contribution Benjamin and Sarah could make to traditional IRAs for 2009?

22. Delores frequently interacts with and watches over other children who are visiting the Reddings' children in the Reddings' home. Are Benjamin and Sarah adequately protected against a possible liability exposure if Delores negligently injures one of those children?

23. What are the tax consequences to Benjamin of the group term insurance policy?

24. Assume that Julie purchased a long-term care policy 5 years ago. The policy provides a daily benefit of $200 using a pool-of-money concept, with an elimination period of 60 days. The policy is tax-qualified (meets HIPAA requirements). The policy does not have an inflation rider.
    a. How can Julie qualify for the benefits under the policy?
    b. Assume Julie qualifies for long-term care benefits and enters a qualifying long-term care facility for a period of 7 years. She incurs costs for the entire 7-year period at today's rates. For how long will her policy provide benefits?

25. The Reddings' homeowners policy has an 80% coinsurance clause which provides for reduced loss settlement if the Reddings carry less than 80% of the replacement cost value on their home. Assume the replacement cost of the Reddings' house is estimated by the insurance company to be $150,000. How much coverage should the Reddings purchase on the home for Coverage A-Dwelling?

26. Assuming the Reddings refinance their home and use the proceeds to retire debt, what is the tax consequence in the current tax year if a point is paid to secure the interest rate?

Nicholas and Whitney Clement

Today is January 1, 2009. Nicholas and Whitney Clement have come to you, a financial planner, for help in developing a plan to accomplish their financial goals. From your initial meeting together, you have gathered the following information.

Personal Background and Information

Nicholas Clement (Age 27)

Nicholas is an assistant in the marketing department for Energy Tech, Inc., a small company with 15 employees. His annual salary is $39,000.

Whitney Clement (Age 24)

Whitney is a legal research assistant with the law firm of Laurent, Heine & Merritt, LLC. Her annual salary is $30,000.

The Children

Nicholas and Whitney have no children from this marriage. Nicholas has two children, Grant, age 4, and Blake, age 3, from a former marriage. Grant and Blake live with their mother, Kelly.

The Clements

Nicholas and Whitney have been married for two years. Nicholas must pay $500 per month in child support until both Grant and Blake reach age 18. The divorce decree also required Nicholas to create an insurance trust for the benefit of the children and contribute $175 per month to the trust. The trustee is Kelly's father. There are no withdrawal powers on the part of the beneficiaries. The trust is to be used for the education and maintenance of the children in the event of Nicholas's death. The trustee has the power to invade any trust principal for the beneficiaries at the earlier of the death of Nicholas or Blake reaching age 18.

Personal and Financial Objectives

1. They want to save for an emergency fund.

2. They want to eliminate debt.

3. They want to save for a 20% down payment on their first home. The current value of the house is $150,000. Property taxes would be $1,800 annually, and the annual insurance premium would be $1,125. Both taxes and insurance are expected to increase with inflation.

4. They want to contribute to tax-advantaged savings.

5. They plan to have additional children in seven years.

6. They both plan to retire in 29 years.

Economic Information

■ Inflation is expected to be 4.0% annually.

■ Their salaries should increase 5.0% annually.

■ There is no state income tax.

■ The after-tax investment rate of return is 6%.

■ Bank lending rates are as follows: 6.0% for a 15-year mortgage, 6.5% for a 30-year mortgage, and 8% for a secured personal loan.

Insurance Information

Life Insurance

	Policy A	Policy B	Policy C
Insured	Nicholas	Nicholas	Whitney
Face amount	$250,000	$117,000[2]	$30,000
Type	Whole life	Group term	Group term
Cash value	$2,000	$0	$0
Annual premium	$2,100	$267	$75
Who pays premium	Trustee	Employer	Employer
Beneficiary	Trust[1]	Kelly	Nicholas
Policyowner	Trust	Nicholas	Whitney
Settlement options clause selected	None	None	None

[1] Grant and Blake are beneficiaries of the trust.

[2] This was increased from $50,000 to $117,000 January 1, 2009.

Health Insurance

Nicholas and Whitney are covered under Nicholas's employer plan, which is an indemnity plan with a $200 deductible per person per year and an 80/20 major medical coinsurance clause with a family annual stop loss of $1,500.

Long-Term Disability Insurance

Nicholas is covered by an own-occupation policy with premiums paid by his employer. The benefits equal 60% of his gross pay after an elimination period of 180 days. The policy covers both sickness and accidents and is guaranteed renewable. In the event of disability, the policy will pay benefits up to age 65.

Whitney is not covered by disability insurance.

Renters Insurance

The Clements have a HO-4 renters policy without endorsements. Content Coverage: $25,000; Liability: $100,000.

Automobile Insurance

Both Car and Truck*

Type	Personal Auto Policy
Bodily injury	$25,000/$50,000
Property damage	$10,000
Medical payments	$5,000 per person
Uninsured motorist	$25,000/$50,000
Comprehensive deductible	$200
Collision deductible	$500
Premium (annual)	$4,950

*The Clements do not have any additional insurance on Whitney's motorcycle.

Investment Information

The Clements think that they need six months of cash flow net of all taxes, savings, vacation, and discretionary cash flow in an emergency fund. They are willing to include in the emergency fund the savings account and Nicholas's 401(k) balance because it has borrowing provisions.

The Federal Express stock was a gift to Nicholas from his Uncle Frank. At the date of the gift (July 1, 1994), the fair market value of the stock was $3,500. Uncle Frank's tax basis was $2,500, and Uncle Frank paid gift tax of $1,400 on the gift.

The K&B stock of 100 shares was a gift to Whitney last Christmas from her Uncle Mike. At the date of the gift (December 25, 2008), the fair market value was $8,000, and Uncle Mike had paid $10,000 for the stock in 1996 (his tax basis).

The growth mutual fund (currently valued at $13,900) had been acquired by Nicholas over the years 2003, 2004, 2005, 2006, 2007, and 2008 with deposits of $1,000, $1,000, $2,000, $2,000, $2,500, and $3,000. The earnings were all reinvested and reported via Form 1099 each year:

Year	Reinvested Earnings
2003	$0
2004	$200
2005	$400
2006	$400
2007	$650
2008	$750

The growth mutual fund has a transfer-on-death provision. The account is in Nicholas's name, and the beneficiary designation is Nicholas's mother. This provision was made prior to his marriage to Whitney.

Income Tax Information

The filing status of the Clements for federal income tax is married filing jointly. Both the children (Grant and Blake) are claimed as dependents on the Clements' tax return as part of the divorce agreement. Their marginal tax rate is 22.65% (the federal marginal tax rate is 15%; FICA taxes are 7.65%). The Clements live in a state that does not have state income tax.

Group Term Life Insurance Section 79 Uniform Premium Schedule	
Under age 25	0.05 per month per $1,000
Age 25 to 29	0.06 per month per $1,000

Retirement Information

Nicholas currently contributes 3% of his salary to his 401(k). The employer matches each $1 contributed with $0.50 up to a total employer contribution of 3% of salary.

Gifts, Estates, Trusts, and Will Information

Nicholas has a will leaving all of his probate estate to his children.
Whitney does not have a will.
The Clements live in a common-law state that has adopted the Uniform Probate Code.

STATEMENT OF CASH FLOWS
Nicholas and Whitney Clement
January 1, 2008 to December 31, 2008
(Expected to be similar in 2009)

CASH INFLOWS

Salaries		
Nicholas—salary	$39,000	
Whitney—salary	30,000	
Investment income*	1,635	
Total inflows		$70,635

CASH OUTFLOWS

Savings—house down payment	$ 1,800	
Reinvestment of investment income	1,635	
401(k) contribution	1,170	
Total savings		$ 4,605

FIXED OUTFLOWS

Child support	$ 6,000	
Life insurance payment (to trustee)	2,100	
Rent	9,900	
Renters insurance	720	
Utilities	1,080	
Telephone (home)	540	
Telephones (cell)	900	
Auto payment principal and interest	5,400	
Auto insurance	4,950	
Gas, oil, maintenance	3,600	
Student loans	3,600	
Credit card debt	4,500	
Furniture payments	1,952	
Total fixed outflows		$45,242

VARIABLE OUTFLOWS

Taxes—Nicholas FICA	$ 2,984	
Taxes—Whitney FICA	2,295	
Taxes—federal tax withheld	7,393	
Food	4,800	
Clothing	1,500	
Entertainment/vacation	1,920	
Total variable outflows		$20,892
Total cash outflows		$70,739
Discretionary cash flows (negative)		$ (104)

*$510 from dividends and $1,125 from other investment sources.

STATEMENT OF FINANCIAL POSITION
Nicholas and Whitney Clement
As of January 1, 2009

ASSETS[1]		LIABILITIES AND NET WORTH	
Cash and equivalents		**Liabilities[2]**	
Cash	$ 500	Credit card 1	$ 8,000
Savings account	1,000	Credit card 2	1,862
Total cash and equivalents	$ 1,500	Student loan—Nicholas[3]	45,061
		Auto loan—Whitney	21,179
Invested assets		Furniture loan	2,300
Federal Express stock (100 shares)[4]	$ 5,000	*Total liabilities*	$78,402
K&B stock (100 shares)	7,200		
Growth mutual fund	13,900		
401(k) account	1,500	**Net worth**	($78)
Total invested assets	$27,600		
Use assets			
Auto—Whitney	$26,474		
Truck—Nicholas	4,000		
Motorcycle—Whitney	1,000		
Personal property and furniture	17,750		
Total use of assets	$49,224		
Total assets	$78,324	**Total liabilities and net worth**	$78,324

Notes to Financial Statements

[1] Assets are stated at fair market value.

[2] Liabilities are stated at principal only as of January 1, 2009, before January payments.

[3] Nicholas's parents took out the student loans, but he is repaying them. Nicholas paid $2,732 in interest in 2008.

[4] Federal Express's current dividend is $3.40 per share.

Information Regarding Assets and Liabilities

Home Furnishings

The furniture was purchased with 20% down and 18% interest over 36 months. The monthly payment is $162.69.

Automobile

The automobile was purchased January 1, 2008, for $26,474 with 20% down and 80% financed over 60 months with payments of $450 per month.

Stereo System

The Clements have a fabulous stereo system with a fair market value of $10,000. They asked and received permission to alter their apartment to build speakers into every room. The agreement with the landlord requires the Clements to leave the speakers if they move because the speakers are permanently installed and affixed to the property. The replacement value of the installed speakers is $4,500, and the non-installed components are valued at $5,500. The cost of the system was $10,000, and it was purchased last year.

QUESTIONS

1.   What does *guaranteed renewable* mean with regard to Nicholas's disability policy?

2.   What are the deficiencies in the Clements' disability insurance coverage?

3.   If the Clements wanted to cover their personal property for replacement value, what would they need to do?

4.   If the Clements were burglarized and had their movable stereo system components stolen, would it be covered under the HO-4 policy, and if so, for what value? (See Exhibit 9 in the Appendix for HO chart.)

5.   If there were a fire in the Clements' apartment building and their in-wall speaker system was destroyed, would they be covered under the HO-4 policy, and if so, to what extent?

6.   If a fire forced the Clements to move out of their apartment for a month, would the HO-4 policy provide any coverage?

7.   Is Whitney covered for liability under the personal auto policy while driving her motorcycle?

8.   Who will actually collect the proceeds of Nicholas's term life insurance if he were to die today, given that the Clements live in a Uniform Probate Code state?

9.   How much must Nicholas's employer include in Nicholas's W-2 for 2008 for the group term life insurance? How much must be included in 2009?

10. In 2009, Whitney sustains injuries while playing with Grant and Blake. Medical expenses totaled $1,800, of which $1,600 were covered. The insurance company paid medical expenses in what amount? (Assume that the Clements had no other 2009 medical claims prior to this claim.)

11. Using a human life value approach net of federal and state income taxes, how much additional life insurance is needed on Nicholas's life? (Round to the nearest $50,000 and assume that the marginal tax rate remains constant.)

12. Assume that Nicholas is in a serious automobile accident during 2009 and is unable to perform the duties of his occupation for 208 consecutive days. What benefits will he receive under his long-term disability insurance policy? What will be the income tax consequences of receiving these benefits?

13. Assume that Nicholas is laid off from his job at Energy Tech, Inc., in 2009. How many months of continuation health insurance coverage are the Clements entitled to under COBRA? If Nicholas and Whitney get a divorce in 2009, how many months of continuation coverage is Whitney entitled to?

14. Assume that in 2009, Nicholas is driving his car on a foggy night and the car collides with a deer in the road. As a result, Nicholas incurs medical expenses of $1,000, and his friend, Bill, who is riding with him, incurs medical expenses of $2,000. The front bumper of the car also sustains damage of $1,500. If Nicholas files a claim for these items under his personal auto policy (PAP), what amount will the policy pay?

15. Nicholas's son, Grant, is playing on the trampoline with a friend in the Clements' back yard. Both of them attempt a daring back flip and land on the ground next to the trampoline. Each child sustains medical bills of $900 for emergency room x-rays. What coverage is provided under the homeowners policy for this incident?

ADDITIONAL QUESTIONS

1. List the Clements' financial strengths and weaknesses.

2. After reading the case, what additional information would you request from the Clements to complete your data-gathering phase?

3. Calculate the following financial ratios for the Clements.

$$\frac{\text{Liquid Assets}}{\text{Monthly Nondiscretionary Expenses}}$$
$$\frac{\text{Liquid Assets}}{\text{Current Debt Payments}}$$
$$\frac{\text{Net Worth}}{\text{Total Assets}}$$
$$\frac{\text{Total Debt}}{\text{Total Assets}}$$
$$\frac{\text{Total Debt}}{\text{Annual Gross Income}}$$
$$\frac{\text{Annual Housing and Debt Payments}}{\text{Annual Gross Income}}$$
$$\frac{\text{Annual Housing Costs}}{\text{Annual Gross Income}}$$
$$\frac{\text{Investment Assets}}{\text{Annual Gross Income}}$$
$$\frac{\text{Annual Savings}}{\text{Annual Gross Income}}$$

4. Comment on any of the above ratios that you think are important.

5. Describe the Clements' current financial condition.

6. If Nicholas and Whitney sell the K&B stock on January 1, 2009, for the fair market value, what are the income tax consequences?

7. Assuming that Nicholas and Whitney decide to sell the Federal Express stock on January 15, 2009, for a total price of $5,500, what are the tax consequences of such a sale?

8. How many payments have been made on the furniture purchased as of January 1, 2009?

9. Calculate the original purchase price of the furniture.

10. What is the approximate 2008 federal adjusted gross income (AGI) for the Clements?

11. How much more money must Nicholas and Whitney save to meet their emergency fund objective?

12. If the Clements sell the growth mutual fund for the Statement of Financial Position value, what will be the income tax consequences?

13. Assuming that the Clements are planning to buy their dream house seven years from now and expect housing costs to increase at the same rate as the general economic inflation rate, how much will they have to save at the end of each month to make the down payment if they plan to earn the assumed after-tax investment rate of return?

14. Do the payments of $175 a month to the trustee of the insurance trust for the children constitute a taxable gift?

15. Nicholas is considering borrowing from his 401(k), which has a loan provision. What are the requirements for such a loan?

16. Nicholas and Whitney are contemplating contributing to individual retirement accounts (IRAs) for 2008 (by April 15, 2009). What do you advise them?

17. Nicholas is trying to determine which is the better choice: the traditional IRA or the Roth IRA. Which do you recommend?

18. What is the implied growth rate of the Federal Express dividend based on the constant dividend growth model? Assume that the Clements' required rate of return is 10%.

19. In the event of Nicholas's death, who would receive the growth mutual fund? Would the monies go through probate?

20. The Clements want to start improving their financial situation in anticipation of buying their dream house. What effect would it have on their net worth and cash flows if they liquidated enough of their invested assets to pay off their credit card debt and furniture loan?

21. How much federal income tax do the Clements owe on the $510 in dividends they received in 2008? Assume that all the dividends were received from stock in domestic corporations and that the Clements owned the stock for the entire year. The ex-dividend date was October 15.

22. Kelly is dissatisfied with the divorce decree and persuades the court to issue a new order stating that, in addition to the $175 monthly trust contribution, Nicholas must pay a total of $750 per month to Kelly until Kelly remarries. The $400 per month payment will terminate when Blake reaches age 18 whether or not Kelly remarries. The $750 payment under this new order replaces the former child support payments of $500. If Kelly dies before Blake reaches the age of 18, the new order states that only $400 per month will be paid to the children until Blake reaches the age of 18, at which time all payments cease. What are the tax consequences of the new order to Kelly and Nicholas?

23. Nicholas and Whitney disclose in a meeting with you that they find woodworking relaxing. For the past five years, they have built and painted wooden Christmas lawn decorations on weekends in their backyard and have sold them to friends and family. The Clements have not been reporting income and expenses to the IRS. They incurred the following for the past five years:

Year	Income	Expenses
2004	$400	$450
2005	$375	$400
2006	$600	$500
2007	$750	$800
2008	$1,000	$600

They want to know how the income and expenses will be treated for tax purposes. What do you advise them?

3

Archie and Elaine Peyton

Today is January 1, 2009. Archie and Elaine Peyton have come to you, a financial planner, for help in developing a plan to accomplish their financial goals. From your initial meeting together, you have gathered the following information.

Personal Background and Information

Archie Peyton (Age 47)

Archie Peyton is an executive in the ABC Company, a closely held corporation. His salary is $100,000, and he expects increases of 5% per year.

Elaine Peyton (Age 50)

Elaine Peyton is Archie's administrative assistant. Her present salary is $24,000. She expects raises of 5% per year.

This is a second marriage for Elaine. Her first husband, Jerry, died five years ago. Elaine was the beneficiary of Jerry's $250,000 life insurance policy with which she created her investment portfolio.

The Peytons

Archie and Elaine have been married for three years. They do not reside in a community property state.

The Children

Elaine has two children from her first marriage, Jerry Jr., age 16, and Christopher, age 12. Archie and Elaine have one daughter, Kelsey, who is now 2 years old. All of the children live with them. The children are cared for during the day by their paternal grandmother who lives next door.

When they were first married, Archie wanted to adopt Jerry Jr. and Christopher, but the children did not agree. Since then, Archie and the two boys have been in continual conflict. As a result, Elaine expects to use her investment portfolio to pay for the boys' education, without any assistance from Archie.

Personal and Financial Objectives

1. The Peytons want to aggressively begin planning for their children's college education. They plan for each child to attend a private institution for five years beginning at age 18 with a cost of $25,000 a year per child (today's cost). The expected educational inflation rate is 6%.

2. Archie and Elaine expect to need 80% of their current pre-tax income during retirement. Elaine would like to retire at age 65 and Archie at age 62. They expect their retirement period to be 30 years, each.

3. Archie wants to review both his and Elaine's life insurance needs and have estate planning documents drafted for both of them.

4. They would like to minimize any estate tax liability.

5. Archie and Elaine plan to travel extensively during retirement.

6. They want to be free of all debt by the time they retire.

7. They want to pay off their credit card in the upcoming year.

Economic Information

▓ Inflation has averaged 4% over the last 20 years.

▓ Inflation is expected to be 3.5% in the future.

(Assumed)
Treasury Yield Curve

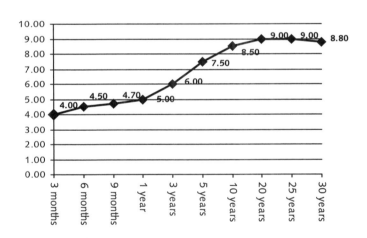

Current Yields for Treasury Securities

3 Months	6 Months	9 Months	1 Year	3 Years	5 Years	10 Years	20 Years	25 Years	30 Years
4.0%	4.5%	4.7%	5.0%	6.0%	7.5%	8.5%	9.0%	9.0%	8.8%

Current Mortgage Rates

■ 8.75% for 30-year loans

■ 8.25% for 15-year loans

Closing costs of 3% will not be included in the refinancing of the existing mortgage.

Economic Outlook—Investments

	Expected Returns (Pre-tax)	Expected Standard Deviation
Aggressive stocks	15%	15%
Growth stocks	12%	10%
S&P 500	10%	8%
Bonds	7%	3%
Insurance contracts	6%	2%
Money markets	5%	1%
T-bills	4%	1%

Insurance Information

Life Insurance

	Policy A	Policy B	Policy C	Policy D
Insured	Archie	Archie	Elaine	Elaine
Owner	Archie	Archie	Elaine	Elaine
Beneficiary	Archie's mother	Estate of Archie	Jerry Jr. & Christopher	Jerry Jr. & Christopher
Original amount	$200,000	$100,000	$48,000	$50,000
Type	Group term	30-year decreasing term	Group term	Modified premium whole life
Cash value	$0	$0	$0	$0
Annual premium	$250	$100	$60	$420
Premium payor	Employer	Archie	Employer	Elaine
Date purchased	Annually	2000	Annually	2005
Current coverage	$200,000	$75,000	$48,000	$50,000

Health Insurance

The entire family is covered under the ABC Company health plan. The Peytons currently pay $200 per month for the employer-provided indemnity plan. The deductible is $500 per person up to a maximum of three persons. There is a stop loss of $5,000 per year and an 80/20 coinsurance provision.

Disability Insurance

Archie has a personally owned disability insurance policy that covers accident and sickness and has an own occupation definition with a 180-day elimination period. The policy pays benefits of 60% of current gross income until Archie reaches age 65.

Homeowners Insurance

	HO-2 Policy
Dwelling	$150,000
Other structure	$ 15,000
Personal property*	$ 75,000
Loss of use (20% of dwelling)	$ 30,000

*There is no rider for replacement value on personal property. There is an endorsement for furs and jewelry (premium $30 annually).

Scheduled Personal Property Endorsement

This Endorsement Changes the Policy. Please Read Carefully.

For an additional premium, we cover the classes of personal property indicated by an amount of insurance. This coverage is subject to the DEFINITION, SECTION 1—CONDITIONS, SECTIONS I AND II—CONDITIONS and all provisions of this endorsement. The Section I deductible as shown on the Declarations does not apply to this coverage.

Class of Personal Property	Amount of Insurance	Premium
1. **Jewelry**, as scheduled.	$10,000	$30
2. **Furs** and garments trimmed with fur or consisting principally of fur, as scheduled.	Same as 1	
3. **Cameras**, projection machines, films, and related articles of equipment, as listed.	5,000	30
4. **Musical instruments** and related articles of equipment, as listed. You agree not to perform with these instruments for pay unless specifically provided under this policy.		
5. **Silverware**, silver-plated ware, goldware, gold-plated ware, and pewterware, but excluding pens, pencils, flasks, smoking implements, or jewelry.		
6. **Golfer's equipment** meaning golf clubs, golf clothing, and golf equipment.		
7. **Fine arts**, as scheduled. This premium is based on your statement that the property insured is located at the following address.		
8. For an additional premium, paragraph 5.b. under Perils Insured Against is deleted only for the articles marked with a double asterisk (**) in the schedule below.		
9. **Postage stamps**		
10. **Rare and current coins**		

SCHEDULE*

Article	Description	Amount of Insurance
Diamond Bracelet	12 pure 1/3k diamonds, 14k white gold setting	$3,000
Diamond Necklace	18" 14k gold chain, pure 2k diamond pendant	$7,000
T-Max 90	35 mm body	$ 500
300Z lens		$3,000
Hasenbladt	camera body + 2 lens	$1,500

THE AMOUNTS SHOWN FOR EACH ITEM IN THE SCHEDULE ARE LIMITED BY CONDITION 2. LOSS SETTLEMENT ON PAGE 3 OF THIS ENDORSEMENT

* Entries may be left blank if shown elsewhere in this policy for this coverage

HO 04 61 04 91

Automobile Insurance

PERSONAL AUTO POLICY DECLARATIONS PAGE
COVERAGES

	Auto 1	Auto 2	Semiannual Premium
Part A—Liability	100/300	100/300	$400
Part B—Medical payments	$10,000	$10,000	$100
Part C—Uninsured motorists	100/300	100/300	$150
Part D—Damage to your auto			
Collision	$500 deductible	$500 deductible	$100
Other than collision	$250 deductible	$250 deductible	$ 70
Towing and labor	$100 maximum	$100 maximum	$ 10
Total semiannual premium			$830

Investment Information

During Elaine's marriage to Jerry, an education fund was established for both Jerry Jr. and Christopher. Since Jerry died, Elaine has no longer contributed to this fund. At the present time, the fund balance is $22,747. The money has been invested at 6%, and the Peytons have the option of renewing the short-term certificate of deposit (CD) in April at an interest rate of 4%.

When Elaine received the life insurance proceeds of $250,000 from Jerry's death, she asked a broker to help her manage the money. Her broker, John, placed her funds in an investment account over which he has full discretion. John's record regarding Elaine's investment portfolio over the last five years is as follows.

	2004	2005	2006	2007	2008
Load-adjusted total return	(10.0)	?	(8.5)	12.0	3.0

Elaine did not have the information for 2005 and has been unable to obtain it from John.

Elaine considers herself to be a conservative to moderate investor and has little experience or education in the area of investments. Archie believes that he is a more moderate investor, and he has more experience with investments than Elaine.

Income Tax Information

The Peytons are in the 25% marginal tax bracket for federal income tax and 6% for state income tax.

Retirement Information

Both Elaine and Archie plan to retire when Elaine turns 65. They expect their retirement portfolio to earn a 10% pre-tax average annual return. They also expect their retirement to last 30 years. Social Security retirement benefits for Archie are expected to be $26,000 annually at age 67, while Elaine's Social Security benefit will be $9,600 annually at her age of 66 years and 8 months.

Archie has not contributed to the traditional IRA in several years.

ABC Company sponsors a profit sharing plan and a 401(k) plan. The 401(k) plan allows participants to defer up to 20% of salary with a 3% employer match when participants save 6%. The maximum dollar limit is $16,500 (2009). Neither Archie nor Elaine has ever participated in the 401(k) plan, but both have vested balances in the profit sharing plan, as follows.

	Vested Balance January 1, 2009
Archie	$80,000
Elaine	$12,000

The ABC Company's profit sharing plan allows the participant to choose between self-directing the retirement assets through the available mutual funds or having the company's fund manager manage the assets. The Peytons, not being confident in their ability to manage assets, have chosen to let the fund manager invest their assets. The 401(k) plan can only be self-directed.

ABC Company has recently established a phantom stock plan in which Archie is a participant. Archie's interest is 1% of ABC as of year-end 2008.

The investment options for the 401(k) plan are as follows.

XYZ Small Company Growth Fund

Fund objective:	The Fund seeks long-term growth of capital.
Portfolio concept:	The Fund invests primarily in common stock of small-and medium-size companies that are early in their life cycle and have the potential to become major enterprises.

XYZ Growth Fund

Fund objective:	The Fund seeks growth of capital and, secondarily, income.
Portfolio concept:	The Fund seeks to invest in equity securities (stocks) placing primary emphasis on those securities that Fund Management believes to be undervalued. The Fund may invest up to 20% in foreign securities.

XYZ Index Fund

Fund objective:	The Fund seeks to approximate the total return of the S&P 500 Composite Stock Price Index.
Portfolio concept:	The Fund invests primarily in a portfolio of equity securities (stocks) that are included in the S&P 500 Index.

XYZ Foreign Fund

Fund objective:	The Fund seeks long-term capital growth through investments in stocks and debt obligations of companies and governments outside the United States.
Portfolio concept:	The Fund generally invests in common stocks; however, it may also invest in preferred stocks and certain debt securities, rated or unrated, such as convertible bonds and bonds selling at a discount.

XYZ Balanced Fund

Fund objective:	The Fund seeks the highest total investment return consistent with prudent risk.
Portfolio concept:	The Fund has a fully managed investment policy utilizing equity, debt, and convertible securities.

XYZ Income Fund

Fund objective:	The Fund seeks a high level of income, consistent with the prudent investment of capital, through a flexible investment program emphasizing high-grade bonds.
Portfolio concept:	The Fund invests primarily in a broad range of high-grade, income-producing securities, such as corporate bonds and government securities.

XYZ Money Market Fund

Fund objective:	The Fund seeks preservation of capital, current income, and liquidity.
Portfolio concept:	The Fund is a money market mutual fund that seeks capital preservation, current income, and liquidity through investment in a portfolio of high-quality, short-term money market instruments, including securities is issued by the US government, its agencies, or instrumentalities.

The company has made the following contributions to the profit sharing plan for Archie and Elaine for each of the related years.

	Archie	Elaine
2009	None yet	None yet
2008	$15,000	$3,600
2007	$ 0	$ 0
2006	$13,605	$3,265
2005	$10,366	$2,488
2004	$ 8,954	$2,369
Balance 1/1/04	$25,000	$ 0

All contributions are made December 31 of the indicated year.

ANNUALIZED RETURNS OF RETIREMENT FUNDS

	1998	1999	2000	2001	2002	2003	2004	2005	2006	2007	2008
XYZ Small Co. Growth Fund	—	—	—	—	—	—	—	—	4.83%	41.14%	15.01%
XYZ Growth Fund	—	—	—	32.96%	0.03%	25.20%	9.97%	32.37%	1.77%	36.82%	14.50%
XYZ Index Trust	—	—	—	—	—	—	—	9.66%	1.02%	37.23%	13.25%
XYZ Foreign Fund	28.77%	24.75%	21.99%	30.53%	–3.01%	18.25%	0.10%	36.82%	0.35%	11.15%	7.08%
XYZ Balanced Fund	19.89%	4.60%	17.04%	22.98%	1.08%	24.69%	5.03%	13.71%	0.91%	32.87%	11.60%
XYZ Income Fund	14.75%	0.74%	8.91%	12.75%	8.32%	17.32%	6.74%	12.58%	–4.43%	18.54%	9.21%
XYZ Money Market Fund	4.21%	3.87%	4.01%	5.02%	5.40%	4.75%	5.00%	5.25%	6.01%	6.71%	5.20%

Gifts, Estates, Trusts, and Will Information

They do not have any estate planning documents at this time.

STATEMENT OF CASH FLOWS
Archie and Elaine Peyton
For January 1, 2008 to December 31, 2008
(Projected to be similar for 2009)

CASH INFLOWS

Salaries

Archie's		$100,000	
Elaine's		24,000	
	Total salaries	$124,000	

Investment income

ML Brokerage Account		$ 3,050	
Elaine's investment portfolio		4,771	
Savings account		618	
Elaine's education fund		1,062	
	Investment income	$ 9,501	
	Total cash inflows		$133,501

CASH OUTFLOWS

Living expenses

Food		$ 4,300	
Clothing		4,000	
Entertainment		6,500	
Utilities, cable, and phone		5,000	
Auto maintenance		1,200	
Church		2,000	
Home mortgage		14,934	
Auto loans		18,818	
Credit card		4,300	
	Total living expenses	$ 61,052	

Insurance

Health		$ 2,400	
Auto		1,660	
Life		520	
Homeowners with endorsements		950	
Disability		1,677	
	Total insurance	$ 7,207	

Taxes

Property (residence)		$ 4,452	
Federal income (withholdings)		36,840	
State income		4,000	
Payroll (FICA) (Schedule 1)		$ 9,486	
	Total taxes	54,778	

Total Cash outflows			$123,037
Discretionary cash flow			$ 10,464

Schedule 1: Payroll Taxes

Old-Age, Survivors, and Disability Insurance

Archie	$100,000 × 6.2%	=	$6,200
Elaine	$ 24,000 × 6.2%	=	$1,488
			$7,688

Medicare

Archie	$100,000 × 1.45%	=	$1,450
Elaine	$ 24,000 × 1.45%	=	$ 348
			$1,798
Total			**$9,486**

2009 Tax Limits		
	Income	Tax Rate
OASDI	$106,800	6.2%
Medicare	Unlimited	1.45%

STATEMENT OF NET WORTH
Archie and Elaine Peyton
As of January 1, 2009

	Assets[1]			Liabilities[2] and Net Worth	
	Liquid assets			**Short-term liabilities**	
JT	Checking[3]	$ 7,500	W	Credit cards	$ 4,300
JT	Savings[4]	15,450			
	Total liquid assets	$ 22,950		**Long-term liabilities**	
	Invested assets		JT	Home mortgage	$144,981
H	First Mutual Growth Fund[5]	$ 7,950	H/W	Auto loans	40,069
H	ML Brokerage Account[6]	100,000	H	Margin loan[7]	7,500
W	Elaine's investment portfolio	210,000		**Total long-term**	$192,550
W	Elaine's education fund	22,747			
H	Archie's profit sharing plan	80,000		**Total liabilities**	$196,850
W	Elaine's profit sharing plan	12,000			
H	Archie's individual retirement account (IRA)[8]	9,000			
	Total invested assets	$441,697			
	Use assets				
JT	Home	$185,000		**Net worth**	$552,797
H	Truck	32,000			
W	Car	21,000			
H	Boat	10,000			
W	Furs and jewelry	10,000			
JT	Furniture and household	27,000			
	Total use assets	$285,000		**Total liabilities**	
	Total assets	$749,647		**and net worth**	$749,647

Notes to financial statements

[1]All assets are stated at fair market value.

[2]Liabilities are stated at principal only.

[3]The checking account is a noninterest-bearing account.

[4]The savings account earns 4% per year.

[5]See detail of fund.

[6]ML Brokerage Account is stated at gross value, which does not include margin loan of $7,500.

[7]Margin loan is for ML Brokerage Account. Interest rate is currently 8%.

[8]Archie's IRA is currently invested in CDs at a local bank.

Title designations

H = Husband

W = Wife

JT = Joint tenancy

Information Regarding Assets and Liabilities

Investment Income

ML Brokerage Account	
Money market	$ 300
Bonds	3,350
Margin interest	(600)
	$3,050
Elaine's investment portfolio	
Bonds	$1,300
Stocks	3,471
	$4,771
Savings account	$ 618
Elaine's education fund	$1,062
TOTAL	**$9,501**

House

Principal residence	January 1, 2006 (purchase)
Fair market value (current)	$185,000
Original loan	$148,000
Term	30 years
Interest rate	9.5%
Payment	$1,244.46
Remaining mortgage	$144,981
Remaining term	27 years

Boat

The boat is a 90-horsepower fishing boat that was originally bought for $10,000 and is owned outright.

Automobiles

	Archie's 2007 Truck	Elaine's 2006 Car
Purchase price	$40,000	$35,000
Down payment	$0	$10,000
Term	48 months	48 months
Interest rate	7%	8%
Monthly payment	$957.85	$610.32
Payments remaining	33	20
Balance	$28,677.07	$11,392.23

ML Brokerage Account

Account Name: Archie Peyton
Account Number: AB100402

Balances

Money Market	Price/ Share	Shares	Current Yield	Fair Market Value
Money market	$ 1.00	6,667.00	4.5%	$6,667.00

Bonds	Maturity	Coupon	Cost Basis	Fair Market Value
$10,000 US Treasury note	5	7.5%	$10,351.18	$10,000.00
$15,000 US Treasury bond	25	6.0%	13,138.64	10,579.83
$50,000 US Treasury bond	30	0.0%	4,093.40	3,982.02
$20,000 Davidson debenture	20	8.5%	17,455.93	16,288.44
			$45,039.15	$40,850.29

Stocks	Price/share	Shares	Cost Basis	Fair Market Value
Stock 1*	$ 5.20	2,000	$10,000	$10,400
Stock 2*	$ 4.85	1,500	6,750	7,275
Stock 3*	$26.00	500	11,250	13,000
			$28,000	$30,675

* These stocks do not currently pay dividends.

Mutual Funds	Price/share	Shares	Cost Basis	Fair Market Value
Emerging growth fund	$21.00	500	$12,250	$10,500
Balanced fund	$18.00	425	8,925	7,650
Municipal bond fund	$12.00	250	3,500	3,000
			$24,675	$21,150

Note: All distributions from these funds are reinvested.

Options	Number of Options Contracts	Option Premium	Exercise Price	Option Expiration	Fair Market Value
Stock 2 call options	5	$3.00	$ 5.50	July 09	$486.37
Stock 3 put options	5	$5.00	$24.00	March 09	$171.34
MARGIN BALANCE					
OUTSTANDING BALANCE					$7,500
NET ACCOUNT VALUE					**$92,500**
TOTAL ACCOUNT VALUE					**$100,000**

First Mutual Growth Fund

Account Name: Archie Peyton
Account Number: AB100357

Transaction	Date	Amount	Price/ Share	Shares	Total Shares	Total Value
Buy	04/01/07	$ 2,500	$25.00	100	100	$ 2,500
Buy	08/01/07	$ 4,000	$20.00	200	300	$ 6,000
Reinvest dividend	12/01/07	$ 500	$12.50	40	340	$ 4,250
Buy	02/01/08	$ 3,000	$15.00	200	540	$ 8,100
Buy	04/01/08	$ 2,000	$20.00	100	640	$12,800
Buy	06/01/08	$ 1,500	$25.00	60	700	$17,500
Sell	12/01/08	$11,880	$27.00	(440)	260	$ 7,020
Reinvest dividend	12/01/08	$ 1,080	$27.00	40	300	$ 8,100
BALANCE	12/31/08	—	$26.50	—	300	$ 7,950

Note: All income from this fund is reinvested.

Elaine's Investment Portfolio

Bonds

Bonds	Term	Duration	Current Fair Market Value
$10,000 US Treasury bonds	10	7.12 years	$10,000
$5,000 US Treasury bonds	20	9.95 years	$ 5,000
		Total value of bonds	$15,000

Stocks

Shares	Stock	$\bar{X}$	Beta	σ	R^2	P/E Ratio	Dividend Yield	Basis	Fair Market Value
1,000	Stock A	6%	0.65	11%	75%	13.0	3.0%	$30,000	$ 38,000
575	Stock B	11%	0.75	9%	65%	14.0	3.7%	$45,000	$ 46,000
200	Stock C	7%	0.65	10%	30%	15.1	3.7%	$20,000	$ 17,000
500	Stock D	3%	0.70	8%	45%	25.2	0.0%	$11,000	$ 8,500
1,000	Stock E	25%	0.95	15%	70%	14.4	0.0%	$20,000	$ 18,000
1,250	Stock F	22%	1.10	18%	20%	11.1	0.0%	$23,000	$ 25,000
							Total value of stocks		$152,500

Mutual Funds

Shares	Mutual Fund	Style	$\overline{X}$	Alpha	Beta	σ	R^2	Front-End Load	Expense Ratio	Basis	Fair Market Value
210	Fund A	MG	14%	3%	1.1	12%	57%	4.5%	.71%	$ 2,500	$ 2,625
300	Fund B	LG	11.5%	.5%	0.94	8%	81%	4.5%	1.0%	$ 5,000	$ 5,100
443	Fund C	MV	6%	(4%)	0.65	8%	42%	4.5%	2.25%	$10,000	$11,075
1,000	Fund D	MG	−6%	(10%)	0.70	20%	4%	4%	1.85%	$ 8,000	$ 7,500
320	Fund E	LG	4%	(3%)	1.1	5%	60%	5%	1.75%	$ 9,500	$ 8,000
410	Fund F	LG	7%	(2.5%)	0.9	3%	78%	3%	1.5%	$10,000	$ 8,200
									Total value of mutual funds		$42,500

Note: All income distributions from the mutual funds is reinvested.

TOTAL PORTFOLIO VALUE   **$210,000**

Key	
$\overline{X}$	5-year average return
σ	Standard deviation
R^2	Coefficient of determination
L	Large
M	Medium
G	Growth
V	Value

QUESTIONS

1. As of December 1, 2008, what is the internal rate of return for the First Mutual Growth Fund since the Peytons' first purchase on April 1, 2007?

2. How does a change in the price of the below-listed stocks affect the profit/loss of the related option? Each change (A–D) is independent.

ML Brokerage Account

	Stock	Price Changes To
Change A	Stock 2	$ 6.00
Change B	Stock 2	$ 4.00
Change C	Stock 3	$29.00
Change D	Stock 3	$20.00

3. Calculate the geometric average return since inception for each of the funds in the ABC Company retirement plan.

4. Determine the Sharpe and Treynor ratios for each mutual fund in Elaine's investment portfolio. Assume a risk-free rate equal to the one-year T-bill rate.

5. Rank each of the funds in Elaine's investment portfolio by the Sharpe and Treynor ratios. Comment on the results and the meaning of the numbers.

6. What is the coupon rate for each of the two bonds in Elaine's portfolio?

7. Comment on the allocation of mutual funds in Elaine's portfolio.

8. Comment on Elaine's broker's choice of mutual funds in her portfolio.

9. How have Archie and Elaine's ABC Company profit sharing plan investments performed since January 1, 2004?

10. a. Comment on the Peytons' decision to let ABC Company's money manager have control over their retirement assets. What should they do now?
    b. If the Peytons had earned an average return equal to that of the XYZ Balanced Fund on their ABC profit sharing plan account, how much better off would they be?

11. What is the expected value of the following bonds in the ML Brokerage Account if all interest rates decrease by 1%? Assume interest is paid semiannually.
    - $10,000 US Treasury note
    - $15,000 US Treasury bond
    - $50,000 US Treasury bond

12. Is the current yield curve consistent with the Liquidity Premium Theory? Why or why not?

13. Is the current yield curve consistent with the Market Segmentation Theory? Why or why not?

14. What was the rate of return on Elaine's investment portfolio in 2005?

15. If the interest rates for all maturities increase by 1.0%, what will be the approximate value of the bonds in Elaine's investment portfolio?

16. What is the total percentage and dollar investment gain related to Stock 2 that Archie would realize if the price of Stock 2 increases to $7.50 (in Brokerage Account)?

17. Has Archie done an effective job of immunizing Stock 3 from downside risk? Why or why not?

18. Explain the coefficient of determination and its purpose.

19. Elaine has heard the terms "unsystematic risk" and "diversification" several times and would like you to explain what these terms mean for an investor.

20. What is the weighted duration for the bond portfolio portion of Elaine's investment portfolio?

21. What is the holding period return (HPR) for Elaine's stock portfolio portion held in her investment portfolio?

22. What is the weighted beta of Elaine's mutual funds located in her investment portfolio?

ADDITIONAL QUESTIONS

1. List the Peytons' financial strengths and weaknesses.

2. After reading the case, what additional information would you request from the Peytons to complete your data-gathering phase?

3. Calculate the following financial ratios for the Peytons.

$\dfrac{\text{Liquid Assets}}{\text{Monthly Expenses}}$
$\dfrac{\text{Liquid Assets}}{\text{Current Monthly Debt Payments}}$
$\dfrac{\text{Net Worth}}{\text{Total Assets}}$
$\dfrac{\text{Total Debt}}{\text{Total Assets}}$
$\dfrac{\text{Total Debt}}{\text{Annual Total Income*}}$
$\dfrac{\text{Housing (PITI)**}}{\text{Monthly Gross Income}}$
$\dfrac{\text{Housing and Monthly Debt Payments}}{\text{Monthly Gross Income}}$
$\dfrac{\text{Investment Assets}}{\text{Annual Gross Income*}}$
* Annual total income is the same as annual gross income. ** PITI: principal, interest, taxes, and insurance.

4. Comment on any of the above ratios that you think are important.

5. What is the taxable gain on the sale of the 440 shares of First Mutual Growth Fund (December 1, 2008), and how will it be classified for income tax purposes? Assume that the tax basis in the shares sold is determined by using a first in, first out (FIFO) method.

6. What are other methods of determining the tax basis of the 440 shares of First Mutual Growth Fund sold on December 1, 2008?

7. As of January 1, 2009, what is the average cost basis per share for the shares remaining of First Mutual Growth Fund, assuming the FIFO method was used for determining the sale of the 440 shares?

8. Under the loss of use coverage, for an HO-2 policy, what is usually provided?

9. Elaine has decided that the educational fund and her investment account will be used for funding the cost of college for the boys. Elaine wants to set aside enough of these assets to fund their education with the remainder being used to fund Kelsey's college education. Ignoring the transaction costs of selling the current assets, how much does she need to set aside for the boys' college education if she wants to invest in an even mix of 5-year and 10-year Treasury bonds? Assume all taxes will be paid out of current expenditures.

10. Elaine wants to know how much she and Archie need to contribute over the next 15 years for Kelsey's education. Their first contribution will be in one year, and they will invest in a portfolio that is split equally between the S&P 500 and 5-year Treasury bonds. This allocation will be maintained by rebalancing every six months. Assume the tax on earnings will be paid from their salary and not from the education fund.

11. a. If Archie were to become disabled on May 30, 2009, when would he collect benefits and how much would he receive in benefits during 2009?
    b. What are the tax consequences of receiving disability benefits?

12. How much of their current gross income, in dollars and percentages, are the Peytons currently saving toward their retirement goal?

13. Ignoring Social Security benefits, how much money should the Peytons have accumulated using a capital needs analysis and the following approaches?

    a. The annuity approach.

    b. The capital preservation approach.

    c. The purchasing power preservation approach.

14. What do the Peytons need to do now to meet their retirement income goal? The Peytons do not want to consider Social Security benefits in their retirement planning.

15. Will the Peytons benefit from itemizing deductions on their 2008 income tax return? If so, what type of interest deductions can they take?

16. Discuss the Peytons' current life insurance situation.

17. Calculate Archie's gross estate were he to die today.

18. What are the current estate planning deficiencies?

19. Do they qualify for refinancing their home mortgage?

20. Calculate the payments and savings from the alternative ways to refinance.

21. What would their payments be if the Peytons kept their current mortgage loan and amortized it over the remaining 15 years?

22. What is a phantom stock plan?

23. Assuming Archie bought the balanced fund in 2005, what would be the income tax consequence for him by selling all the shares in 2008 using the average cost basis method? What is his loss/gain per share on the sale? What is his total loss/gain on the sale of the fund?

24. Elaine Peyton was recently in a car accident with the Smith family, in which she was found to be at fault, and has provided her automobile insurance company with the following bills:

   $ 12,000 damage to the Smiths' vehicle—actual cash value

   $ 7,500 damage to Elaine's vehicle—actual cash value

   $ 15,000 medical bills for Elaine

   $125,000 medical bills for the Smiths (Mr. Smith: $75,000; Mrs. Smith: $50,000)

   Based on the information provided, what would be the total amount of coverage provided by the Peytons' automobile policy?

25. Discuss the Peytons' homeowners and personal property coverage, including the boat.

Clara Morrish

Today is January 1, 2009. Clara Morrish has come to you, a financial planner, for help in developing a plan to accomplish her financial goals. From your initial meeting together, you have gathered the following information.

Personal Background and Information

Clara Morrish (Age 69)

Clara is a retired homemaker. She is a recent widow. Clara's 70th birthday will be April 1, 2009.

Tim Morrish (deceased)

Clara was married to Tim Morrish, who died November 1, 2008, at the age of 69, after a brief battle with cancer. His date of birth was June 1, 1939.

Tim's estate is in probate. Tim was employed 45 years as a supervisor at ABC Co., Inc. (ABC) before retiring at age 65.

The Morrishes

They were married 50 years. Clara's health is fair.

The Morrishes' Children

Clara has two children from her marriage to Tim: George (age 50) and Vince (age 49). George and Vince are each married, healthy, employed, and self-sufficient.

The Morrishes' Grandchildren

George and his wife, Kathy, have one daughter, Sarah (age 18). Sarah is currently a senior in high school and will be a freshman at a university in September. The cost of tuition for the university is currently $20,000. Clara would like to pay Sarah's tuition for this year. As a graduation gift, Clara is paying for Sarah's trip to Europe this summer. The cost of this trip is $3,000.

Vince and his wife, Laena, have one son, Kirby (age 17). Kirby is a junior in high school. Kirby is in need of orthodontic work that will cost $6,000. Clara would like to pay for Kirby's orthodontic work. Clara is also considering gifting stock worth $9,000 to Kirby.

Personal and Financial Objectives

1. Clara wants to have sufficient income at retirement ($30,000 per year in today's dollars including Social Security benefits).

2. Clara will consider acquiring a smaller residence.

3. Clara wants to explore long-term nursing care alternatives (annual cost in today's dollars $40,000).

4. Clara wants to donate to the American Cancer Society.

5. Clara wants to provide for her children and grandchildren.

6. Clara wants to pay Sarah's university tuition ($20,000).

7. Clara wants to gift stock to Kirby ($9,000).

8. Clara wants to pay for Kirby's orthodontic work ($6,000).

9. Clara wants to send Sarah to Europe ($3,000).

Economic Information

■ Inflation is expected to be 4% annually.

■ There is no state income tax.

■ Stocks are expected to grow at 9.5%.

■ Bank lending rates are as follows: 6.5% for a 15-year mortgage, 7.5% for a 30-year mortgage, and 10.0% for a secured personal loan.

Life Expectancies from Table III, Uniform Lifetime

Age	Life Expectancy Factor
70	27.4
71	26.5
72	25.6

Insurance Information

Life Insurance
Irrevocable Life Insurance Trust (ILIT)

Tim created an ILIT 10 years ago. The only asset in the trust is a permanent life insurance policy with a face value of $200,000. The income beneficiary of the ILIT is Clara. She is also the trustee and has a general power of appointment over the trust assets. The remainder beneficiaries are the grandchildren. Clara currently receives an annual income of $10,000 based on a return on the inherited assets of 5%.

Health Insurance

Tim and Clara were both covered under Medicare Part A and B until the time of his death. Clara is still covered under Medicare Part A and B.

Investment Information

Clara's investment risk tolerance is low.

Income Tax Information

The Morrishes filed as married filing jointly for 2007. Clara and Tim have always lived in a community property state.

Clara has been making and selling jewelry for six years with some success. Since Tim's death last year, she has devoted more time to her craft and enjoys it tremendously. Her grandson, Kirby, created a Website for her last year and Clara is amazed at the sales results. While she had been traveling to jewelry shows for most of her sales, the online sales this year have eliminated the need to travel. Because Clara will be itemizing her deductions this year, she believes she can report her income and expenses on Schedule C. Her gross sales from the jewelry business this year are $19,500. Her expenses are:

Cost of goods sold	$12,900
Supplies	$ 500
Web-related costs	$ 600
Web advertising	$ 200
Postage/delivery costs	$ 1,200

She has kept detailed records from the beginning and can track her profit and loss from each year. In Year 1 she had a loss of $2,000; Year 2 was a loss of $1,000; Year 3 showed a profit of $3,000; Year 4 had another loss of only $500; Year 5 was a good year with a profit of $6,000.

Retirement Information

Tim had a pension sponsored by ABC with Clara designated as the beneficiary. The pension has a present value of $150,000 as of January 1, 2009. As the beneficiary, Clara chose to receive a life annuity from the pension. The life annuity is projected to pay $12,307 per year for 17.8 years.

Clara currently has an individual retirement account (IRA) with Tim as the named beneficiary. Clara is the named beneficiary on Tim's IRA. They had both decided to defer IRA withdrawals until they are mandatory after age 70½. Clara has no plans to change this since Tim's death. She will rollover Tim's IRA into an inherited IRA in her name as the sole beneficiary early in 2009. Both Tim and Clara began receiving Social Security benefits on their respective 65th birthdays. Tim's benefit for 2009 would have been $1,200 per month, and Clara's benefit for 2009 was estimated to be $600 per month.

Gifts, Estates, Trusts, and Will Information

Tim's will left all probate assets to Clara. The grandchildren are named as contingent beneficiaries (equally). Clara does not have a will.

STATEMENT OF FINANCIAL POSITION
Tim (deceased) and Clara Morrish
As of January 1, 2009

	Assets[1]			Liabilities and Net Worth		
	Cash and equivalents			**Liabilities[2]**		
CP	Cash	$ 25,000		Credit cards[3]		$ 20,000
CP	Savings account	20,000				
	Total cash and equivalents	$ 45,000				
	Invested assets					
H	Stocks[6]	$ 20,000		*Total liabilities*		$ 20,000
CP	IRA - Clara's	40,000				
CP	IRA - Tim's	50,000				
CP	Pension[7]	150,000		Net worth		$ 980,000
	Total invested assets	$ 260,000				
	Personal use assets					
CP	Primary Residence[4]	$ 400,000				
W	Vacation Home[5]	200,000				
CP	Auto	18,000				
CP	Furniture and personal property	77,000				
	Total use assets	$ 695,000				
	Total assets	$1,000,000		**Total liabilities and net worth**		$1,000,000

Notes to financial statements
[1]Assets are stated at fair market value.
[2]Liabilities are stated at principal only as of January 1, 2009, before January payments. All liabilities are community property.
[3]Interest rate 18.3%.
[4]The primary residence was originally purchased for $110,000. There have been no additions or upgrades.
[5]The vacation home was inherited by Clara from her mother. Adjusted taxable basis is $125,000.

[6]Inherited from a sibling.

[7]Present value of Tim's pension

Other notes to financial statements
The $200,000 ILIT is the separate property of Tim. The income beneficiary is Clara. Remainder beneficiaries are the grandchildren. Clara has general power of appointment over trust assets. The trustee has power to invade for the health, education, maintenance, or support (HEMS) for the grandchildren. The ILIT is not listed on the Statement of Financial Position.

Title designations:
H - Husband
W - Wife
CP - Community property

Information Regarding Assets and Liabilities

Primary Residence

- Purchased April 1, 1972
- Market value $400,000 as of November 1, 2008, and January 1, 2009
- Original purchase price $110,000

Vacation Home

- This home is owned by Clara (fee simple).
- It was inherited from her mother who paid $75,000 for the home. The fair market value at the date of transfer to Clara was $125,000 in July 1991.
- The current fair market value is $200,000.
- The vacation home is located in a noncommunity property state. All payments for repairs and maintenance have been made by using community property assets.

QUESTIONS

1. What is Clara's federal income tax filing status for the years 2008, 2009, 2010, and 2011?

2. On November 1, 2009, Clara decides to sell her personal residence for the fair market value as of January 1, 2009. What will be her tax consequences? Disregard the vacation home.

3. What amount, if any, of Clara's pension annuity will be included in her gross income?

4. How should Clara report her jewelry business?

5. Ten years ago, Tim and Clara gave their grandchildren stock in a US domestic corporation that is publicly traded. The earnings have been steady but unremarkable over the years, returning dividends of about $1,200 for each grandchild last year. Because of an important advance in technology in the last year, the company is growing rapidly and in 2009 will pay about $2,100 in qualified dividends to each child. What are the kiddie tax implications of the dividends on the income of the grandchildren in 2009? To their parents (assume a marginal tax rate of 35%)? To Clara?

6. Rather than let the vacation home sit unused during Tim's last illness, it was rented to vacationers for 180 days in 2008. However, Clara used her vacation home for the last 40 days of the year after Tim's death in 2008. The only expenses for the home were utilities, taxes, and maintenance. How much of these expenses may she deduct? Where does she report the income and expenses on her tax return in 2008?

7. How much of Tim's IRA must Clara include in taxable income in 2008?

8. How much of Clara's Social Security is taxable in 2009?

9. What is Clara's taxable income in 2009?

10. Assume that in 2010 Clara decides to sell the stock she inherited from Tim that now has a fair market value of $24,000. She directs the broker to make the check payable to her sons, George and Vince, because she does not need the extra income from the sale. What are the tax consequences to Clara, George, and Vince as a result of this stock sale in the year of the sale?

11. A thief entered Clara's home while she was on vacation and stole an antique gun that had been one of Tim's treasures that he had purchased for $3,500. Unfortunately, while Clara had the gun appraised after Tim's death, she did not specifically insure it and only recovered $200 for the gun that had been valued at $4,500. How much may Clara claim as a casualty loss on her tax return this year?

12. Clara's best friend, Marlene, who is 67 and legally blind, is in poor health and has only a meager Social Security income of $6,250 annually. Clara invited her to live with her beginning January 1, 2009, and is providing more than 50% of her total support. How will this affect Clara's filing status and standard deduction in 2009?

13. Sarah, Clara's granddaughter, has a qualified tuition plan (QTP) currently valued at $195,000. Contributions from various family members were $145,000 over the years. Sarah has the following expenses for her first year at the university:

Tuition	$20,000
Room and board	$ 4,000
University fees	$ 900
Books for classes	$ 600
Laptop required by the university	$ 2,500
Auto to use on campus	$11,000
Total 1st year expense	$39,000

If Sarah pays for all of her expenses using a distribution from her qualified tuition plan, what effect does it have on her gross income?

14. On April 2, 2009, Clara received a refund of $4,800 from the hospital where Tim died. She had paid the hospital $5,600 late in the prior year for the medical bill and planned to add the expense to the rest of the unreimbursed medical expenses from Tim's death. Her son, Vince, told her to allow the estate to reimburse her when she paid the bill because the estate could deduct the expense from the gross estate, but Clara chose to forego reimbursement. Faced with the check from the hospital, Clara fears she may have made a mistake in how she handled the expense. She consults her financial planner about the $4,800 refund. Neither the 2008 income tax return nor the Form 706 for Tim's estate have been filed. How should the financial planner advise Clara?

15. George and Kathy vacationed in Guatemala in 2008 and after a visit to a local orphanage, decided to adopt a three-year-old little boy. George and Kathy felt their annual AGI of $225,000 could adequately provide for another child and that their time and cost would be greatly rewarded. Sarah is excited about her new little brother and looks forward to his arrival in the US. In February 2009, Marcus came to live with the family and his adoption became final in August 2009. The couple incurred qualified adoption costs in 2008 of $9,000 and a further $7,500 in 2009. How much of an adoption credit can the couple use on their income tax return in 2009? Assume they file MFJ.

16. Clara is considering selling the vacation home she inherited from her mother. Her mother paid $75,000 for the home 20 years before she died and Clara inherited it. If Clara sells it today for its full fair market value of $200,000, how much would her taxable gain be on the sale of the house?

17. Assume a forest fire destroyed Clara's mountain vacation retreat in May 2009. Clara's basis in the property is $100,000. The insurance company paid Clara $226,000 in July 2009 to rebuild. Clara decided not to rebuild in such a remote area and bought a vacation home near a lake in November 2011 for $220,000. How should Clara treat the gain, if any, on this involuntary conversion?

ADDITIONAL QUESTIONS

1. List Clara's financial strengths and weaknesses.

2. After reading the case, what additional information would you request from Clara to complete your data-gathering phase?

3. Calculate the following financial ratios for Clara.

    $$\frac{\text{Net Worth}}{\text{Total Assets}}$$

    $$\frac{\text{Total Debt}}{\text{Total Assets}}$$

    $$\frac{\text{Investment Assets}}{\text{Total Assets}}$$

4. Comment on any of the above ratios that you think are important.

5. What are Clara's options with regard to Tim's IRA?

6. Clara plans to delay the initial distribution from her IRA account until April 1, 2010. How much will she have to distribute, at a minimum, in the year 2010, assuming she uses the MDIB table and the IRA has the following account balances? (For the purposes of this question, disregard the Worker, Retiree, and Employer Recovery Act of 2008.)

	2008 (Year-End)	2009 (Year-End)	2010 (Year-End)
IRA account balance	$40,000	$50,000	$60,000

7. Calculate Clara's probate estate as of today, assuming the pension plan is left by Clara to George and Vince.

8. Calculate Clara's gross estate as of today, assuming the pension plan is left by Clara to George and Vince.

9. Which postmortem devices should Clara seriously consider with regard to Tim's estate?

10. What effect does the use of community assets to pay for repairs on the vacation home property have on the titling of the vacation home at Tim's death?

11. Clara is considering establishing a charitable trust for the American Cancer Society but wants the grandchildren to receive income from the property for a 20-year period. Which devices would be appropriate to meet Clara's objective?

12. If Clara instead exercised her right to take a lump-sum cash distribution from Tim's pension plan, how much money would she actually receive from the plan?

13. For which Social Security benefits does Clara currently qualify?

14. What happens to Clara's IRA upon her death, assuming she makes no changes to the account?

15. How could Clara benefit each grandchild equally without incurring any transfer taxes or using her applicable exclusion amount?

16. At her death, Clara wants to maximize her benefit to the American Cancer Society and, at the same time, maximize benefits to her children and grandchildren. Which assets would be best left to the American Cancer Society?

17. Assuming that Clara has taken instead a lump-sum distribution from Tim's pension plan, what combination of investments is appropriate for Clara?

18. How much will Clara's monthly Social Security benefit be in 2009?

19. Clara is enrolled in Medicare Part B. Which benefits are covered under Medicare Part B?

20. Clara has a Medicare Part B policy but is still concerned about the deductibles and co-payment requirements. She is considering either purchasing a Medigap policy or joining a Medicare health maintenance organization (HMO). What are the advantages of an HMO over a Medigap policy in Clara's situation?

21. Clara is worried that she will need long-term custodial care because although her mother lived at home until age 95, she needed assistance in bathing, dressing, and toileting once she became 75 years old. Clara is worried that there will be no family member around to care for her. What insurance would provide Clara with such continued assistance in her home?

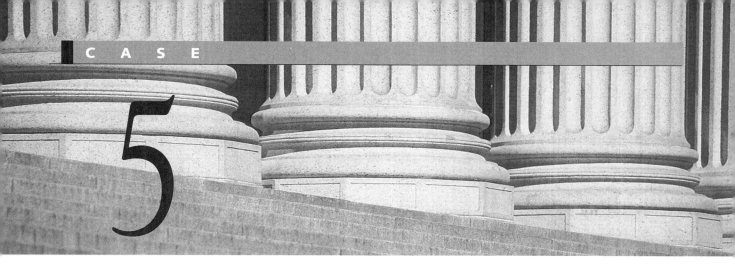

5

Michael and
Michelle Williams

Michael and Michelle Williams believe they have a solid financial future; however, they are concerned about actions they need to take to ensure college educations for two of their children and a secure future for a third child with special needs. They have come to you for assistance in determining how they can achieve these goals. Today is January 1, 2009.

Personal Background and Information

Michael Williams (Age 35)

Michael is a doctor who specializes in internal medicine. He is an employee of Lakeside Hospital. The salary that Michael earns compensates him for patients seen at both the hospital and the Lakeside-owned clinic. Michael is starting his sixth year of practice. He has been discouraged lately with the medical economic environment. Given the proliferation of managed care, he sees only a limited ability to increase his salary in the future and is concerned that his salary increases are not likely to exceed inflation.

Michelle Williams (Age 35)

Michelle grew up in a middle class family and lost both of her parents to cancer in their early 50s. Michelle is a nurse but has not worked in her profession since her children were born. Michelle is fascinated with all things technological. She is a seller on an online auction site. Michelle has an uncanny sense for shopping for unique items that she buys, adds a markup, and resells. She marks up an item 100%, does not sell the item for less than its marked-up price, and charges the online buyer for all related shipping costs. In 2009, she has changed the dynamic of her business and expects to generate up to $90,000 net income from the business this year.

Children

Michelle and Michael have three children: Beau (age 7), Lizabeth (age 5), and Madison (age 2). Madison has Down syndrome.

Michael's Family

Michael is an only child and has been his parents' pride and joy. Michael's parents (Frank and Isabelle) are first-generation immigrants from England. They immigrated before Michael was born and operate a small neighborhood deli. Michael and Michelle met at the deli when Michelle worked there during her college years. The ebb and flow of community life through the deli still fascinates Michelle, and she often visits Michael's parents there. The elder Williamses own the building (fair market value, $150,000) that houses the deli. The neighborhood has seen needed renovations in recent years, and the future outlook for continued renewal is good. The deli enjoys a steady stream of loyal customers and has generated moderate wealth for Michael's parents. They are both 60 years old and are in fair health. Frank and Isabelle have no family in this country except for Michael. As they approach retirement, their primary concerns are the high costs of long-term residential and medical care for the elderly.

Michelle's Family

Michelle's parents are both deceased. Michelle is close to her only sibling, Joan (age 40). Joan is unmarried and has no children. Joan is particularly close to the Williamses' children. In the past, Joan has mentioned to Michelle that she would consider assisting with the educational and maintenance needs of the children. Joan has given up her job as a business education teacher to be a full-time author of financial self-help books and works out of her home. To date she has enjoyed tremendous success and has raised her annual income from $35,000 a year to $100,000.

Personal and Financial Objectives

1. The Williamses want to provide Beau and Lizabeth with up to $25,000 (today's dollars) per year for four years of college education. The children will be on their own for the costs of any graduate work.

2. They want to assist Michael's parents in their retirement years, as needed.

3. They want to be free of mortgage indebtedness by the time Michael is 55 years old.

4. They want to design a retirement plan that will provide an income to replace 70% of Michael's preretirement income.

5. They want to make necessary arrangements for Madison so that she will be cared for throughout her adult life.

6. They want to maintain an adequate emergency fund of six months' living expenses.

7. They want to prepare proper wills and an estate plan.

Economic Information

- They expect inflation to average 3%.

- They expect an educational consumer price index (CPI) of 5%.

- They expect Michael's salary to increase 3% annually.

- Rates are 7% for a 15-year fixed mortgage and 7.5% for a 30-year fixed mortgage.

- They are in a 28% federal income tax bracket and a 6% state income tax bracket.

Any refinancing will incur 3% of the mortgage as a closing cost which will not be financed.

Insurance Information

Health Insurance

Health insurance is provided for the entire immediate family through Lakeside Hospital. Michael is staunchly opposed to health maintenance organizations (HMOs), as he has seen firsthand how quality of care can suffer under these contracts. Lakeside Hospital's health insurance is through a preferred provider organization (PPO). The contract has a family deductible of $500 per year. If preferred contract physicians are used, the contract is an 80/20 major medical coinsurance plan. The family annual stop-loss limit is $2,000. There is no prescription drug, eye, or dental coverage included in the plan. The plan has unlimited lifetime benefits.

Life Insurance

Michael has elected $50,000 group term life insurance through the hospital. The hospital pays the premium as a benefit to Michael. Michelle has maintained a $10,000 whole life insurance policy her parents purchased for her as a child. The cash value of the whole life policy is $6,000 and policy is paid up.

Disability Insurance

The hospital does not provide disability insurance for its employed physicians. Michael has purchased a policy through the American Medical Association. The policy provides own-occupation coverage for disability resulting from either sickness or accident, pays a benefit of 60% of gross pay after an elimination period of 180 days, covers a term of 60 months with residual benefits, and is guaranteed renewable.

Malpractice Insurance

The hospital provides Michael with malpractice insurance and pays the premium. The policy covers Michael's work at both the hospital and in the clinical practice.

Homeowners Insurance

The Williamses currently have an HO-3 policy with a replacement value on contents endorsement. The policy covers all risk and replacement value. The deductible is $250 with a premium of $2,000 per year.

Automobile Insurance

Michael and Michelle have full coverage on both cars, including:

- $100,000 bodily injury for one person
- $300,000 bodily injury for all persons
- $50,000 property damage
- $100,000 uninsured motorist
- $10,000 medical payments

Deductibles are:

- $500 comprehensive
- $1,000 collision

Investment Information (Assumptions)

	Expected Return	Beta
Aggressive stocks	13.5%	1.7
Growth stocks	10%	1.2
S&P 500	9%	1.0
Value stocks	8.5%	0.9
Bonds (corporate)	6.5%	0.6
Money market (bank)	1.75%	0.2

The Williamses consider themselves to be moderate risk-taking investors.

Retirement Information

Michael and Michelle would like to retire on or before age 67. They both expect to live to age 92. They would like to have a standard of living equal to 70% of their preretirement income. They do not want to rely on Social Security benefits in planning for their retirement.

Last year Michael began participating in a 401(k) plan available through Lakeside Hospital. Under the plan, the hospital matches $.50 for every dollar contributed, up to 6% of his salary. The plan allows for deferrals up to a maximum of 7% of salary.

Gifts, Estates, Trusts, and Will Information

Neither Michael nor Michelle has a will. They realize the importance of having a will; however, Michael's schedule seems to preclude any time for finalizing one. They are most concerned about guardian care for Madison, while at the same time minimizing as much estate tax as possible.

STATEMENT OF CASH FLOWS
Michael and Michelle Williams
For the Year Ended December 31, 2008

CASH INFLOWS

Salary—Michael	$170,000	
Gift from Michael's parents	20,000	
Michelle's self-employment income	4,000	
Interest	900	
Total inflows		**$194,900**

CASH OUTFLOWS

401(k) savings	$ 11,900	
Mortgage payment	20,700	
Property taxes (residence)	1,800	
FICA and self-employment tax	9,021	
Federal income tax withholding	68,000	
State income tax withholding	6,734	
Utilities	3,980	
Disability insurance premium	900	
Homeowners insurance	2,000	
Auto notes	10,789	
Auto expense and maintenance	1,200	
Auto insurance	2,400	
Housekeeping service	2,400	
Educational loan repayment	6,915	
Clothing and dry cleaning	5,600	
Food	5,750	
Entertainment	3,970	
Miscellaneous	5,998	
Total outflows		**$170,057**
Discretionary cash flow		**$ 24,843**

STATEMENT OF FINANCIAL POSITION
Michael and Michelle Williams
January 1, 2009

Assets[1]			Liabilities and Net Worth[2]	
Cash/cash equivalents			**Current liabilities**	
Checking account	JT	$2,500	Credit card balances	$ 550
Money market account[3]	JT	5,000	Auto loan (Audi)	25,000
(1.75% interest rate)			Auto loan (Toyota)	18,000
Total cash/cash equivalents		**$7,500**	*Total current liabilities*	**$43,550**
Invested assets			**Long-term liabilities**	
CD	JT	$15,000	Home mortgage	$225,000
401(k) plan	H	10,000	Student loans	50,500
Cash value of life insurance	W	6,000		
Coin collection	H	10,000	**Total long-term liabilities**	**$275,500**
Total investments		**$41,000**		
Personal use assets			**Net worth**	**$73,950**
House (appraised 7/01/07)[4]	JT	$275,000		
Auto (Toyota)	JT	22,500		
Auto (Audi)	JT	47,000		
Total personal use		**$344,500**		
Total assets		**$393,000**	**Total liabilities and net worth**	**$393,000**

Note to financial statements
[1]Assets are stated at fair market value.
[2]Liabilities are stated at principal only and are all joint obligations except the student loans which belong to Michael.
[3]The money market account is currently serving as their emergency fund.

[4]Land value was determined to be $50,000 and the home value $225,000.
Title designations
JT = Joint tenancy with right of survivorship
H = Husband's separate property
W = Wife's separate property

The Williamses primarily use cash, check, and debit cards for personal expenditures.

QUESTIONS

1. Assume that Michelle is self-employed. What are her retirement plan options?

2. By using the annuity approach, calculate the capital needed at retirement (age 67) for the Williamses. Assume a 9% after-tax rate of return. Base the calculation on Michael's salary only.

3. By using the capital preservation approach, calculate the capital needed at retirement for the Williamses.

4. By using the purchasing power preservation approach, calculate the capital needed at retirement for the Williamses.

5. Explain the key differences among the three approaches in Questions 2–4.

6. Use the capital need you computed in Question 2 to determine whether the Williamses will be able to retire at age 67 with their current annual savings. For current annual savings, use Michael's 401(k) contribution plus the employer's match and assume that Michelle saves all that she currently earns on an annual basis. Assume that all investment assets (regardless of how they are currently invested) will earn a 9% after-tax rate of return. Consider the checking account, money market account, and coin collection as nonretirement assets.

7. What changes, if any, would you recommend to the Williamses regarding their retirement planning?

8. If Michael and Michelle include the receipt of Social Security benefits in their retirement planning, could they retire at age 67 without increasing their annual savings? Assume that at age 67 (in today's dollars) Michael's Social Security benefit would be $29,820 and Michelle's would be $14,910. Use Michael's salary only.

9. If the Williamses choose to rely on Social Security benefits in their retirement planning, how much earlier than age 67 can they retire? (Assume all other facts as given in Question 8).

Use the following information for questions 10 through 14.

Michelle's online auction business has taken off this year, and she had to hire two employees. She has a website on which she sells products in a manner similar to other stores. The most unusual and valuable items in her inventory are available through Internet auction only. Her store is linked to the online auction website and several search engines. She is projecting net income of $90,000 from the business in 2009. Michelle wants to keep her workforce stable by offering them benefits, including a retirement plan. More importantly, she needs to maximize her retirement savings in order to help meet the retirement goals she and Michael have set. She does not want to factor the increase in her business income into their retirement needs calculations. Both Michelle and Michael believe the plan based primarily on his income will be sufficient for their retirement. Michelle wants to make contributions to the employees' retirement accounts as a benefit to them. She has heard a lot about the testing of retirement plans and wants a plan that will minimize the testing and administration burden.

Her employees make $20,000 and $25,000 each. She is considering a Keogh (HR-10) plan, a SEP IRA, a SIMPLE IRA, and a SIMPLE 401(k).

10. Describe a Keogh (HR-10) plan and discuss the advantages and disadvantages in adopting this type of plan.

11. Describe a SEP IRA and discuss the advantages and disadvantages in adopting this type of plan.

12. Describe a SIMPLE IRA and discuss the advantages and disadvantages in adopting this type of plan.

13. Describe a SIMPLE 401(k) and discuss the advantages and disadvantages in adopting this type of plan.

14. Of the four plans discussed, which is the best fit for Michelle's new business?

15. Other than child care costs and unreimbursed medical expenses, what expenses can Michael pay for with pre-tax dollars through his FSA?

ADDITIONAL QUESTIONS

1. List the Williamses' financial strengths and weaknesses.

2. What additional information would you request from the Williamses to complete your data-gathering phase?

3. Comment on the Williamses' use of debt.

4. Assuming a 9% after-tax rate of return, calculate the amount needed today to fund the children's college education.

5. By using life insurance industry rules of thumb, how much life insurance should Michael carry?

6. In general, what issues must be decided when purchasing a long-term care policy?

7. Frank and Isabelle are thinking of retiring in five years and are considering transferring the deli to Michelle. They believe that such a transfer would be wise, for it would remove the value of the deli from their gross estate. Moreover, they would like to see Michelle receive it, given her love for it. Frank and Isabelle are wondering what the value of the deli might be.

   Calculate the value of the deli by using the following approaches.
   a. Capitalized earnings model
   b. Present value analysis of the earnings and the building (assume the residual value of the earnings is $1,314,570)

8. Frank and Isabelle have identified five possible ways that they could effect the transfer of the deli to Michelle. Describe the transfer method and the advantages and disadvantages to the parties.
   a. Outright gift
   b. Private annuity
   c. Self-canceling installment note (SCIN)
   d. Grantor retained annuity trust
   e. Family limited partnership

9. The Williamses wish to establish a special needs trust for Madison. What factors and benefits should be contained in such a trust? How should it be funded?

10. Assume that the state in which they live has a fairly onerous probate system. What can the Williamses do to avoid the probate process?

11. Michael and Michelle wish to refinance their home mortgage. Will they qualify for the 15-year or the 30-year mortgage? What will be the total principal and interest payments for the 15-year and the 30-year mortgage?

12. Are there federal income tax implications regarding the group term life insurance benefit that Michael receives from the hospital if the coverage is increased to two times his salary? If so, what are they? Be sure to include any calculated amounts, and say how and where they would be reported.

13. Lakeside Hospital has just begun offering employees a flexible spending account (FSA) benefit. Michael is considering contributing to the FSA for assistance in covering child-care costs. Recently, however, a CPA friend of Michael's told him about the federal income tax dependent care credit. Assume that Michael approaches you, a financial planner, for advice on which approach would be best to use—FSA or the dependent care credit. Can the Williamses use both the FSA and the dependent care credit?

14. If Michelle only conducts a few online auction transactions will the transactions qualify as a trade or business? Discuss the tax consequences of Michelle's online auction transactions assuming: a) the transactions do not constitute a trade or business, and b) the transactions do constitute a trade or business. For each alternative, specify how transaction gains and losses would be treated for federal income tax purposes, and identify the tax schedule on which the activity would be reported.

15. Assuming a 9% after-tax rate of return, calculate the amount the Williamses need to save annually at year-end to fund the children's college education. Assume payments are made until the second child starts college.

16. What are the Williamses' present insurance portfolio deficiencies?

17. Using a human value approach net of state and federal income taxes and assuming a 9% after-tax rate of return, how much additional life insurance is needed on Michael's life?

18. Michelle's sister wishes to pay for Madison's daycare, schooling, and medical costs. How can she pay these costs so the payment is not considered a taxable gift?

19. Assume that Michael's 401(k) balance is equally invested in two mutual funds. Mutual Fund A has a standard deviation of 8%, and Mutual Fund B has a standard deviation of 11%. Assume the correlation coefficient of the funds is 75%. Calculate the standard deviation of the two-asset portfolio.

20. What is the residual benefits feature in Michael's disability policy?

21. Should Frank and Isabelle Williams purchase a long-term care insurance policy? Would any premiums paid for the long-term care policy be income tax deductible?

22. In the order of importance, what are the ten primary actions the Williamses should take immediately regarding their financial security?

23. What issues are involved in the selection of a guardian for Michael and Michelle's children?

24. Assuming the following annual expenses, what is the minimum amount of life insurance Michelle should have today? Use the needs approach.

    - Final expenses of $20,000

    - Annual childcare costs of $15,000 per year for 10 years

    - College funding for Beau ($62,721) and Lizabeth ($58,202)

    - Mortgage $225,000

    - Auto loans of $43,000

    - Student loans of $50,500

    - Credit card debt of $550

    - Return on invested money is 9%

    - Expected inflation rate is 3%

    - Emergency fund need of roughly $24,064 ($30,564 need – $6,500 cash)

25. If the Williamses average $2,000 in annual dental and vision care expenses, how much would they save/exclude from taxes by using pre-tax dollars?

6

Robert and Lisa Franklin

Today's date is January 1, 2009. Robert and Lisa Franklin have come to you, a financial planner, for help in developing a plan to accomplish their financial goals. From your initial meeting together, you have gathered the following information.

Personal Background and Information

Robert Franklin (Age 65)

Robert Franklin's date of birth is May 11, 1943. He was employed for 20 years as a partner at Franklin Securities (Franklin). He participates in a Keogh plan at Franklin. He was previously employed for 20 years as a broker with Smith Brothers, Inc., where he participated in a 401(k) plan.

Lisa Franklin (Age 65)

Lisa Franklin's date of birth is January 10, 1943. She has volunteered at Children's Hospital and the American Red Cross for the past 15 years.

The Franklins

They have been married 42 years. Both Robert and Lisa are currently in good health, although Robert had a mild heart attack eight years ago. Their joint life expectancy is 26.2 years.

Children

		Grandchildren
Pam	Age 39	Two children
Elise	Age 36	Five children
Jackie	Age 30	Four children
Vicki	Age 29	Three children
Robert Jr.	Age 18	No children

All of the daughters are healthy, employed, married, and not living with Robert and Lisa. Robert Jr. is unemployed, single, a high school graduate, and lives with his parents until he begins college in the fall.

Personal and Financial Objectives

1. Robert plans to retire now and begin his retirement by traveling around the world with Lisa.

2. Robert plans to sell his share of the securities business. He wants to sell half of his share of the business to his key employee, Mark Newhart. He wants to sell the other half to his daughter, Elise, who is the senior broker in the firm.

3. After traveling around the world, Robert plans to return to the business as a self-employed consultant on a fee basis beginning January 1, 2010.

4. Robert Jr. will be starting at a private university in the fall of 2009.

5. Robert's grandchild, Greg, Pam's youngest child, was born with a serious physical disability. Robert plans to give Greg $2.5 million through a trust for his care and benefit.

Economic Information

-   The couple expects inflation to average 4% annually. The expected stock market returns are 10% annually, as measured by the S&P 500 Index, with a standard deviation of 15%.

-   Tuition is currently $30,000 per year at the private university. The expected education inflation rate is 5%.

-   The 30-day T-bill is yielding 3.5%. The 30-year Treasury bond is yielding 7.5%.

-   Current mortgage rates are 7.5% for 15 years and 8.0% for 30 years. In addition, closing costs (3% of the mortgage) will be paid at closing and not financed.

Insurance Information

Life Insurance

Neither spouse has life insurance.

Health Insurance

Robert's business provides health coverage for both Lisa and himself during employment and during retirement.

-   Major medical 80/20

-   $250 deductible per person

-   $1 million cap

-   $2,000 family stop-loss provision

Disability Insurance

Neither Robert nor Lisa has disability insurance.

Homeowners Insurance

They have HO-3 policies on their primary residence and vacation homes. The vacation homes are located on the US Gulf coast and in the mountains.

	Residence	Vacation Home US Gulf Coast	Vacation Home Mountains
Dwelling	$975,000	$700,000	$600,000
Coinsurance requirement	80%	80%	80%
Deductible—all other covered losses	$250	$250	$250
Deductible—hurricane	n/a	$10,500	n/a

Umbrella Liability Policy

They have $5 million of coverage.

Automobile Insurance

They have liability coverage, $250,000/$500,000/$100,000. They also carry comprehensive and collision on their autos.

Insurance Premiums

- Car insurance: $6,000 per year for all three of Robert and Lisa's automobiles

- Homeowners insurance: $8,500 per year (includes all homes)

- Boat insurance: $1,200 per year (covered under the umbrella policy)

- Umbrella policy: $1,000 per year

Investment Information

- The Franklins have a required rate of return of 8%.

- The couple can tolerate medium to high amounts of risk but have little need to take excessive risks because of their net worth.

■ Robert's 401(k) plan investments are secure in a well-diversified but relatively volatile group of small-cap value stocks. The funds in his 401(k) plan are still in Smith Brothers' Retirement Plan.

■ Robert has a single premium deferred annuity that was purchased on July 1, 1981, for $60,000 and is currently worth $233,047. The expected return over the next year and the 15 years of the fixed term of the annuity is 6%. The start date of the monthly annuity is January 1, 2010, when the expected fair market value will be $247,030.

■ Robert plans to sell 4,468 shares of Dollar Mart stock to his daughter, Vicki, who is employed by Dollar Mart. Robert anticipates the stock will greatly appreciate in the upcoming years. (The stock was purchased in 2003 for $26.66 per share and is currently trading for $11.25 per share.)

Income Tax Information

■ Robert and Lisa are currently in the highest federal income tax bracket (35% marginal rate).

■ They also pay state taxes of 5% for a total of 40%.

■ For personal income tax reporting, Robert has a $700,000 salary.

■ They do not reside in a community property state.

Retirement Information

■ The 401(k) plan has a balance of $600,000 consisting of a portfolio of small-cap value stocks. The portfolio is projected to average a return of 16% over the next 20 years with a standard deviation of 8%.

■ Robert's anticipated Social Security retirement benefit is $24,000 per year in 2009 and will increase at the expected consumer price index (CPI) of 4%.

■ Robert has a profit sharing type of Keogh plan. His company contributes $12,000 per year to the profit sharing plan. The contributions to this plan have been made out of the company's profits. The balance in his account is a result of an annual contribution of $12,000, with a 7% approximate average return since July 1, 1987.

■ Robert and Lisa will continue to collect $200,000 per year in rental proceeds from Commercial Property A.

■ Robert and Lisa will receive $50,000 per year from the charitable remainder annuity trust (CRAT) that owns Commercial Property B for Robert's lifetime.

Gifts, Estates, Trusts, and Will Information

Gifts

The following are the Franklins' only lifetime gifts.

- In 2007, Robert gave each of his five children $52,000 ($40,000 taxable and $12,000 annual exclusion) and paid gift tax of $82,000 in 2007.

- In December 2007, Robert transferred $3 million of property to a grantor retained annuity trust (GRAT). Robert hoped to save on gift and estate taxes by transferring this portion of his interest into a trust while retaining the right to a fixed ordinary annuity for a term of 10 years. He transferred this $3 million interest and kept the right to receive $298,059 per year for 10 years. The Franklins' five children are the remainder beneficiaries of the GRAT. Upon the death of a remainderman, the interest will pass to the remainderman's descendants. If a remainderman dies without heirs, then the remainderman's interest will pass to the other children (remaindermen) pro rata. Robert paid no gift tax in 2007 on this gift. This was his first taxable transfer. Because the Section 7520 rate was 8%, the taxable gift was $1 million.

- Lisa has made no taxable gifts during her lifetime nor have any gifts been split.

- A 5% CRAT was established by Robert in 2008 by donating a piece of real estate (an apartment building, Commercial Property B) inherited from his grandfather. The initial valuation of the trust was $1 million with the initial income in the first year projected to be $50,000 beginning in 2009. The charitable remainder beneficiary is the Chicago Art Institute.

- He plans to donate $2.5 million to an irrevocable trust for his grandchild, Greg, the youngest child of Pam.

Estates

The last illness and funeral expenses combined with estate administration expenses are estimated at $400,000 each.

Wills

Robert and Lisa have simple wills. They have left all probate assets to each other. Each will also include a six-month survivorship clause. Debts and taxes are to be paid from the residue of the estate.

Will

Excerpts from Robert Franklin's Statutory Last Will and Testament

I, ROBERT FRANKLIN SR., being of sound mind and wishing to make proper disposition of my property in the event of my death, do declare this to be my Last Will and Testament. I revoke all of my prior wills and codicils.

1.1　I have been married but once, and only to Lisa Franklin with whom I am presently living.

1.2　Out of my marriage to Lisa Franklin, five children were born namely Pam Franklin, Elise Franklin, Jackie Franklin, Vicki Franklin, and Robert Franklin Jr.

1.3　I have adopted no one nor has anyone adopted me.

3.1　I give my entire estate to Lisa Franklin, my wife.

3.2　In the event that Lisa Franklin predeceases me or fails to survive me for more than six months from the date of my death, I give my entire estate to my children Pam Franklin, Elise Franklin, Jackie Franklin, Vicki Franklin, and Robert Franklin Jr., in equal and undivided one-fifth shares.

3.3　In the event that any of the named heirs or legatees should predecease me, die within six months from the date of my death, disclaim or otherwise fail to accept any property bequeath to him and said legatee has no descendants, his share of all of my property of which I die possessed shall be given to the surviving named legatees.

5.1　I name Lisa Franklin to serve as my executrix of my succession, with full seisin and without bond.

5.2　I direct that the expenses of my last illness, funeral, and the administration of my estate shall be paid by my executrix as soon as practicable after my death.

5.3　All inheritance, estate, succession, transfer, and other taxes (including interest and penalties thereon) payable by reason of my death shall be apportioned in accordance with the law.

STATEMENT OF CASH FLOWS
Robert and Lisa Franklin
January 1, 2008 to December 31, 2008

CASH INFLOWS		
Salary		
Robert's salary	$700,000	
Total salary		$700,000
Rental income		200,000
Dividend income		
Robert	5,000	
Lisa	1,500	
Total dividend income		6,500
Interest income[1]		1,000
Total income		$907,500
CASH OUTFLOWS		
Mortgage payments		
Primary residence	$ 37,030	
Vacation home 1	45,181	
Vacation home 2	79,308	
Total mortgage payments		$161,519
Insurance Premiums		
Homeowners	$ 8,500	
Auto	6,000	
Boat	1,200	
Umbrella	1,000	
Total insurance premiums		$ 16,700
Misc. expenses		
Credit card payments	$ 2,400	
Entertainment	50,000	
Food	14,400	
Clothes	30,000	
Utilities	24,000	
Charity	90,000	
Total misc. expenses		$210,800
Tax		
Property tax	$ 84,000	
Income tax	408,375	
Total tax		$492,375
Total outflows		$881,394
Discretionary cash		$ 26,106

Notes to financial statements

[1] Because the initial income from the CRAT of $50,000 and GRAT of $298,059 is projected for January 1, 2009 (2008 payment), it was omitted from the 2008 Statement of Cash Flows.

STATEMENT OF FINANCIAL POSITION
Robert and Lisa Franklin
As of January 1, 2009

Assets[1]			Liabilities and Net Worth		
			Liabilities[2]		
			Current liabilities		
Cash/cash equivalents					
JT	Cash	$ 100,000	W	Credit card 1	$ 1,000
			W	Credit card 2	15,000
	Total cash/cash equivalents	$ 100,000	**Total current liabilities**		$ 16,000
Invested assets			**Long-term liabilities**		
JT	Franklin Securities	$ 5,000,000	JT	Mortgage—primary	$ 258,630
W	Lisa's portfolio	500,000	JT	Mortgage—vac GC	369,428
H	Deferred annuity	233,047	JT	Mortgage—vac mts	687,444
H	401(k) plan	600,000			
H	Keogh	526,382	**Total long-term liabilities**		$ 1,315,502
H	Robert's portfolio	4,000,000			
JT	Commercial Property A	1,500,000	**Total liabilities**		$ 1,331,502
Total investments		$12,359,429			
Personal use assets			**Net worth**		$15,087,927
JT	Primary residence	$ 1,300,000			
JT	Vacation home—US Gulf coast	800,000			
JT	Vacation home—mountains	700,000			
JT	Personal property/furniture	875,000			
H	Auto 1	80,000			
H	Auto 2	55,000			
W	Auto 3	40,000			
W	Boat	110,000			
Total personal use assets		$ 3,960,000			
Total assets		$16,419,429	**Total liabilities and net worth**		$16,419,429

Notes to financial statements
[1]Assets are stated at fair market value (rounded to whole dollars).
[2]Liabilities are stated at principal only (rounded to whole dollars).

Title designations
JT - Joint tenancy with right of survivorship
H - Husband separate
W - Wife separate

Information Regarding Assets and Liabilities

Franklin Securities (Robert is a 50% partner)

- The fair market value of Robert's interest is $5 million.

- The current adjusted taxable basis is $1 million.

- Details of the transfer of the business (sale) are as follows.

  - 50%: a 10-year installment sale to Mark Newhart for a down payment of 20% on January 1, 2009, and monthly payments beginning February 1, 2009, at 10% annual interest

  - 50%: self-canceling installment note (SCIN) or private annuity to Elise

Primary Residence

- Purchased in 1991

- Joint-owned (joint tenants with right of survivorship)

- Market value $1.3 million

- Original purchase price $300,000

- Current mortgage at 12% interest; payment: $3,085.84 (30 year) per month

Vacation Home—US Gulf Coast

- Joint-owned; purchased in 2006

- Market value $800,000

- Original purchase price $400,000

- Current mortgage at 7.75%; payment: $3,765.10 (15 year) per month

Vacation Home—Mountains

- Joint-owned; purchased in 2007

- Market value $700,000

- Original purchase price $700,000

- Current mortgage at 7.8%; payment: $6,608.99 (15 year) per month

Commercial Property A

- Original site of the business
- Fair market value $1.5 million
- Adjusted basis $200,000

Single Premium Deferred Annuity

- Robert purchased this annuity on July 1, 1981, for $60,000. The current fair market value is $233,047.
- An earnings rate of 6% compounded annually is expected in the near term.
- Annuity start date is January 1, 2010, at which time the fair market value is projected to be $247,030 and will consist of 180 monthly payments (15 years).
- If Robert dies before the annuity start date, Lisa is named beneficiary (100% joint and survivor annuity).

Summary of Indebtedness

Asset	Date 1st Payment	Amount of Mortgage	Term/ Years	Interest	Monthly Payments	Remaining Payments	Remaining Balance
Primary residence	4/1/93	$300,000	30	12.00%	($3,085.84)	183	$ 258,629.70
Vacation home GC	1/1/06	$400,000	15	7.75%	($3,765.10)	156	$ 369,427.86
Vacation home mts	7/1/07	$700,000	15	7.80%	($6,608.99)	174	$ 687,443.56
							$1,315,501.12

Detailed Investment Portfolios

Robert's Portfolio

Description	Acquired	Shares	Adjusted Basis	Beta	Current FMV
Sears	8/00	16,325	$201,633	0.9	$ 830,214
Dollar Mart	1/03	4,468	$119,117	1.2	$ 50,265
Canon, Inc.	2/05	22,249	$400,188	1.4	$2,230,462
*RC, Inc.	9/05	3,742	$ 67,181	1.5	$ 222,600
WW Grainger	10/07	4,257	$221,435	1.2	$ 311,293
Circuit City stores	9/07	10,561	$304,062	1.2	$ 355,166
					$4,000,000

*The RC, Inc., stock is Section 1244 Small Business Stock. The beta is determined by industry standards.

Lisa's Portfolio

Description	Acquired	Shares	Adjusted Basis	Beta	Current FMV
Tenet Health Care	1/01	2,542	$ 30,504	0.6	$ 50,209
Bay Bank, Inc.	2/05	1,500	$120,000	0.5	$167,250
Microsoft	9/05	589	$ 53,010	0.7	$ 66,189
Zenith	10/06	22,190	$177,520	0.8	$216,352
					$500,000

QUESTIONS

1. Assume that Robert decided it was necessary to donate $2.5 million as a taxable gift to his grandson, Greg, in an irrevocable trust in 2008. How much cash did Robert pay out in total for such a gift, including the gift itself and all related taxes? Robert has made no previous gifts to any grandchild. Robert's total previous taxable gifts have amounted to $1.2 million, with $82,000 in previous gift tax paid. What is the projection of his total cash outflow from the above transaction? What would be the cash outflow if he had waited until 2009 to make the gift?

2. Which of the following transfers will not result in a taxable gift from Robert in 2009, assuming he makes no other gifts?
   a. Robert pays each grandchild's private school tuition ($6,000 each).
   b. Robert pays City Hospital for the hospital bill of a friend ($15,000).
   c. Robert pays a distant cousin's law school tuition ($16,000).
   d. Robert pays the tuition for Robert Jr. to private university ($30,000).

3. What is the impact of the survivorship clause in Robert's will?

4. Robert and Lisa are considering the purchase of a joint and survivor (second-to-die) life insurance policy for the purpose of wealth replacement for the assets that were transferred to the CRAT and to help to create estate liquidity. Discuss the most appropriate way to own the joint and survivor life insurance to ensure that the proceeds are not included in their estate.

5. Assume that Robert dies January 1, 2010, and Lisa survives him by six months. What is true regarding the installment sale to Mark Newhart with respect to estate and income taxation?

6. Discuss the Franklins' estate planning deficiencies.

7. What estate planning recommendations would you make to the Franklins?

8. Explain the benefits of the grantor retained annuity trust (GRAT) established by Robert.

9. What are the drawbacks to establishing a GRAT?

10. What are the advantages of using a charitable remainder trust (CRT)?

11. Calculate Robert's federal estate tax liability if he died in 2009. For this question, assume that Robert created the $2.5 million irrevocable trust for his grandson Greg in 2008 and that the financial statement of January 1, 2009, reflects the Franklins' assets after the trust was established.

12. Discuss private annuities and SCINS and how the use of each would affect Robert Franklin and his daughter Elise in the sale of half of his share of Franklin Securities to her instead of in an installment sale.

13. The Franklins want to set up an irrevocable trust for the rest of their grandchildren and fund it with $2 million of their wealth. All previous gifts have been made by Robert. What are the generation-skipping transfer tax and gift tax liabilities this gift will incur?

14. What kind of tax will the grandchildren pay on the income distributed to them from this irrevocable trust created by their grandparents?

ADDITIONAL QUESTIONS

1. If Robert took a lump-sum distribution from his retirement plan, could he elect 10-year averaging?

2. List the Franklins' financial strengths and weaknesses.

3. After reading the case, what additional information would you request from the Franklins to complete your data-gathering phase?

4. Assume that Robert sells the Dollar Mart stock to Vicki for the current fair market value. What are Robert's tax consequences from this transaction?

5. Assume that Robert sells the Dollar Mart stock to Vicki for the fair market value as of January 1, 2009, and Vicki resells the Dollar Mart stock at $16.50 per share on December 15, 2009. What are the income tax consequences to Vicki?

6. What is the tax treatment if Robert sells all of his RC, Inc. stock this year at the current fair market value?

7. Assume that on August 15, 2009, Robert has the following sales in his stock portfolio. Assume that these are the Franklins' only stock transactions for the year.

Sale Date	Stock	Number of Shares	Sale Price Net Commissions
8/15/09	Sears	16,325	$840,000
8/15/09	WW Grainger	4,257	$320,000
8/15/09	Circuit City	10,561	$190,000

What are the income tax consequences of these transactions?

8. Evaluate Robert and Lisa's insurance situation.

9. Assuming that Robert begins his single premium deferred annuity on the start date of January 1, 2010, what will be his tax consequences from the annuity payments received in 2010?

10. In 2010, when Robert returns from traveling and begins his consulting career, he expects to have taxable earned income of $100,000 per year. Describe the impact of his consulting activities on Social Security benefits and the taxation of Social Security benefits received.

11. By using the capital asset pricing model, determine the expected return for Lisa's portfolio, assuming the market has a return that is 20% better than expected.

12. If the Franklins were to refinance their primary residence at current mortgage rates for 15 years, how much would their monthly payment decline?

13. In 2010, Robert will begin his consulting. Discuss his ability to defer taxes by using a qualified retirement plan.

14. With regard to the installment sale portion of the interest in Franklin Securities to Mark Newhart, how much, if any, of the down payment is taxable to the Franklins in 2009, and what is the character of the down payment?

15. Rounding to the nearest dollar, calculate the total monthly installment payments that will be made to the Franklins by Newhart during 2009.

16. In 2009, how much will Robert have to claim as ordinary income from the installment sale of Franklin Securities?

17. Robert has paid his general liability insurance premiums for Franklin Securities for two years in advance (January 1, 2009, to December 31, 2010). The premium for the two years was $144,000. At the time of his sale of the firm to Newhart and Elise, there will be a prepaid insurance amount. Robert plans to assign the insurance policy to the new partnership of Elise and Newhart and wants them to pay him for the remaining prepaid insurance premiums. Discuss the validity and effectiveness of the assignment of the policy.

18. What is the likelihood that Robert's 401(k) will yield a return that is below the Franklins' required rate of return?

19. What investment planning recommendations would you make to the Franklins?

20. How much will the Franklins have to set aside today to fund tuition for Robert Jr. for six years at the university if he begins attending in 2009?

21. Because the Franklins will be traveling for the next year, they will not be using the vacation homes very often. The vacation home on the Gulf Coast in particular is used by the Franklins as their children all prefer the larger vacation home in the mountains that is in a desirable resort area. The couple is considering renting the house to vacationers for at least the next year. How would the rental income affect the Franklins' income tax return for 2009?

22. The Franklins have decided to sell the vacation home on the Gulf Coast, instead of renting it to others, for the FMV of $800,000. They have owned the home and used it for vacations since 2006. How much of the gain on the sale of the home can the couple exclude from gross income in 2009, the year the sale is finalized?

23. What steps should the Franklins take now concerning Social Security and Medicare?

24. While driving home from work, Robert gets into a car accident with a deer that causes $1,500 in damage to his vehicle. In addition, after hitting the deer, Robert's car careens off the road and into a neighbor's garage, causing $12,500 worth of damage to the structure. What is the amount of insurance that Robert's policy will pay regarding the two incidents?

Alex and Amanda Silver

Alex and Amanda Silver have great aspirations for their future; however, they have recently realized that they are not as financially well-off as they had thought. As a result, they have come to you for advice on how to solve their current cash flow problems and to help them plan to achieve their financial goals. Assume today is January 1, 2009.

Personal Background and Information

Alex Silver (Age 37)

Alex is a bank vice president. He has been employed at the bank for 12 years and has an annual salary of $70,000.

Amanda Silver (Age 37)

Amanda is a full-time homemaker.

The Silvers

Alex and Amanda have been married for eight years. They have two children, and Amanda is nine months pregnant. They have always lived in this community and expect to remain indefinitely in their current residence.

Children

Joey is 6 years old.
Jane is 3 years old.
The unborn child is due at any time now.

Personal and Financial Goals

1. They want to save for college tuition.

2. They want to pay off all debt by retirement.

3. They want to retire at age 62 with 80% of preretirement salary at the time of their retirement.

4. They want to prepare an estate plan including wills.

5. They want to purchase a new car in two years, in 12 years, and at retirement (total of three cars).

6. They want to evaluate both investment and insurance risk and improve their overall risk management.

Economic Information

■ The Silvers expect medical inflation to be 6% annually and the annual general consumer price index (CPI) to average 3% over both the short term and long term. The average interest rate on their credit cards is approximately 16%.

■ Current mortgage rates are 8.0% for 30-year fixed mortgages and 7.5% for 15-year fixed mortgages. Closing costs are approximately 3.0% of any mortgage refinanced and will be paid at closing and not financed.

■ Alex expects salary increases of 4.0% per year for the foreseeable future.

Insurance Information

Health Insurance

The entire family is insured under Alex's PPO (Preferred Provider Organization). There is a $200 family deductible and a $25 co-payment for in-network doctor's visits. The plan has a $500,000 lifetime limit for each family member. Alex's employer pays the entire premium.

Life Insurance

Alex has a term life insurance policy with a face amount of $25,000 provided by his employer. The policy's beneficiary is Amanda.

Disability Insurance

Alex has a private disability insurance policy with an own occupation definition of disability. The policy covers accidental disability, has a 90-day elimination period, and has a $2,000 monthly benefit payable to age 65.

Homeowners Insurance

The Silvers have a HO-3 policy with dwelling extension and replacement cost on contents. There is a $1,000 deductible. The annual premium is $950.

Automobile Insurance

The Silvers have automobile liability and bodily injury coverage of $100,000/$300,000/$100,000. They have both comprehensive coverage (other than collision) and collision. The deductibles are $500 (comprehensive) and $1,000 (collision), respectively. The annual premium is $900.

Investment Information

The bank offers a 401(k) plan in which Alex is an active participant. The bank matches contributions dollar-for-dollar up to 3% of Alex's salary. Alex currently contributes 3% of his salary. Alex's maximum contribution is 16%.

In the 401(k), the Silvers have the opportunity to invest in a money market fund, a bond fund, a growth and income fund, and a small-cap stock fund. The Silvers are expecting a retirement period of 30 years. (They expect to live to 92 years of age.) The Silvers have a moderate investment risk tolerance.

The bank has recently implemented an employee stock purchase plan (ESPP) and a stock option plan which includes nonqualifying stock options (NQSOs) and incentive stock options (ISOs), both for which Alex will qualify. The NQSOs and the ISOs may be exercised by using a cashless exercise provision. To date, Alex has not participated in the ESPP or the stock option plan.

Alex's current 401(k) portfolio is as follows:

Balance

	Money Market	Bond	Growth and Income	Small Cap	Total
Current balance	$12,000	$12,000	$12,000	$0	$36,000*
Current deposits monthly	$100	$150	$100	$0	$350/month includes match

*Loan of $7,000 from 401(k) balance to buy boat (balance is net of the loan)

Expected Returns

	Geometric Mean	Arithmetic Mean	Standard Deviation
Common stocks	10.41%	12.4%	20.8%
Small company stocks	12.1%	17.5%	35.3%
Long-term corporate bonds	6.2%	6.4%	8.7%
Long-term gov't bonds	5.4%	5.7%	8.5%
Intermediate-term gov't	4.8%	5.1%	8.6%
Bonds	5.1%	5.3%	5.6%
US Treasury bills	3.7%	3.8%	3.4%
Inflation	3.1%	3.2%	4.7%

Income Tax Information

Alex and Amanda are in the 15% federal income tax bracket. There is no state tax assessed by the state in which they reside. They pay $820 annually in local income taxes.

Retirement Information

Alex wants to retire at age 62. He wants to retire with income equal to 80% of his preretirement income. He expects to receive Social Security benefits of $24,000 (today's dollars) for himself and $12,000 for Amanda (today's dollars) at full retirement age 67. They will receive 70% of the full benefit at age 62.

His estimated Social Security retirement benefits at age 62, 67, and 70 are shown below in the excerpt from Alex's recent *Social Security Statement* (Form SSA-7005).

Your Estimated Benefits

Retirement	You have earned enough credits to qualify for benefits. At your current earnings rate, if you stop working and start receiving benefits:	
	At age 62, your payment would be about......................	$1,390 a month
	If you continue working until:	
	your full retirement age (67 years), your payment would be about.................................	$2,000 a month
	age 70, your payment would be about.............	$2,494 a month
*Disability	You have earned enough credits to qualify for benefits. If you became disabled right now, your payment would be about..	$1,854 a month
*Family	If you get retirement or disability benefits, your spouse and children also may qualify for benefits	
*Survivors	You have earned enough credits for your family to receive survivors benefits. If you die this year, certain members of your family **may** qualify for the following benefits:	
	Your child..	$1,401 a month
	Your spouse who is caring for your child.........................	$1,401 a month
	Your spouse, if benefits start at full retirement age..........	$1,868 a month
	Total family benefits cannot be more than.......................	$3,270 a month
	Your spouse or minor child may be eligible for a special one-time death benefit of $255.	
Medicare	You have enough credits to qualify for Medicare at age 65. Even if you do not retire at age 65, be sure to contact Social Security three months before your 65th birthday to enroll in Medicare.	

* Your estimated benefits are based on current law. Congress has made changes to the law in the past and can do so at any time. The law governing benefit amounts may change because, by 2041, the payroll taxes collected will be enough to pay only about 78% of scheduled benefits.

(Continued on next page)

We based your benefit estimates on these facts:	
Your date of birth (please verify your name on page 1 and this date of birth)..	June 15, 1971
Your estimated taxable earnings per year after 2008............................	$70,000
Your Social Security number (only the last four digits are shown to help prevent identity theft)..	XXX-XX-1234

Education Information

Joey is 6 years old and currently attending first grade at a private school. He will attend private school through high school. Alex and Amanda have $2,500 in certificates of deposit (CDs) that they contribute to once a year ($500 each year) for Joey. This account will be used to pay for high school tuition and is in Joey's name.

Jane is 3 years old. She will attend private school from pre-kindergarten through high school. Alex and Amanda have $1,000 in CDs to which they contribute once a year ($500 each year) for Jane. This account will be used to pay for high school tuition and is in Jane's name.

Alex and Amanda plan to contribute to CDs for the unborn child's high school education beginning next year.

They have set up college funds through CDs. The current balance of the college fund is $15,000 ($7,500 for each child), and the rate of return is 6%. They would also like to be able to send their children to college for five years instead of the traditional four years. The extra year could be used to get a master's or graduate degree. They are currently making no additional contributions to the fund.

The current cost of a public university (including room, board, tuition, and books) is $15,000 annually per child. The Silvers expect their children to start college at age 18. They expect college costs to increase 5% annually.

Gifts, Estates, Trusts, and Will Information

Alex's will leaves everything to Amanda conditioned on a six-month survivorship clause. Otherwise, everything is equally split in separate trusts for Joey and Jane.

Amanda does not have a will.

STATEMENT OF CASH FLOWS
Alex and Amanda Silver
For the Year 2009 (Expected)

CASH INFLOWS		
Salary—Alex		$ 70,000
Investment income		
Interest (taxable)	$ 900	
Dividends	150	
Total investment income		$ 1,050
Total cash inflows		$ 71,050
CASH OUTFLOWS		
Planned savings		
Reinvestment interest/dividends	$ 1,050	
401(k)	2,100	
High school fund (Joey and Jane)	1,000	
Total savings		$ 4,150
Ordinary living expenses		
Food	$ 6,000	
Clothing	3,600	
Baby sitters	600	
Entertainment	1,814	
Utilities	3,600	
Auto maintenance	2,000	
Church	3,500	
Total ordinary living expenses		$ 21,114
Other payments		
401(k) repayment	$ 1,703	
Credit card payments	960	
Mortgage payment	21,954	
Boat loan	3,040	
Total payments		$ 27,657

(Continued on next page)

STATEMENT OF CASH FLOWS
Alex and Amanda Silver
For the Year 2009 (Expected)
(Continued)

Insurance premiums		
Automobile	$ 900	
Disability	761	
Homeowners	950	
Total insurance premiums		$ 2,611
Tuition and education expenses		$ 1,000
Taxes		
Federal income tax (W/H)	$7,500	
State (and city) income tax	820	
FICA	5,355	
Property tax for real estate (principal residence)	1,000	
Total taxes		$14,675
Total Cash Outflows		$71,207
Discretionary Cash Flow (Deficit)		$ (157)

STATEMENT OF FINANCIAL POSITION
Alex and Amanda Silver
As of January 1, 2009

ASSETS[1]

Liquid assets

Checking account	$ 1,500	
Savings account	1,000	
Total liquid assets		$ 2,500

Investments

ABC stock[2]	$ 13,000	
CDs (college fund)	15,000	
401(k) plan	43,000	
Total investments		$ 71,000
Personal real estate—residence		$250,000

Other personal assets

Automobiles	$ 15,000	
Boat	20,000	
Jewelry	13,500	
Furniture/household	60,000	
Total other personal assets		$108,500
TOTAL ASSETS		$432,000

LIABILITIES[3] AND NET WORTH

Current liabilities—credit cards		$ 4,000

Long-term liabilities

401(k) loan	$ 7,000	
Mortgage on residence	197,888	
Boat loan	13,559	
Total long-term liabilities		$218,447
Total liabilities		$222,447
NET WORTH		$209,553
TOTAL LIABILITIES AND NET WORTH		$432,000

Notes to financial statements

[1]Assets are stated at fair market value.

[2]The ABC stock was inherited from Amanda's aunt on November 15, 2007. Her aunt originally paid $20,000 for the stock on October 31, 2007. The fair market value at the aunt's death was $12,000.

[3]Liabilities are stated at the principal amount only.

Information Regarding Assets and Liabilities

Home

The Silvers own a home in the city that was purchased two years ago for $250,000. The value of the house has appreciated. Because the Silvers paid more than the value of the home at the time of the sale, however, the current value is equal to the price paid. At the time of purchase, a $50,000 down payment was made, and the remaining amount was financed at 10.5% over 30 years.

Automobiles

The Silvers own two automobiles, which have values of $10,000 and $5,000, respectively.

Boat

The Silvers own a 100-horsepower speedboat valued at $20,000. They purchased the boat paying 20% down, with a term of 36 months. The monthly payment, due on the 30th of each month, is $253.33.

Antique Furniture

On June 1, 2008, Amanda's parents gave Alex and Amanda antique furniture valued at $10,000. Amanda's parents had owned the antique furniture for three years.

Baseball Card Collection

On March 1, 2008, Alex inherited Uncle Travis's baseball card collection. Alex gave it to his nephew on his 18th birthday (September 1, 2008). The value of the baseball card collection at the time of the gift was $20,000.

Other Debt

Asset	Acquired	Price	Initial Debt	Interest Rate	Term	Current Monthly Payment	Balance of Debt
Credit card				16.0		$80.00*	$4,000.00
401(k)	05/01/07		$ 7,000.00	8.0	5 year	$141.93	$6,319.64

*This is the minimum payment. The Silvers charge about $100 per month on the credit cards.

QUESTIONS

1. List the Silvers' financial strengths and weaknesses.

2. After reading the case, what additional information would you request from the Silvers to complete your data-gathering phase?

3. Calculate the following financial ratios for the Silvers.

$$\dfrac{\text{Liquid Assets}}{\text{Current Debt Payments}}$$
$$\dfrac{\text{Net Worth}}{\text{Total Assets}}$$
$$\dfrac{\text{Total Debt}}{\text{Annual Gross Income}}$$
$$\dfrac{\text{Housing}}{\text{Monthly Gross Income}}$$
$$\dfrac{\text{Housing and Monthly Debt Payments}}{\text{Monthly Gross Income}}$$
$$\dfrac{\text{Investment Assets}}{\text{Annual Gross Income}}$$
$$\dfrac{\text{Monthly Savings}}{\text{Monthly Gross Income}}$$

4. Comment on any of the ratios from the previous question that you think are important.

5. Can the Silvers qualify to refinance their home for the following?
   (Do not include 401(k) loan payment.)
   a. 15-year loan
   b. 30-year loan

6. Should the Silvers refinance their existing home mortgage?

7. What will be the monthly savings from refinancing over the term of the loan?

8. Is the term of the refinanced loan the appropriate term over which to evaluate the savings from refinancing?

9. Calculate the education funding needs for the time periods listed below. (Assume the first payment will be made in one year.)
   a. To college start date (determine separately for Joey and Jane)
   b. For Jane only, through the end of college
   c. For Jane only, at Alex's age 45

10. Are the Silvers currently saving enough in CDs to provide for the education needs?

11. Are CDs the appropriate investment vehicles for education funding?

12. Assume that the antique furniture has been refinished and has increased 12% in value as of January 1, 2009. What is the value of the furniture as of January 1, 2013, if its value increases by 5% annually?

13. Assume that Alex and Amanda purchased their home for $250,000 in December 2007. If they had made a $25,000 down payment and financed the balance at 10.5% for 15 years, their monthly payment (principal and interest) for that mortgage would be $2,487. The FMV as of January 1, 2009, is $250,000, because their house was over-valued when they purchased it. Their mortgage payment is 43% of their total monthly income. The Silvers find that they can no longer pay their monthly mortgage payment of $2,487 and are very close to losing their home. What might you suggest to the Silvers to save their home?

14. Assuming the same facts in Question #13 above. according to the Hope for Homeowners Act of 2008, what is the result if, four years after the new mortgage, the Silvers' home value increases to $300,000 and they sell the property in that year?

ADDITIONAL QUESTIONS

1. Calculate Alex and Amanda's approximate adjusted gross income for federal tax liability for the current year.

2. What are Alex's current life insurance needs? Assume for this question that any last ill-ness, funeral, and administrative expenses will be $25,000. Use the two industry stan-dards:

   a. the 6-times approach, and
   b. the 10-times approach.

3. Discuss the life insurance needs for Amanda.

4. What are the deficiencies of Alex's disability insurance coverage?

5. What are the risks that the Silvers may face with respect to their health insurance cov-erage?

6. Discuss any other insurance deficiencies that the Silvers have.

7. Calculate capital needs for retirement at age 62 using the annuity model. Assume a 10% pre-tax investment rate of return.

8. Calculate capital needs for retirement using the capital preservation model. Assume a 10% pre-tax investment rate of return.

9. Calculate capital needs for retirement using the purchasing power preservation model.

10. How much should the Silvers save at the end of each month to meet their retirement objectives? Assume an annual investment return of 10%.

11. Should Alex opt to begin Social Security benefits at age 62 or age 67?

12. What is the maximum that participants may borrow from a 401(k) plan?

13. What is the payback period for loans from a 401(k) plan?

14. How is the 401(k) loan balance treated if Alex quits his job?

15. What is the effect of the six-month survivorship clause in Alex's current will?

16. What will provisions should the Silvers include in their revised/new wills?

17. Discuss the need for a durable power of attorney and explain the purpose of such a document.

18. What is the Silvers' tax basis in the ABC stock?

19. What is the tax consequence of selling the ABC stock for the current fair market value?

20. If the Silvers sell the ABC stock for less than their original basis and then repurchase the same stock within the same month, do they have a deductible loss for income tax purposes? How does this loss affect basis?

21. What is an ESPP? Describe its characteristics.

22. Are there any limits on the amount that can be granted for NQSOs and ISOs?

23. What is a cashless exercise for NQSOs and ISOs?

24. Suppose Amanda and Alex decide to put the college funding accounts in the children's names despite your recommendation to keep the funds in their names. They increase their savings for the college accounts to where Joey accumulates $36,000 by age 11. If the account is earning a 6% annual return, what are the income tax consequences?

25. The Silvers have very little savings in light of their financial goals. As their financial planner, you discuss risk tolerance with the Silvers, who now realize that their risk tolerance is actually higher than they first assumed. While they are working on increasing their cash flow and discretionary income, how can they improve their investment returns and increase diversification without taking on an inordinate amount of risk?

Zachary and Kayla Garrett

Zachary and Kayla Garrett have come to you, a financial planner, for help in developing a plan to accomplish their financial goals. From your initial meeting together, you have gathered the following information. Assume today is January 1, 2009.

Personal Background and Information

Zachary Garrett (Age 26)

Zachary Garrett is employed as a salesperson for a rapidly growing air conditioning and heating services company. He has been employed with this company for five years. Zachary has tremendous potential and has positioned himself for advancement.

Kayla Garrett (Age 26)

Kayla Garrett is a Canadian citizen and is employed as an interior design consultant for a home-decorating center. Kayla is studying for her interior design license and plans to become an independent design consultant in three years. Kayla is pregnant with twins. She started paid maternity leave for six months beginning late September 2008 and ending two months after the twins are expected to be born.

Children

The Garretts' son, Brennan, was born January 1, 2007. The twins are expected to be born in late January 2009. Brennan is perfectly healthy, and there is no history of pregnancy-related complications in either Kayla's or Zachary's family.

Zachary's Parents

Zachary's parents, David and Julie, are financially secure and live in California. All of their property is owned as community property. They have known Kayla for many years and any gifts that they make will be to both Zachary and Kayla. David and Julie have made no previous taxable gifts.

The Garretts expect Zachary's parents either to lend (interest free) or to give them a $30,000 down payment (27% of the purchase price) to purchase a house.

Personal and Financial Objectives

1. Zachary wants to start his own business in 10 years. In the meantime, he plans to advance in his current job. He wants to open a business similar to that of his current employer and expects to need $100,000 in today's dollars to start the company.

2. The Garretts want to buy a house for approximately $110,000 in a rural area with little or no crime. They expect taxes and homeowners insurance to average $200 per month combined.

3. Kayla would like to pursue an interior design license. Zachary wants to sharpen his business skills by attending a local MBA program, which he expects to begin in September 2009. He will pay for the program himself. The expected cost is $18,000 ($600 per credit hour in today's dollars).

4. They want each of their children to receive a private school education and would like to create a fund for this purpose. The current cost of the desired school is $2,500 per child annually for elementary and $5,000 per year for middle and high school. College tuition is expected to be $8,000 per year (see Economic Information).

5. They want to purchase a new car within the next six months in a price range between $20,000 and $25,000.

6. They would like to buy new furniture for the new house (valued at $8,000–$10,000 today's dollars).

7. They plan to create an emergency fund of at least six months' salary ($24,000). Currently, they only have a small savings balance; therefore, this amount needs to be saved in installments over the next four years.

8. They plan to retire in 30 years and travel.

9. They expect their income to increase by an average of 3.5% over their remaining work life expectancy.

10. They both expect to live to age 90.

Economic Information

■ Expected inflation will average 3.5% annually.

■ Expected return for the S&P 500 Index is 11%.

■ T-bills are currently yielding 5%. The long-term risk-free rate is 7% (Treasury bonds).

■ Current mortgage rates are 7.5% for a fixed 15-year and 8.0% for a fixed 30-year.

■ Home closing costs are expected to be 3% of any new mortgage.

■ Savings accounts currently yield 1.5% annually, compounded monthly.

■ One-year CDs are currently yielding 5%.

■ The unemployment rate is currently 6%.

■ College tuition is expected to be $8,000 per year (expected to increase by 5% per year).

Insurance Information

Life Insurance

Insured	Zachary
Owner	Zachary
Beneficiary	Kayla
Face amount	$50,000
Cash value	$0
Type of policy	Term
Settlement option	Lump Sum
Premium	Employer Paid

Assumptions for Life Insurance Needs Calculations

- The surviving spouse will continue working at his or her present job.

- An education fund needed is $50,000 in today's dollars.

- An emergency fund of $24,000 is needed for the survivor.

- Funeral and debt expenses will be $50,000 as needed (including any probate costs).

- Survivor income needs are $3,200 per month in today's dollars for 22 years at which time either spouse would be age 48. This is $1,200 more than is currently earned by either spouse.

- From age 48 to 67, survivor needs will be $3,000 per month ($1,000 above either spouse's earnings in today's dollars). At age 67, Social Security will provide $1,078 per month in today's dollars.

- Retirement needs from age 67 to 90 for the survivor are $2,400 per month in today's dollars.

- Life insurance proceeds will be invested at the long-term risk-free rate of return.

- If one of the Garretts dies before retirement, the other will continue working until age 67.

- Social Security benefits during the dependency period will be a family maximum of $1,603 per month (based on current earnings).

Health Insurance

Premium	Employer-paid for Zachary—Kayla and the children are dependents under Zachary's policy
Coverage	Major medical with a $500,000 lifetime limit and an 80/20 coinsurance provision
	Maternity coverage also has 80/20 coinsurance provision
	Dental coverage is not provided
Deductible	$250 per person (three person maximum)
Family out-of-pocket limit	$2,500

Disability Insurance

Neither Zachary nor Kayla has disability insurance.

Automobile Insurance

Premium	$1,000 total annual premium for both vehicles
Bodily damage and property damage	$10,000/$25,000/$5,000 for each vehicle
Comprehensive	$250 deductible
Collision	$500 deductible

Renters Insurance

Type	HO-4
Contents coverage	$35,000
Premium	$600 annually
Deductible	$250
Liability	$100,000
Medical payments	$1,000 per person

HO-4 Policy Declaration Page

Policy Number: **H04-123-ZA-996**
Policy Period: **12:01 a.m. Central Time at the residence premises**
From: January **1, 2009** To: **December 31, 2009**

Name insured and mailing address:

Zachary and Kayla Garrett
Uptown Apartments
1324 Oak Lane, Apartment 100
Anytown, State 00001

The residence premises covered by this policy is located at the above address unless otherwise indicated.

Coverage is provided where a premium of limit of liability is shown for the coverage.

SECTION I COVERAGES	Limit of Liability	Premium
A. Dwelling	N/A	N/A
B. Other structures	N/A	N/A
C. Personal property	$35,000	$475
D. Loss of use	N/A	N/A

SECTION II COVERAGES		
A. Personal liability: each occurrence	$100,000	$100
B. Medical payments to others: each occurrence	$1,000	$25
Total premium for endorsements listed below		
Policy Total		$600

Forms and endorsements made part of this policy:

Number	Edition Date	Title	Premium
Not applicable.			

DEDUCTIBLE—Section I: **$250**
In case of a loss under Section I, we cover only that part of the loss over the deductible stated.
Section II: Other insured locations: **Not applicable.**

[Mortgagee/Lienholder (Name and address)]
Not applicable.

Countersignature of agent/date	Signature/title—company officer

Investment Information

Both Zachary and Kayla have a high risk tolerance. They currently have a balance of $3,840 in Zachary's 401(k) plan provided by his employer. He is currently deferring 4% of his salary, while the maximum deferral allowed by the plan is 10%. The 401(k) plan offers a variety of mutual funds ranging from aggressive growth stock funds to Treasury money market funds. Zachary currently has 100% invested in the growth fund.

Three years ago, Zachary's grandmother gave him shares of ABC stock. The fair market value of the stock at the date of the gift was $6,000 and the annual exclusion was unavailable. Zachary's grandmother originally paid $2,000 for the stock and paid gift tax of $600 on the transfer.

The Garretts' required rate of return for investments is 1% below the S&P 500 Index return.

Income Tax Information

Zachary and Kayla file a joint tax return. Their total tax rate is 24.65% (federal income tax average rate is 15%; the state income tax rate is 2%; FICA tax rate is 7.65%).

Retirement Information

Zachary is a participant in his employer's 401(k) plan.

Kayla would like to contribute $5,000 to an individual retirement account (IRA) in early 2009.

Gifts, Estates, Trusts, and Will Information

Zachary and Kayla have simple handwritten wills leaving all probate assets to each other.

Last Wills and Testaments

Kayla

Last Will and Testament
January 15, 2008

I, Kayla Campeaux Garrett, a citizen of Canada domiciled in the United States of America, declare this to be my last will and testament. I revoke all of my prior wills and codicils.

I hereby give all of the property of which I die possessed to Zachary Garrett, my husband.

Kayla Campeaux Garrett

Zachary

Last Will and Testament
January 15, 2008

I, Zachary Garrett, a citizen of and domiciled in the United States of America, declare this to be my last will and testament. I revoke all of my prior wills and codicils.

I hereby give all of the property of which I die possessed to Kayla Garrett, my wife.

Zachary Garrett

STATEMENT OF CASH FLOWS
Zachary and Kayla Garrett
Monthly Statement of Cash Flows for 2008
(Expected to be similar for 2009)

CASH INFLOWS

Salary—Zachary[1]	$2,000	
Salary—Kayla[2]	2,000	
Interest income	15	
Total inflows[3]		$4,015

CASH OUTFLOWS

401(k) deferral savings	$ 80	
Rent	650	
Groceries	370	
Utilities	70	
Water	25	
Telephone	40	
Auto fuel	100	
Auto repair	50	
Cable TV	35	
Child care	200	
Entertainment	300	
Vacations[4]	375	
Auto insurance	84	
Life insurance	0	
Medical insurance	0	
Renters (HO-4) insurance	50	
State withholding	80	
Federal withholding	600	
FICA	306	
Student loan—Zachary 1	144	
Student loan—Zachary 2	111	
Student loans—Kayla	45	
Credit card 1—Zachary	51	
Fuel card—Zachary	9	
Credit card 2—Kayla	42	
Credit card 3—Kayla	165	
Credit card 4—Kayla	33	
Total outflows		$4,015
Discretionary cash flow		$ 0

Notes to financial statements
[1] $2,000 per month salary = $24,000 per year
[2] $2,000 per month salary = $24,000 per year
[3] Dividend income is reinvested and therefore not listed.
[4] Vacation = two vacations costing $4,500 per year; $4,500 ÷ 12 months = $375

STATEMENT OF FINANCIAL POSITION
Zachary and Kayla Garrett
As of January 1, 2009

Assets[1]		Liabilities[2] and Net Worth	
Cash/cash equivalents		**Current liabilities[3]**	
Checking[4]	$ 750	Credit card 1 (Zachary)[5]	$ 1,500
Savings[6]	1,000	Credit card 2 (Kayla)[5]	1,200
Certificate of deposit[7]	3,000	Credit card 3 (Kayla)[5]	4,800
EE savings bonds[8]	500	Credit card 4 (Kayla)[5]	950
Total cash/cash equiv.	$ 5,250	Fuel card 1 (Zachary)[5]	200
Invested assets		*Total current liabilities*	$ 8,650
ABC stock	$10,000	**Long-term liabilities[3]**	
Stock portfolio[9]	22,000	Student loans[5]	
Zachary's 401(k)	3,840	Zachary 1	20,000
Total invested assets	$35,840	Zachary 2	15,000
		Kayla 1	6,000
Personal use assets		*Total long-term liabilities*	$41,000
Auto 1	$ 7,500		
Auto 2	4,500	**Total liabilities**	**$49,650**
Furniture	6,000		
Personal property	7,000	**Net worth**	**$16,440**
Total personal use assets	$25,000		
Total assets	**$66,090**	**Total liabilities and net worth**	**$66,090**

Notes to financial statements
[1]All assets are stated at fair market value.
[2]Liabilities are stated at principal only.
[3]All liability payments are as indicated on monthly cash flow statement.
[4]Checking is a noninterest-bearing account.
[5]The average interest rate for student loans is 10% and for all credit cards is 25%.
[6]Savings interest of 1.5% annually, compounded monthly.
[7]Certificate of deposit maturing December 1, 2009; interest of 4.5% annually, compounded monthly.
[8]EE savings bonds, five bonds with present value of $100 each; interest of 6% annually; maturity date of 2033.
[9]Stock portfolio in stock account managed by Zachary.

Information Regarding Assets and Liabilities

Detailed Investment Portfolio

Zachary's 401(k) Plan

Description	Shares	Price/Share	Total Value	2007 Returns	2008 Returns
Growth fund	93.00	$41.29	$3,840	13%	7%

Stock Portfolio

Stock	Date Acquired	Cost Basis	Fair Market Value as of 1/1/09	Beta	Current Dividend	Growth of Dividend
A	1/01	$ 300	$ 2,800	1.3	$ 200	3.50%
B	3/03	3,000	700	1.6	33	5.00%
C	5/08	5,000	7,000	1.0	400	4.00%
D	6/08	12,000	2,500	1.1	197	2.00%
E	7/08	9,000	9,000	1.2	500	4.25%
TOTAL		$29,300	$22,000	N/A	$1,330	N/A

Miscellaneous

The Garretts like to take two vacations each year with an average cost of $2,250 per vacation. Zachary and Kayla also enjoy going out with friends or entertaining weekly.

QUESTIONS

1. List the Garretts' financial strengths and weaknesses.

2. After reading the case, what additional information would you request from the Garretts to complete your data-gathering phase?

3. Calculate the following financial ratios for the Garretts:

$\dfrac{\text{Liquid Assets}}{\text{Monthly Expenses}}$
$\dfrac{\text{Liquid Assets}}{\text{Current Debt Payments}}$
$\dfrac{\text{Net Worth}}{\text{Total Assets}}$
$\dfrac{\text{Total Debt}}{\text{Total Assets}}$
$\dfrac{\text{Total Debt}}{\text{Annual Total Income*}}$
$\dfrac{\text{Housing and Monthly Debt Payments}}{\text{Monthly Gross Income}}$
$\dfrac{\text{Housing}}{\text{Monthly Gross Income}}$
$\dfrac{\text{Investment Assets}}{\text{Annual Gross Income}}$
$\dfrac{\text{Monthly Savings}}{\text{Monthly Gross Income}}$

*Annual Total Income is the same as Annual Gross Income.

4. Comment on any of the above ratios that you think are important.

5. Will the Garretts qualify for either a 15- or 30-year home mortgage loan, assuming that they make a down payment of $30,000?

6. Assuming that the Garretts qualify for a home mortgage loan, calculate the monthly payment for each of the following:
   a. 15-year loan
   b. 30-year loan

7. Assuming they have no current savings set aside, how much should be saved at the end of each month, beginning this month, to be able to acquire Zachary's business? Assume they will invest in a no-load S&P 500 Index fund and will pay all current taxes out of their regular budget. They will reinvest all earnings in this account.

8. Rounding to the nearest $100,000, how much additional life insurance should be purchased on Zachary's life by using the needs approach method?

9. Rounding to the nearest $25,000, how much additional life insurance should be purchased on Kayla's life by using the needs approach method?

10. The Garretts want to establish a fund that will provide for each child's four-year college education. Any postgraduate education will be the responsibility of each child. If they can earn an after-tax rate of return equal to the expected return of the S&P 500 Index, how much do they need to save at the end of each year to be able to fund their children's education by the end of 10 years? Assume that the children will all attend college at age 18 and tuition is paid at the beginning of each year. (Round to the nearest dollar.)

11. What are the Garretts' present insurance needs?

12. What are the Garretts' insurance deficiencies?

Use the following information for questions 13 through 17.

While on a vacation at Josephine Lake, the Garretts had several unfortunate incidents.

▪ A large pigeon collided with the windshield of their automobile causing $800 worth of damage while driving to the lake.

▪ Zachary rented a 100-horsepower jet ski. While skiing, his wallet was stolen, but he thought he had lost the wallet in the lake so he did not report the loss to the credit card company until he returned home a week later.

▪ While Zachary was jet skiing, Kayla was taken to the emergency room where she gave birth to twins. Mother and children are doing fine.

▪ While jet skiing, Zachary noticed the ambulance taking Kayla to the hospital. While he was looking at the ambulance, he skied into a boat causing damage to the jet ski, the boat, and to himself. The boat owner, Mr. Frank, had minor medical injuries.

▪ Upon returning home with the twins and their older child, the Garretts discovered that their apartment building had been destroyed by fire.

13. How much will Zachary's insurance company pay to have his windshield repaired from the collision with the pigeon?

14. When Zachary received his credit card statements, he discovered that the following amounts had been charged to his credit cards by the thief.

Credit card 1	$200
Credit card 2	$450
Credit card 3	$ 35
Credit card 4	$ 60

How much of the new charges is Zachary's responsibility?

15. The hospital costs for delivery of the twins was $15,000. How much will the insurance company pay?

16. A fire that destroyed the Garretts' apartment building also destroyed all of their personal property. Although the depreciated or actual cash value of all their property is $5,000, it would cost the Garretts about $37,000 to replace all of their lost items. How much will the insurance company pay for this loss?

17. In the jet ski accident, Zachary incurred medical expenses of $1,450. Discuss which of the Garretts' insurance policies, if any, will cover these expenses.

ADDITIONAL QUESTIONS

1. What would be the deduction for Kayla's IRA contribution for last year?

2. If Zachary were to sell the ABC stock today, what would be the current tax consequences to the Garretts?

3. Assume Zachary has the following transactions in his stock trading account for the current year:

Sold Stock	Current Year	Sales Price/Net of Commissions
A	August 15	$ 2,750
B	August 15	$ 600
C	April 1	$ 8,000
D	April 1	$ 3,000
		$14,350 Total proceeds

What are the net gains or losses from the above stock transactions during the current year?

4. If the stock market yields 17%, what is the expected return for the Garretts' stock portfolio under the capital asset pricing model, based on the value as of the January 1 balance sheet?

5. Based on the constant dividend growth model, which of the stocks in the Garretts' stock portfolio (A–E) is(are) overvalued as of the January 1 balance sheet?

6. If Zachary's parents donate a 20% down payment on the house, what are the gift tax consequences?

7. Assuming that David and Julie decide to loan a 20% down payment to Zachary and Kayla instead of giving it to them, what are the tax consequences to David and Julie? Assume that the federal rate for imputed interest is 9%.

8. Discuss the Garretts' current estate planning deficiencies.

9. What estate planning recommendations would you make to the Garretts?

10. What tax planning recommendations would you make to the Garretts?

11. Which of the following would be appropriate for the Garretts to consider to reduce their current income tax liability for the year 2009?

    a. Hope Scholarship Credit

    b. Coverdell Education Savings Accounts

    c. Child Tax Credit

12. Can the Garretts deduct the interest on student loans for federal income tax purposes?

13. Zachary's parents, David and Julie, live in California and are financially well off. They purchased their current residence 20 years ago for $500,000. Today, it is worth $1.5 million. If David passes away and Julie sells their residence for $1.8 million, how much of the gain can she exclude from income?

14. Assume it is five years from now, and David's 401(k) vested account balance totals $50,000. Can David rollover these funds from his qualified plan directly to a Roth IRA?

15. Zachary and Kayla purchased a new home. Six months later they incur major medical expenses, a downturn in the stock market, and an adjustable rate mortgage with a dramatically increased interest rate. They determine that they cannot afford to continue making their mortgage payments and cover all of their other expenses as well.

    a. What 401(k) withdrawal option might be available to them?

    b. What is the maximum amount of elective contributions that can be distributed as a hardship distribution from a 401(k) plan?

    c. What are the consequences of taking a hardship distribution of elective contributions from a 401(k) plan?

16. The company that Zachary works for acquired $560,000 of personal property used 100% in the operation of the business in 2009. Assuming that income is not a limitation, what is the amount of a Section 179 deduction available to the company in 2009?

Joel and Candy Jones

Today is January 1, 2009. Joel and Candy Jones have come to you, a financial planner, for help in developing a plan to accomplish their financial goals. From your initial meeting together, you have gathered the following information.

Personal Background and Information

Joel (Age 43)

Dr. Jones is a research scientist with GaAs, Inc., where he has been employed for three years. He spends the majority of his time writing articles, teaching, and developing computer programs to simulate and optimize gallium arsenide (GaAs) devices. He holds many patents, is developing an international reputation in his field, and has recently been approached to coauthor an engineering text. This is his second career; he spent the previous 14 years working as a geophysicist with OnShore, Inc.

A lawsuit over the Jones family inheritance splintered Joel's family. Joel disclaimed his portion of the estate and maintains limited contact with only one family member, his sister Jane.

Joel appears to be in good health but seeks medical attention only when required to do so by his employer.

Candy (Age 43)

Candy is a certified public accountant by profession and has held various financial management positions. She supported Joel's academic efforts and gave up her consulting practice three years ago to relocate with Joel to Arizona. Once there, Candy began studying for a second career as a financial analyst. She plans to reenter the work force in three years.

Candy's parents recently outlined an estate plan in which they identified their wish to grant her a general power of appointment over family assets of approximately $1.5 million. Candy has specified that she will disclaim any inheritances in favor of her direct descendants (one daughter and one grandchild).

Candy appears to be in good health, though she underwent two surgeries last year. Complications from the first (major) surgery required a second (outpatient), but she has begun swimming and cycling to rebuild her endurance. She expects a full recovery and has resumed studying for her second career.

The Joneses

Joel and Candy Jones have been married for 14 years. They came to you to identify estate planning opportunities. The achievement of personal and financial goals has positioned the Joneses to benefit from a comprehensive financial review. They live in Ahwatukee, Arizona. Arizona is a community property state.

Joel and Candy discuss all financial matters. They have very different risk tolerances. Candy executes all investment decisions, manages their separate and combined wealth, pays all bills, and prepares personal financial statements and tax returns.

Joel and Candy executed wills 10 years ago in Texas. Prior to the recent surgeries, Candy updated her will and asked Joel to do the same. Candy told Joel they should meet with an estate planner. Joel felt it was unnecessary to update his will, and disagreed as to the need for estate planning. The Joneses have sweetheart wills (all property left to each other) except for a $50,000 life insurance policy on Candy that is left to her daughter. Beneficiaries (Candy for Joel; Joel for Candy) have been listed on all retirement accounts. Most nonretirement assets are community property. Personal items are separately identified in a side letter and given to various family members.

Personal and Financial Objectives

Joel's Goals (in order of priority)

1. He wants to continue making the maximum contribution (10% of salary) to employee stock purchase plan (ESPP).

2. He wants to continue maximizing contributions to 401(k) plan.

3. He wants to spend $7,500 per year for hardware and software updates to the home office.

4. He wants to become debt-free in five years but will consider refinancing first as mortgage rates are dropping.

5. He wants to review and reposition the investment portfolio (accumulated mainly over past 10 years).

6. He wants to minimize their federal income tax burden.

7. He wants to retire at age 67 (approximately 23.5 years from now) with $120,000 per year in today's dollars from all sources.

Candy's Goals (in order of priority)

1. She wants to minimize contributions to Joel's employee stock purchase plan.

2. She wants to continue maximizing contributions to 401(k) plan.

3. She wants to spend $2,000 annually for books and travel costs related to education.

4. She wants to spend $5,000 annually for one major vacation and regular visits with relatives.

5. She wants to replenish the emergency fund back to $22,000, which was used by Joel to pay cash for nonemergency items.

6. She wants to establish an education fund for her daughter (married, age 22, who dropped out of college).

7. She wants to review and reposition the investment portfolio (accumulated mainly over past 10 years).

8. She wants to exercise Joel's nonqualifying stock options (NQSOs) when the tax impact is less onerous.

9. She wants to make additional principal payments on the current mortgage after meeting other financial goals.

10. She wants to plan for estate issues arising from changes in net worth and from the current titling of assets.

Funding of Goals

Joel and Candy disagree as to the adequacy of their emergency fund, as well as funding alternatives for their stated goals. Candy is willing to consider a combination of savings and available cash flow, depending on the nature of the item to be funded. Joel wants to accomplish only those goals that can be funded by excess cash flow from regular salary. Joel thinks that they can meet emergency needs by selling part of Candy's stock portfolio. Candy, however, has a buy/never sell philosophy about the portfolio, except when repositioning the portfolio or when it receives a step-up in adjusted taxable basis.

Economic Information

■ Inflation has averaged 3% over the past 20 years and is expected to continue at this rate.

■ Educational inflation is expected to be 6%.

■ The 30-year mortgage rate is 6.75%. The 15-year mortgage rate is 6.25%. Refinancing costs are 2% and could be added to the amount of the mortgage or paid separately at closing.

■ Annualized investment returns to be used for 1-, 3-, 5-, and 10-year periods ending 12/31/08 are as follows:

— Dow—(6.2%); 10.9%; 16.1%; 15.2%

— Nasdaq—(39.1%); 16.3%; 18.6%; 20.8%

— S&P 500—(10.1%); 10.8%; 16.5%; 15.0%

Insurance Information

Auto

$100,000/$300,000/$100,000

Life

There is a $240,000 term policy on Joel; Candy is the beneficiary. There is a $50,000 universal life policy on Candy, owned by Candy, listing Candy's daughter as the beneficiary.

Health

The Jones family has a major medical policy with a 50/50 coinsurance provision provided by Joel's employer. The plan has a $2,000 annual deductible per individual, a $3 million lifetime coverage cap per person, and a $10,000 stop loss limit.

Disability

Joel pays 100% of the premium on a long-term disability policy offered through his employer. It includes 60% benefit coverage for both accident and sickness with a 180-day elimination period and defines disability as any occupation.

Homeowners Policy

Joel and Candy have a typical HO-3 policy—no separate endorsements.

Inland Marine Policy

This covers Joel's laptop computer that he uses for work both at home and the office.

Umbrella Policy

They have $1 million in coverage.

Investment Information

Investments (see Various Subsections)

Joel and Candy agree that their investments are widely dispersed and were accumulated without any particular plan. Filing and record keeping has become a full-time, uncompensated job for Candy. As part of your comprehensive financial review, they want you to make recommendations about the structure of the portfolio and the holdings.

Candy executed a trustee-to-trustee rollover of the entire balance of one of her individual retirement accounts (IRAs) to a technology value fund.

Retirement Information

Joel and Candy are both fully insured for Social Security retirement benefits. Joel's SSA 7004 (earnings and benefits statement) indicates that he will receive a monthly benefit of $2,436. Candy's SSA 7004 indicates she will receive approximately $1,229.

Joel's current employer offered him a choice between a portable or traditional defined benefit plan. Joel chose the traditional defined benefit plan that includes a five-year cliff vesting schedule. If Joel retires from GaAs, Inc., at age 67, he will be entitled to an annual benefit of $120,000 in future dollars for the remainder of his life.

Candy included in their retirement assets a present value for Joel's vested monthly benefit after Social Security offset on a single-life annuity from OnShore, Inc. She used a 5.75% discount rate and a 20-year retirement life expectancy. Joel does not believe the vested benefit is an asset or that it should appear on their financial statement.

STATEMENT OF NET WORTH
Joel and Candy Jones
As of January 1, 2009

Assets

Cash and cash equivalents

CP	Cash reserves—money market mutual fund		$ 16,800
CP	Joint checking and savings		13,300
W	Cash reserves—brokerage		5,032
W	Cash surrender value of universal life insurance		3,647
	Total cash and cash equivalents		$ 38,779

Investments

	Technology		$ 161,035
	GaAs stock—brokerage	$ 10,811	
	GaAs stock—ESPP	6,228	
	GaAs ESPP—cash balance	4,669	
	GaAs NQSOs	5,303	
	Technology—GaAs		27,011
	Cyclical (Section 1202 Stock)	3,093	
	Interest sensitive—bank	1,295	
	Drug delivery	2,450	
CP	Total individual stocks		$ 6,838
CP	Domestic mutual funds		84,782
	Total investment assets		**$ 279,666**

Retirement assets

CP	401(k)—OnShore, Inc.—cash	$ 14,411	
CP	Profit sharing—OnShore, Inc.—cash	7,915	
			$ 22,326
CP	Annuity—403b	$ 34,450	
CP	Annuity—457	8,530	
CP	Annuity—nonqualified	12,639	
			$ 55,619
CP	401(k)—GaAs—company stock		4,735
H	IRAs—domestic mutual funds	$ 104,515	
W	IRAs—domestic mutual funds	81,271	
CP	Profit sharing—OnShore, Inc.—domestic mutual funds	199,716	
CP	401(k)—OnShore, Inc.—domestic mutual funds	118,171	
CP	401(k)—GaAs—domestic mutual funds	36,973	
			$ 540,646
W	IRAs—international mutual funds	$ 11,461	
CP	401(k)—OnShore, Inc.—international mutual funds	34,524	
			$ 45,985
CP	Vested defined benefit—OnShore, Inc.		38,462
	Total retirement assets		**$ 707,773**

(Continued on next page)

STATEMENT OF NET WORTH
Joel and Candy Jones
As of January 1, 2009 *(Continued)*

Use assets				
CP	Home			$ 204,920
CP	Vehicles			26,000
CP	Other—computer (hardware/software/network)	$	18,000	
W	Other—jewelry		10,000	
CP	Other—furniture		20,000	
	Other			$ 48,000
	Total use assets			**$ 278,920**
Total assets				**$1,305,138**
Liabilities				
CP	GaAs Credit Union West—credit card—(7.9%)			0
CP	GaAs Credit Union West—auto—(6.25%)			1,513
CP	Chase Manhattan Mortgage—original balance $150,000—(7.25%)			145,018
Total liabilities				**$ 146,531**
Net worth				**$1,158,607**

Notes to financial statements

All assets are stated at fair market value.

Title designations

H = husband's separate property

W = wife's separate property

CP = community property

STATEMENT OF CASH FLOWS
Joel and Candy Jones
January 1, 2008 to December 31, 2008
(Expected to be similar in 2009)

	Annual	Monthly
INFLOWS[1]		
Salary (H)	$ 120,000	$ 10,000
Patent income (H)[2]	5,772	481
Annual bonus (H)[2]	7,500	625
Interest and dividends (from investments)[3]	3,600	300
Capital gains (from 1099-Div.; Sch. D not required)[3]	12,000	1,000
	$ 148,872	$ 12,406
OUTFLOWS		
GaAs 401(k) contribution (max by H)	$ 15,500	$1,292
GaAs ESPP contribution (10% by H)	12,000	1,000
Credit union—savings	1,536	128
Federal income tax withholding	25,670	2,139
FICA	8,256	688
State income tax	5,300	442
Mortgage payment—(principal, interest, taxes, and insurance)[4]	14,640	1,220
Credit union—vehicle loan	2,580	215
Utilities: Electricity	1,800	150
Phones	1,200	100
Cable	360	30
Water	600	50
Insurance: Auto	800	67
Health	600	50
Disability	120	10
Umbrella	240	20
Inland marine	50	4
Life	180	15
Homeowners ($360/year included in mortgage)		
Hardware/software	3,000	250
Pool service	60	5
Lawn service	70	6
Gasoline	1,265	105
Food	3,120	260
Professional journals/memberships	2,400	200
Travel	1,000	83
Charity	1,200	100
	$ 103,547	$ 8,629
Cash flow available for goals and savings	$ 45,325	$ 3,777

[1]Items not shown include potential new source of income from teaching and royalties and employer matches 4.5% of total compensation of (H).
($133,272 × 4.5% = $5,997)
[2]Income from patents and bonus not guaranteed.
[3]All dividends and capital gains from investments are reinvested.
[4]Qualified property tax estimated at $2,000. Qualified residence interest estimated to be $11,000.

Detailed Investment Account Information

Schedule 1: Analysis of Assets (net of debt) Prepared by Candy Jones

	Investment	Retirement	Use	Total	Asset %
Cash and cash equivalents	$ 38,779	$ 22,326		$ 61,105	5%
Annuities		55,619		55,619	5%
Individual and GaAs stock	194,884	4,735		199,619	17%
Domestic mutual funds	84,782	540,646		625,428	54%
International mutual funds		45,985		45,985	4%
Defined benefit plan		38,462		38,462	3%
Home (net of debt)			$ 59,902	59,902	5%
Vehicles (net of debt)			24,487	24,487	2%
Other			48,000	48,000	4%
(194,884 + 84,782) = 279,666	$ 318,445	$ 707,773	$ 132,389	$ 1,158,607	100%
	27%	61%	11%		

Schedule 2: Domestic Mutual Funds—$625,427 (from Schedule 1)

	Investment	Retirement	Total	Weights	Actual 5-yr. Avg. Ret.	Category 5-yr. Avg. Ret.
Bonds		$ 5,195	$ 5,195	0.83%	6.05%	6.05%
Large cap blend		107,794	107,794	17.24%	14.85%	15.96%
Large cap growth	$64,133	267,386	331,519	53.01%	17.18%	18.11%
Mid cap growth	20,649	22,597	43,246	6.91%	11.03%	17.82%
Mid cap value		22,387	22,387	3.58%	10.53%	14.21%
Small cap value		39,210	39,210	6.27%	16.33%	13.41%
Specialty—real estate		2,409	2,409	0.39%	11.61%	10.34%
Specialty—technology		73,667	73,667	11.78%	42.88%	26.09%
	$84,782	$ 540,645	$ 625,427	100.00%		
	14%	86%				

Schedule 3: Individual and GaAs Stock—$199,620 (from Schedule 1)

	Investment	Retirement	Total	Weights
Technology	$161,035		$161,035	81%
Technology—employer*	27,011	$4,735	31,746	16%
Cyclical	3,093		3,093	2%
Interest sensitive	1,295		1,295	1%
Drug delivery	2,450		2,450	1%
	$194,884	$4,735	$199,619	100%
	98%	2%	100%	

*Reflected on Net Worth Statement

Schedule 4: GaAs Stock (Number of Shares)*

	Shares	Market Price	Ex. Price	FMV
Fair market value				
Shares held in brokerage	303.4580	$ 35.6250		$ 10,811
Long-term shares in ESPP	174.8142	35.6250		6,228
Cash in ESPP				4,669
NQSOs vested, in brokerage	300.0000	35.6250	17.9467	5,303
NQSOs vested, in brokerage	281.2500	35.6250	43.8433	—
Shares held in 401(k)	132.9154	35.6250		4,735
	1,059.522			$ 31,746
Unvested employer shares/value**				
NQSOs unvested, in brokerage	843.750	$ 35.6250	43.843	$ —
NQSOs unvested, in brokerage	1,125.000	35.625	25.000	11,953
	1,968.750			$ 11,953
Total	3,028.272			$ 43,699
	GaAs 52-week high, $62; GaAs 52-week low, $15			

Reflected on Statement of Financial Position
***Not reflected on Statement of Financial Position*

Schedule 5: Summary of Domestic Mutual Funds and Individual Stock Holdings
(Excludes Cash, Annuities, International Mutual Funds, DB Plan, Home, Vehicles, Other)

	1 Value	2 MF Cat. Wt.	3 MF Cat. Beta	4 MF Wt. Beta (2 × 3)
Domestic LC Growth	$ 331,519	53%	1.03	0.55
Domestic LC Blend	107,794	17%	0.70	0.12
Specialty—Technology	73,667	12%	1.67	0.20
Mid Cap growth	43,246	7%	1.17	0.08
Small Cap Value	39,210	6%	0.62	0.04
Mid Cap Value	22,387	4%	0.77	0.03
Specialty—Real Estate	2,409	0%	0.19	0.00
Intermediate Bond	5,195	1%	0.98	0.01
Domestic Mutual Funds*	$ 625,427	100%		1.02
Individual and GaAs Stock**	199,621			1.37
	$ 825,048			

Note: Mutual Fund Weighted R^2 = 69
* *From Schedule 3*
** *From Schedule 4*

Schedule 6: Detail of Combined Funds

Fund	Value	%	R^2	Beta	Wtd. Beta	Return	Wtd. Ret.
Domestic Large Cap Growth Funds (Schedule 5)							
Holding 1	$ 66,344	20.0%	75%	1.0	0.21	17.68%	3.54%
Holding 2	71,270	21.5%	82%	1.2	0.27	17.40%	3.74%
Holding 3	79,200	23.9%	89%	1.0	0.25	17.33%	4.14%
Holding 4	114,706	34.6%	73%	0.9	0.31	16.64%	5.76%
	$331,519	100.0%			1.03		17.18%
Domestic Large Cap Blend Funds (Schedule 5)							
Holding 2	$ 41,655	38.6%	100%	1.0	0.39	18.34%	7.09%
Holding 1	66,138	61.4%	80%	0.5	0.31	12.66%	7.77%
	$107,794	100.0%			0.70		14.85%
Specialty - Technology (Schedule 1)							
Holding 2	$ 64,423	87.5%	35%	1.7	1.45	44.70%	39.09%
Holding 1	9,244	12.5%	45%	1.7	0.22	30.17%	3.79%
	$ 73,667	100.0%			1.67		42.88%
Foreign (Schedule 1)							
Holding 2	$ 34,524	75.1%	61%	0.8	0.63	10.52%	7.90%
Holding 1	11,460	24.9%	27%	0.7	0.18	17.25%	4.30%
	$ 45,984	100.0%			0.81		12.20%

Schedule 7: Average Actual and Expected Five-Year Returns for Domestic Mutual Funds

	Investment	Retirement	Total	Weights	Actual 5 yr. Avg. Ret.	Category 5 yr. Avg. Ret.	Actual Wavg. 5 yr. Ret.	Exp'd Wavg. 5 yr. Ret.
Bonds		$ 5,195	$ 5,195	0.83%	6.05%	6.05%	0.05%	0.05%
Large Cap Blend		107,794	107,794	17.24%	14.85%	15.96%	2.56%	2.75%
Large Cap Growth	$64,133	267,386	331,519	53.01%	17.18%	18.11%	9.11%	9.60%
Mid Cap Growth	20,649	22,597	43,246	6.91%	11.03%	17.82%	0.76%	1.23%
Mid Cap Value		22,387	2,387	3.58%	10.53%	14.21%	0.38%	0.51%
Small Cap Value		39,210	39,210	6.27%	16.33%	13.41%	1.02%	0.84%
Specialty- Real Estate		2,409	2,409	0.39%	11.61%	10.34%	0.04%	0.04%
Specialty- Technology		73,667	73,667	11.78%	42.88%	26.09%	5.05%	3.07%
	$84,782	$540,645	$625,427	100%			18.97%	18.09%
	14%	86%						

Schedule 8: Comparison of Joneses' Mutual Fund Holdings to Established Benchmarks

Domestic Mutual Funds			No. of			Std.				Average Mean Returns at 12/31/08				
	Category	Risk/Return	Stars	P/E	R²	Dev.	Beta	Alpha	Sharpe	YTD	1	3	5	10
Holding	Inter. Bond	Avg/AbAvg	4		96	3.2	1.0	-0.5	0.2	1.64	12.88	5.92	6.05	8.15
Intermediate Bond	Benchmark									1.64	12.88	5.92	6.05	8.15
Holding 1	LC Blend	Low/Avg	4	24.40	80	10.9	0.5	-0.6	0.4	1.06	11.38	9.00	12.66	14.28
Holding 2	LC Blend	Avg/AbAvg	4	31.15	100	20.0	1.0	0.0	0.5	3.55	-0.84	13.19	18.34	17.26
Large-Cap Blend	Benchmark									2.68	-0.49	11.46	15.96	15.41
Holding 1	LC Growth	AbAvg/AbAvg	3	44.48	75	24.2	1.0	2.2	0.5	-0.42	-12.91	15.18	17.68	15.31
Holding 2	LC Growth	High/High	3	44.70	82	28.6	1.2	2.1	0.4	4.90	-10.30	16.27	17.40	19.50
Holding 3	LC Growth	Avg/High	5	36.55	89	22.4	1.0	1.4	0.5	2.66	-4.62	14.71	17.33	19.69
Holding 4	LC Growth	Avg/AbAvg	4	34.27	73	20.9	0.9	1.8	0.5	-3.96	-7.27	13.87	16.64	19.44
Large-Cap Growth	Benchmark									2.29	-8.53	16.88	18.11	
Holding	MC Growth	High/Avg	2	33.80	25	53.2	1.2	10.8	0.3	-9.26	-11.03	19.23	11.03	14.70
Mid-Cap Growth	Benchmark									2.39	-4.06	21.72	17.82	
Holding	MC Value	Avg/Avg	3	15.76	40	23.4	0.8	-3.6	0.0	1.86	20.42	6.24	10.53	15.26
Mid-Cap Value	Benchmark									2.56	25.86	10.10	14.21	15.50
Holding	SC Value	BelowAvg/Avg	4	18.70	52	16.7	0.6	0.3	0.3	6.66	30.43	10.20	16.33	19.33
Small-Cap Value	Benchmark									4.87	27.27	5.99	13.41	14.80
Holding	Spec. R/E	Avg/BelowAvg	2	19.55	5	15.1	0.2	-3.1	-0.2	0.27	32.73	2.73	11.61	13.07
Specialty—Real Estate	Benchmark									0.88	27.91	1.05	10.34	10.71
Holding 1	Spec. Tech	High/High	5	45.74	45	70.5	1.7	27.5	0.6	8.59	-25.06	41.03	30.17	27.63
Holding 2	Spec. Tech	High/High	5	47.78	35	85.2	1.7	41.8	0.6	14.00	-3.90	52.60	44.70	0.00
Specialty—Technology	Benchmark									8.82	-25.93	35.39	26.09	
International Mutual Funds														
Holding 1	Foreign	Avg/High	5	34.07	27	29.0	0.7	7.0	0.4	-1.74	-12.02	16.62	17.25	0.00
Holding 2	Foreign	Avg/Avg	3	28.38	61	20.7	0.8	-2.0	0.2	1.69	-11.94	9.07	10.52	9.35
Foreign										0.59	-10.89	9.98	9.04	

Schedule 9: Joneses' Individual Stock Holdings

Symbol	Industry	52 wk Hi/Low	Div. Yld.	EPS	P/E	Beta	Value	Tax Basis	Gain/Loss	Weight	Wtd Beta
Individual and GaAs Stock											
TECH1	Internet software & services	33-1.75		-1.19		0.0	$ 850	$2,500	$(1,650)	0.43%	0.00
TECH2	Networking— comm. devices	82-27		0.42	67.3	1.6	34,813	10,500	24,313	17.44%	0.28
DRUG	Drug delivery	21-3		-1.41		2.4	2,450	3,200	(750)	1.23%	0.03
CYCLICAL	Sporting goods	23-11	1.3	1.16	19.0	1.2	3,093	1,500	1,593	1.55%	0.02
GaAs	Diversified electronic equip.	62-16	0.9	0.58	32.1	1.3	31,746	20,000	11,746	15.90%	0.21
BANK	Regional— southeast banks	15-9	3.7	1.25	11.4	1.0	1,296	1,000	296	0.65%	0.01
TECH3	Diversified computer syst.	135-80	0.5	4.44	15.9	1.2	57,816	3,500	54,316	28.96%	0.35
TECH4	Semiconductor broad line	76-30	0.2	1.51	22.8	1.5	59,319	13,400	45,919	29.72%	0.45
TECH5	Scientific and tech. instr.	63-17		0.55	38.1	1.0	8,238	3,200	5,038	4.13%	0.04
							$199,621	$58,800	$140,821	100%	1.37

QUESTIONS

1. List the Joneses' financial strengths and weaknesses.

2. After reading the case, what additional information would you request from the Joneses to complete your data-gathering phase?

3. Calculate the following financial ratios for the Joneses.

$\dfrac{\text{Liquid Assets}}{\text{Total Monthly Expenses}}$
$\dfrac{\text{Liquid Assets}}{\text{Current Debt}}$
$\dfrac{\text{Net Worth}}{\text{Total Assets}}$
$\dfrac{\text{Total Debt}}{\text{Total Assets}}$
$\dfrac{\text{Total Debt}}{\text{Annual Gross Income}}$
$\dfrac{\text{Annual Housing Costs}}{\text{Annual Gross Income}}$
$\dfrac{\text{Investment Assets}}{\text{Annual Gross Income}}$
$\dfrac{\text{Annual Savings}}{\text{Annual Gross Income}}$

4. Comment on any of the above ratios that you think are important.

5. Identify areas of conflict between Joel's and Candy's goals.
    a. Whose goals should take priority? On which goals can they compromise?
    b. Do they have enough cash flow to fund all goals?

6. The Joneses are considering three alternatives to retire their mortgage debt in five years. Calculate the total monthly payment for each alternative. Include the savings component in alternative *b* for comparability purposes and comment on the appropriateness and risk of each.
    a. Make equal monthly payments on the existing mortgage to retire the debt in five years.
    b. Deposit a monthly amount in an investment account to retire the existing mortgage in five years. Assume they can earn an average return of 8% per year on this investment account.
    c. Refinance and make equal monthly payments sufficient to retire the mortgage balance in five years.

7. Is the life insurance coverage for Joel and Candy sufficient?

8. Candy's medical bills totaled $18,000. How much of this amount will Candy have to pay?

9. Should Joel have additional disability coverage? Discuss why or why not, and discuss the significant issues. Where might he obtain coverage?

10. Does the HO-3 policy provide sufficient coverage for Candy's jewelry and Joel's hardware and software? If not, what would?

11. Joel wants to drop the personal umbrella liability coverage, and Candy thinks they should keep it. What is your recommendation and why?

12. Joel keeps a laptop with him at all times and is quite concerned about loss or theft. It contains his engineering notes, experiments, intellectual property, and proprietary data belonging to his employer. Do the Joneses need an inland marine policy for Joel's laptop?

13. What is the tax consequence of Joel's term insurance coverage, and how is it reported?

14. Candy is considering two alternatives to provide an education for her daughter. What are the risks, income tax consequences, and gift tax consequences of each of the two (*a* and *b*) alternatives?

    a. Gifting $13,000 per year for five years.
    b. Paying the tuition directly to the institution chosen by her daughter.

15. Do the Joneses have a sufficient emergency fund? Is the sale of stock at the time of an emergency an appropriate way to provide for an emergency?

16. The Joneses are both fully insured for Social Security retirement benefits. Will Candy's absence from the work force affect her Social Security status or final benefit?

17. Project the future value of the Joneses' existing retirement assets, assuming they both retire at age 67 (23.5 years from today) and earn an average return of 8%. Calculate the inflation-adjusted future value as well.

18. Project the future value of the Joneses' existing investment assets, assuming they both retire at age 67 (23.5 years from today) and earn an average return of 8%. Calculate the inflation-adjusted future value as well. What adjustment, if any, should be made to the investment total prior to calculation?

19. The Joneses have asked you to explain beta.

20. The weighted-average beta of the Joneses' individual stock holdings is 1.37. Given that the Joneses' domestic mutual fund and stock portfolio totals $825,048, what is the weighted-average beta of the combined portfolio?

21. What is the general significance of R squared (R^2)? What is the particular significance of R^2 for the large-cap blend, holding 2?

22. Explain alpha to the Joneses and identify the risk measure incorporated in alpha. What does a positive alpha imply?

23. What is the Treynor ratio, and which measure of risk is used in its calculation?

24. What is the Sharpe ratio, and which measure of risk is used in its calculation?

25. The Joneses believe their portfolio contains too many different mutual funds and fund companies. They are willing to change the type and number of funds held. Evaluate the appropriateness of their portfolio in the context of diversification, risk, return, and retirement funding projections.

26. Discuss the risk associated with maximizing contributions to Joel's employee stock purchase plan. Consider the existing portfolio, the likelihood that Joel will continue receiving NQSOs from his employer and will continue allocating 401(k) funds to employer stock, the 52-week fluctuation in market price of GaAs, Inc., the Joneses' emergency fund, and other stated financial goals.

27. You complete the financial analysis and develop a comprehensive plan. When you call the Joneses to schedule a follow-up meeting, Candy informs you she has filed for divorce. The Joneses are now trying to split their assets. You have done the work. Do you present the plan?

28. Can you assist the Joneses in the division of assets related to an impending divorce?

29. What are your ethical responsibilities to the Joneses should one or both of them ask you to represent them after the divorce?

30. Explain standard deviation for historical (actual) returns.

ADDITIONAL QUESTIONS

1. The Joneses file a joint federal income tax return. Are they subject to a phaseout of personal exemptions?

2. Which of the Joneses' expenses qualify as itemized deductions? For simplification purposes, use mortgage interest and property tax information estimated on the statement of cash flows.

3. Should Candy's rollover be reported on the Joneses' federal income tax (Form 1040)? If so, is the rollover amount included in taxable income?

4. Identify timing and tax issues associated with exercising Joel's NQSOs.

5. What was Candy implying when she said she would sell stock from the portfolio when she got a step-up in adjusted taxable basis?

6. Calculate the monthly payment Joel can expect from his vested defined benefit plan with his former employer, OnShore, assuming he will begin taking benefits in 23.5 years.

   Note: Joel is going to begin taking benefits from his previous employer's plan, not from GaAs.

7. Benefit calculations under each of Joel's pension plans are subject to Social Security offset. What is Social Security offset, and does this mean Joel will lose an amount equal to twice the amount of his Social Security benefit?

8. The Joneses would like to retire with the present day equivalent of $120,000 per year from all sources. Assuming the Joneses can achieve an 8% return on these assets, will the projected future value of their existing retirement and investment assets be sufficient to fund their retirement?

9. Joel chose the traditional pension plan with GaAs. The company projects Joel's annual benefit at normal retirement will be $120,000. How should this unvested pension plan benefit be treated in retirement projections for the Joneses?

10. What is the significance of Joel disclaiming his inheritance? What steps must be taken to effectively disclaim?

11. What are the consequences and risks associated with the granting of a general power of appointment being considered by Candy's family?

12. Do the Joneses need estate planning? If so, what should they consider?

13. Discuss the tax implications of selling or consolidating parts of the mutual fund portfolio versus the individual stock portfolio. The Joneses tell you they have tax basis of $58,800 in their stock portfolio ($143,221 long-term capital gains; $2,400 long-term capital losses). They have also reinvested all income and capital gains on mutual fund holdings.

14. The Joneses tell you that, as part of their impending divorce, Joel has agreed to pay Candy alimony for the next three years while she completes her studies to become a financial analyst. Joel has tentatively offered to pay alimony in the following amounts:

    Year 1: $50,000

    Year 2: $50,000

    Year 3: $30,000

    What are the income tax implications of this arrangement for the Joneses?

15. Assume that Joel dies in an automobile accident in 2009. The Joneses' sweetheart wills are still in effect, and Candy inherits all of the Joel's property, including his interest in any assets held as community property. Among these assets are the shares of Drug Delivery stock, which are valued at $3,000 on the date of Joel's death. The Joneses acquired the stock several years ago for $500. What would be the income tax implications for Candy if she sells the Drug Delivery stock for $4,000 seven months after Joel dies?

16. Assume that Candy dies in 2009 and that Joel, as her designated beneficiary, inherits her IRAs when she dies. What distribution requirements will apply to Joel with respect to the IRAs? What distribution requirements would apply if Candy had designated Joel and her daughter as beneficiaries for the IRAs?

17. If Joel died on January 1, 2009, what would be the value of his probate estate?

18. What would be the income tax consequences for the Joneses if they sold the Cyclical stock in 2009 for $5,000? Assume they purchased the stock in 2001 and that their adjusted basis is $2,000.

Ryan and Allison Duke

Ryan and Allison Duke have come to you, a financial planner, for help in developing a plan to accomplish their financial goals. Assume today is January 1, 2009, and you have gathered the following information.

Personal Background and Information

Ryan Duke (Age 56)

Ryan owns his own business, a small jewelry store, with Schedule C net income of $50,000 in 2008. Ryan's only employee is his son, Bill, who works part-time.

Allison Duke (Age 51)

Allison is a professor of physics at a state university where she has been employed full-time since 1987. Her W-2 income, which is $60,000 for nine months of teaching, is paid ratably over 12 months at $5,000 per month.

The Dukes

Ryan and Allison have been married for six years. Both are in excellent health. They provide some financial support to Allison's father, Ralph, who is in an assisted living facility. Ralph is not a dependent of the Dukes for income tax purposes.

The Children

Ryan and Allison have five-year old twins. Ryan has two children from a former marriage. Bill, age 20, attends a state university. All of his college expenses including tuition, books, room and university fees are paid by his aunt Cleo. Alice, age 12, is in 7th grade at a public school. Bill works less than 20 hours per week in the jewelry store.

Personal and Financial Objectives

1. The Dukes want to retire when Ryan is 62 and Allison is 57.

2. They want to increase their tax-advantaged savings.

3. They want to be debt free of all mortgages at retirement.

4. They want to minimize their estate tax liability and avoid the costs of probate.

5. They want to transfer the jewelry business to Bill at their death or retirement.

Economic Information

They expect inflation to average 4% over the long-term. The historical return on the market has been 12% and is expected to continue. The market has had a standard deviation of 14%, which is expected to continue.

T-bills are currently yielding 3%, while T-bonds are yielding 4%.

Insurance Information

Life Insurance

	Policy #1	Policy #2
Person insured	Ryan	Allison
Face amount	$250,000	$250,000
Cash value	$0	$0
Type of policy	Individual Term	Group term
Annual premium	$650	Employer paid
Beneficiary	Allison	Debra (Allison's mother)
Contingent beneficiary	None	None
Policyowner	Ryan	Allison
Settlement option chosen	Life annuity	None chosen

Health Insurance

Persons covered	Family
Type of policy	Comprehensive basic/state university plan
Coverage	Major medical 80/20, $2,500 stop loss
Deductible	$500 family deductible
Annual premiums	Employer paid

Automobile Insurance

Type	Personal auto policy
Liability	$100,000/$300,000/$50,000
Medical payments	$3,000/person/accident
Uninsured motorist	$100,000/accident
Physical damage, own car	Actual cash value
Collision deductible	$500
Comprehensive deductible	$500
Annual premium for two cars	$1,200

Homeowners Insurance

Residence

Type	HO-3 Special Form
Dwelling	$220,000
Personal property	$110,000
Personal liability	$100,000/occurrence
Medical payments	$5,000/person/occurrence
Deductible	$250
Premium (annual)	$1,500
Other	80% coinsurance

Condominium

Type	HO-6 Personal Property
Personal liability	$300,000/occurrence
Medical payments	$2,000 person/occurrence
Deductible	$500
Premium (annual)	$500

Long-Term Disability Insurance

Disability Policy

Insured	Allison
Definition	Own occupation
Premium	Employer pays 60%; Allison pays 40%
	Total premium of $800 per year
Elimination period	90 days
Benefit	60% of gross pay (currently $3,000 per month)

Table I—Group Term Insurance

Age	Monthly Cost/ Thousand
45–49	$0.15
50–54	$0.23
55–59	$0.43

Income Tax Information

The Dukes file married filing jointly. They are in the 25% federal marginal tax bracket. There is no state income tax.

Bill and Alice are claimed as dependents by Ryan's former wife.

Retirement Information

Savings

The Dukes currently save $21,750 annually, consisting of $6,000 ($3,000 each) contributed to their traditional individual retirement accounts (IRAs), $13,750 in reinvested dividends and interest, and $2,000 contributed to Allison's retirement plan.

Titling of Retirement Accounts	Beneficiary Designation
Ryan's IRA (traditional and Roth)	Allison
Allison's IRA (traditional and Roth)	Ryan
Allison's defined contribution retirement plan	Ryan

The Dukes had each contributed $8,000 to their Roth IRA accounts in previous years; however, no conversion had been made.

Social Security Benefits

Ryan's Social Security benefits at full retirement age of approximately 66 years are estimated to be $18,000 per year (in today's dollars). Allison will be able to retire at age 66 years and 6 months with a Social Security benefit of $21,600 (in today's dollars).

Retirement Plan

Allison's state university has a mandatory defined contribution plan and contributes 7% of Allison's salary. She must contribute 3%, but the 3% is currently an after-tax contribution because of her election.

TSA 403(b) Plan

The university has a tax-sheltered annuity plan for Allison. Allison currently does not make use of the 403(b) plan. The plan contains a loan provision.

Gifts, Estates, Trusts, and Will Information

Ryan's Will

Ryan's will leaves the business and his automobile to his son Bill and everything else to his wife Allison. Allison is the executor for the estate. The residuary legatee is to pay all administrative expenses, costs, and taxes. Any indebtedness is attached to the respective asset.

Allison's Will

Allison's will leaves everything to Ryan.

STATEMENT OF CASH FLOWS
Ryan and Allison Duke
January 1, 2008 to December 31, 2008
(Projected to be similar in 2009)

INFLOWS			
Ryan's Schedule C net income	$50,000		
Allison's faculty salary	60,000		
Dividend income from mutual fund*	8,750		
Condo rental income (net of mgt fees)	18,000		
Interest income from bonds	5,000		
Total inflows			$141,750
OUTFLOWS			
Savings and investments		$21,750	
Fixed outflows			
Alimony payment	$ 9,600		
Mortgage—principal residence (principal and interest)	21,270		
Taxes—principal residence	2,070		
Principal residence insurance	1,500		
Mortgage Condo—rental (principal and interest)	17,244		
Condo operating costs	1,400		
Taxes—condo	1,000		
Condo association dues	2,600		
Condo insurance premium	500		
Auto note payment	6,950		
Auto insurance premium	1,200		
Life insurance premium	650		
Disability insurance premium	320		
Total fixed outflows		$66,304	
Variable outflows			
Taxes	$28,455		
Food (including dining out)	6,200		
Transportation	2,600		
Clothing/personal care	3,900		
Entertainment/vacations	4,500		
Medical/dental	2,000		
Utilities and household expenses	2,640		
Church donations	1,720		
Miscellaneous	278		
Total variable outflows		$52,293	
Total outflows			$140,347
Deficit			$ 1,403

Tax detail	FICA Ryan**	$ 7,065
	FICA Allison	4,590
	Federal withholdings	16,800
		$28,455

*Qualified Dividends

**FICA: $50,000 × .1413 = $7,065 (The technical calculation per Schedule SE: .153 × .9235 = .1413)

Note: Allison's salary of $60,000 does not include Section 79 applicable income.

STATEMENT OF FINANCIAL POSITION
Ryan and Allison Duke
As of December 31, 2008

Assets[1]				Liabilities and Net Worth			
Cash and cash equivalents				**Liabilities[2]**			
Cash and checking	JTWROS	$	18,000	Automobile notes payable	JT	$	18,750
Money market	JTWROS		25,000	Mortgage condo[3]			116,981
Total cash and equivalents		$	43,000	Mortgage personal residence			167,034
				Total liabilities		$	302,765
Invested assets							
Proprietorship	H	$	800,000				
IRA	H		40,000				
IRA	W		48,000				
Roth IRA	H		15,000				
Roth IRA	W		18,000				
Equity mutual fund Portfolio (TOD)	H		295,000				
Bond portfolio	W		80,000				
Rental real estate condo[3]	JTWROS		220,000				
Retirement plan	W		90,000				
Total invested assets		$	1,606,000	Net worth			$1,826,235
Use assets							
Personal residence[4] dwelling	JTWROS	$	300,000				
Personal residence land	JTWROS		30,000				
Art collection	W		35,000				
Automobiles	TC		30,000				
Personal property	JTWROS		85,000				
Total use assets		$	480,000				
Total assets			$2,129,000	**Total liabilities and net worth**			$2,129,000

Notes to financial statements
[1]Assets are stated at fair market value.
[2]Liabilities are stated at principal only.
[3]Condo was refinanced in 2005 at 10.5%, original balance was $130,000 at December 15, 2005, and it was financed for 15 years. The first payment was due January 15, 2006. The payment for January 20, 2009 has been made.
[4]Personal residence financed December 1, 2006, for $180,000 at 8.5% fixed for 15 years. The January 20, 2009 payment has not been made.

Title designations
H = Husband (sole owner)
W = Wife (sole owner)
TC = Tenants in common with spouse/No survivorship
JTWROS = Joint tenancy with right of survivorship
TOD = Transfer on death

Information Regarding Assets and Liabilities

Proprietorship

This business was purchased by Ryan in 1998 for $200,000. There have been no additional capital contributions.

Equity Portfolio

Mutual Fund	Shares	Fair Market Value	Basis	Beta	Standard Deviation
A	1,000	$65,000	$25,000	1.3	25%
B	2,000	$80,000	$80,000	1.0	15%
C	6,000	$120,000	$90,000	0.9	20%
D	200	$30,000	$45,000	1.2	18%

Notes to equity portfolio:
[1] The portfolio of mutual funds has a correlation of 0.50 with the market.
[2] The portfolio has had a historical return of 14% with a volatility of approximately 18%, as measured by standard deviation.
[3] The fund is owned by Ryan with a TOD provision to Allison.

Bond Portfolio

The bond portfolio was a gift to Allison from her Uncle Mike in 2001. The value at the time of the gift was $48,000. Mike paid gift tax of $16,000. The bonds currently earn 7.5% annually. Mike had originally paid $53,000 for the bonds.

Rental Property (Condo)

This condo was purchased in January 1980 for $130,000 by Ryan as separately owned property. Ryan retitled the property as joint tenants with rights of survivorship with Allison after their marriage. The depreciation method used was accelerated cost recovery system 15 years. The current adjusted taxable basis of the condo is $0 plus land cost of $15,000. The property is exclusively rental property.

Art Collection

The art collection was acquired from Allison's mother in 2001 as a gift. At the time of the gift, Allison's mother's basis was $10,000 while the fair market value of the collection was $40,000. The annual exclusion was unavailable for this gift. Allison's mother paid gift tax of $8,200.

Divorce Decree

Ryan was divorced from Susan early in 2002, and he remarried the same year. His divorce decree calls for payments to his former spouse (Susan) of $800 per month for support until year 2015, at which time Alice will be 18. The payments will then be reduced to $500 per month for five more years. In the event of Susan's early death, payments are to be made to Susan's estate until 2020.

QUESTIONS

1. List the Dukes' financial strengths and weaknesses.

2. After reading the case, what additional information would you request from the Dukes to complete your data-gathering phase?

3. What is the amount of alimony that Ryan and Allison can deduct as alimony on their 2008 federal tax return?

4. What amount, if any, will be included in Allison's W-2 as a result of her group term life insurance?

5. What are the Dukes' current insurance deficiencies?

6. If Allison were to become disabled on March 31, 2009, and remain disabled for the balance of 2009, how much would she collect in disability benefits during 2009?

7. How much, if any, of Allison's disability benefits for 2009 would be taxable if she were to become disabled on March 31, 2009, and remained disabled for the balance of the year?

8. If the Dukes were to have a fire in their personal residence resulting in a loss of $20,000, how much of the loss would be paid to the Dukes by the insurance company?

9. If Allison were to sell the bond portfolio today for the value on the Statement of Financial Position, what would be the tax consequences?

10. What is Allison's adjusted taxable basis in the art collection?

11. Discuss the investment characteristics of the art collection and its valuation.

12. What is the approximate adjusted gross income for the Dukes for 2008?

13. If the alimony is not deductible, how long do Ryan and Susan have to amend their divorce decree to make the alimony deductible?

14. Susan's parents have gifted the children, Bill and Alice, various investments. Alice has investment income of $4,000 this year (2009) and earned $1,000 babysitting. Bill's investments did not do as well; he only earned $2,000, but his part-time job in Ryan's jewelry store paid him $6,000. Alice deposited all but her babysitting earnings in the bank, but Bill used all of his income to pay for the automobile insurance on his car and his social life (he goes out every weekend during the school year and more often in the summer months). Susan provides more than 50% of each child's support. Given their earnings, can Susan still claim both children as dependents on her tax return this year?

15. Consider the facts in the previous question. How much of each child's income will be taxed at their individual tax rate?

16. Ryan has a large safe in the jewelry store that has a fair market value of $40,000 and an adjusted basis of $15,000. Ryan has taken cost recovery deductions in prior years of $30,000. His friend, Mike, also in the jewelry business, has a larger, walk-in safe to dispose of that has a fair market value of $85,000 and an adjusted basis of $50,000. Mike will exchange it for the smaller safe and $45,000 cash. Ryan thinks this is a good deal, as these types of safes will sell for $125,000 when they are new.

    a. What is Ryan's basis in the new safe after the like-kind exchange?
    b. What is Mike's basis in his new safe?
    c. Calculate the realized gain of both Ryan and Mike.
    d. Calculate the recognized gain of both Ryan and Mike.

17. Instead of using a like-kind exchange, Ryan decides to buy a new safe for $96,000 in January. Ryan is considering using Section 179 to write off the new safe in 2009. How much of the purchase price of the new safe can Ryan write off this year?

18. Ryan flew from New York to London on a jewelry buying trip. London is where he purchases the bulk of his estate jewelry for his business. He spent 14 days on business and five days on personal matters and then flew back to New York. He spent one day flying in each direction. What are Ryan's deductible expenses for this trip?

19. A shortage of parking space on campus has resulted in Allison's university offering employees subsidized parking at a neighboring parking garage. How much can the university pay Allison for the parking without including it in her W-2? What other alternatives can it offer employees as a nontaxable transportation benefit?

20. In 2009, Ryan and Allison paid $6,000 in child care costs for the twins. How much can they claim as a child-care credit in 2009?

21. Allison's father, Ralph, has been in an assisted living facility for the last 30 months and is quite happy there. Allison's mother still lives in their home but will be joining her husband soon. She has asked Allison to sell their small home which has increased in fair market value due to intense development in their old neighborhood. They paid $40,000 for it 50 years ago and have been greatly surprised to receive an offer of $325,000 from a developer interested in the land. Because Ralph has not been living in the home, they are resigned to paying tax on the sale. How much of the gain on the sale of the home is taxable to Allison's parents?

22. Allison had her art collection appraised and discovered that some of the artwork had declined in value since she received them from her mother. She wants to donate some of the pieces to charity. Can she take a charitable deduction for the cost of the appraisal fee?

23. Allison wants to donate a portrait of an ancestor who served in the American Revolution to the museum in her town that houses a collection of Revolution Era items. Her basis in the portrait is $1,750, and it has a fair market value of $2,000. How much can she potentially deduct as a charitable contribution?

24. What is the weighted beta for the Dukes' equity portfolio?

25. Using the Security Market Line, calculate whether the actual historical return on the Dukes' equity portfolio has underperformed, outperformed, or matches the expected return.

26. What is the probability the equity portfolio could have a return between -4% and 50%?

27. How much of the equity portfolio's movement in price can be explained by changes in the market?

ADDITIONAL QUESTIONS

1. What kind of retirement plan would allow Ryan the greatest deductible contribution while providing him with only a small cash flow commitment each year? What would be Ryan's maximum percentage contribution?

2. What are the characteristics of tax-sheltered annuity (TSA)?

3. Discuss the pros and cons of Ryan establishing the following retirement plans.
   a. SEP IRA
   b. 25% profit sharing plan

4. If Ryan were to die today, what would be the value of his gross estate?

5. If Ryan were to die today, what would be the value of his probate assets?

6. Assume Ryan's last medical, funeral, and administrative expenses were $50,000. What would Ryan's estate tax liability be if he died today?

7. Evaluate Ryan's current estate plan.

8. If Allison were to die today, what would be the value of her gross estate?

9. What would be the value of Allison's probate assets if she died today?

10. Assume Allison's last medical, funeral, and administrative expenses were $50,000. What would Allison's estate tax liability be if she died today?

11. Evaluate Allison's current estate plan.

12. Assume Ryan dies today and Allison dies very soon thereafter. Calculate the second-to-die estate tax liability.

13. Evaluate the current overall estate plan.

14. What devices could be used to ensure that they avoid any poor results of the current estate plan?

15. Ryan and Allison have decided to send Alice to a private academy next school year at a cost of $18,000 per year. Assuming no additional contributions, could they use the funds in their Roth IRAs for this purpose, and, if so, what would be the income tax impact?

16. What is a TOD provision? What would it accomplish for the Dukes?

17. Given the Dukes' objectives of retiring in six years, as well as increasing their tax advantaged savings, would advising Allison to participate in the 403(b) available to her through the university be recommended?

    a. What would be the 403(b) contribution limits for Allison?
    b. The Dukes' statement of cash flows shows limited additional discretionary cash flow that would be available for Allison to contribute to the 403(b) plan. How could the Dukes' current savings plan be restructured to allow Allison to take advantage of the 403(b) plan?

Karl and June Monroe

Karl and June Monroe have come to you, a financial planner, for help in developing a plan to accomplish their financial goals. From your initial meeting, you have gathered the following information. Assume today is January 1, 2009.

Personal Background and Information

Karl Monroe (Age 37)

Karl is the owner and manager of a bar named Marlo's. Marlo's is a small, neighborhood bar that is open only at nights and has five part-time employees (less than 1,000 hours each). Karl inherited the bar four years ago from his Uncle Marlo. Karl attended Arizona State University and received a MBA in management. After graduation, he became employed by Texas Energy Resources, Inc., an oil and gas exploration company based in Austin, Texas, where he served as their human resources manager. The company paid for Karl to attend graduate school at the University of Texas-Austin. He attended classes part-time at night and earned his MBA. He was earning $78,500 when he inherited the bar. Because of the volatility in the oil and gas industry, Karl felt that Marlo's afforded him a more stable working environment and a chance for self-employment. He decided to leave Texas Energy Resources, Inc., and dedicate all his efforts to Marlo's.

June Monroe (Age 37)

June is a loan officer at Wood National Bank. She has been employed by Wood for eight years. She attended Texas Christian University and received her BA in finance. She also attended the University of Texas-Austin and earned her MBA. June and Karl resided in an apartment in Austin when Karl was transferred to San Antonio by Texas Energy Resources, Inc. June transferred to San Antonio and maintained her position at the Wood National Bank in San Antonio.

The Monroes

Karl and June have been married for 11 years. They both plan to retire in 25 years. They own a three-bedroom house with a pool, two cars, and a bar (Marlo's) in San Antonio, Texas. They have three children and do not plan on having any more children.

The Children

Sebastian, age 10, attends Davy Crockett Grammar School (the local public school) and is in the fourth grade.

Sandy, age 5, also attends Davy Crockett Grammar School and is in kindergarten. Sandy spends the afternoon at Alamo Day Care Center.

April, age 2, attends Alamo Day Care Center for nine hours a day, Monday through Friday.

The Grandparents

Karl's mother, Gerdi, age 62, was widowed four years ago when her husband died at age 60. Her only income is $600 a month from Social Security and $500 a month from Karl and June. She does not spend the $600 from Social Security; she simply puts it in her money market account. She lives about 100 miles from Karl and June.

June's mother, Maria, age 70, is a lifelong resident and citizen of Colombia and is fully supported by Karl and June. Karl and June contribute $300 each month to support Maria.

Personal and Financial Objectives

The Monroes have the following financial objectives in order of priority.

1. They want to provide a standard of living after retirement of 80% of their pre-retirement earnings.

2. They want to accumulate sufficient assets to send the children to a state university away from home, yet in the state of Texas.

3. They want to minimize their current income tax liability.

4. They want to expand Marlo's to include a daytime grill within the next five years.

5. They want to be mortgage free at retirement.

6. They want to develop an estate plan to minimize estate tax liabilities.

Economic Information

■ The Monroes expect inflation to average 3% annually, both currently and for the long term. They also expect June's salary to increase 5% annually, both currently and long term.

■ Current mortgage rates are 7.5% for 15 years and 8.0% for 30 years. Closing costs would be 3% of the amount financed and would be paid at closing.

Insurance Information

Life Insurance

	Policy 1	Policy 2
Insured	June	Karl
Policy Through	Employer	State Farm
Face Amount	$50,000	$150,000
Type	Term (Group)	Whole
Cash Value	$0	$21,250*
Annual Premium	$102 (Employer Paid)	$2,361
Beneficiary	Karl	June
Contingent Beneficiary	Three children	None
Policyowner	June	Karl**
Settlement Options	None	Life Annuity

*Karl's after-tax earnings rate is 6%. Cash value at January 1 last year was $20,900, and last year's dividend was $100.
**Community property

June also has an accidental death and dismemberment policy through her employer. She is covered for $100,000 under this policy. She pays a premium of $68 per year for this coverage.

Health Insurance

All family members are covered by June's employer under a group health plan with an annual family deductible of $400. After the deductible is met, the plan pays 100% of the first $2,000 of covered hospital charges for each hospital stay and 80% thereafter. There is a stop-loss maximum of $2,000 including the deductible. The plan will then pay 100% of any other covered expenses, as long as they are reasonable and customary and incurred that year no matter how high the amount.

Dental Insurance

The Monroes have dental insurance. The premium is $216 annually.

Disability Insurance

Karl has a personal disability policy with an own-occupation definition that provides a benefit of $2,000 per month disability income and has a 14-day elimination period. The policy was purchased from a local insurance company. This policy covers both accidents and sickness and has a benefit period of five years. His annual premium is $608.

June has an own-occupation definition policy that provides a benefit of 65% of gross pay and has a 90-day elimination period. The policy is provided through her employer. The policy covers both accidents and sickness until age 65. The annual premium is $460, and the employer and June each pay half.

Homeowners Insurance

The Monroes have a HO-3 policy (replacement value) with a $250 deductible and a dwelling value of $97,000 purchased through State Farm Insurance Co. (The premium is $739 per year.) There is a $100,000 liability per occurance.

Automobile Insurance

Both Cars	
Type	Personal Auto Policy
Liability	$100,000/$300,000
Medical Payments	$5,000 per Person/Accident
Physical Damage, Own Car	Actual Cash Value
Uninsured Motorist	$50,000/Accident
Collision Deductible	$100
Comprehensive Deductible	$250
Premium (per Year)	$1,080

Investment Data

The Monroes' tolerance for investment risk on a scale of 1 to 10 (1 being the most risk averse) is a 7. They expect to be more conservative as they get closer to retirement.

Income Tax Information

Their marginal income tax rate is currently 25% for federal income taxes, and there are no state income taxes in Texas.

Retirement Information

The Monroes plan to retire in 25 years when they are 62 years old. They would like to have a standard of living equal to 80% of their preretirement income. At or before retirement, the Monroes plan to sell the bar and put the proceeds toward retirement. They expect to be in retirement for 28 years.

June has a 401(k) plan through Wood National Bank. Wood matches $1 for every $4 contributed by June up to an employer maximum contribution of 2% of salary. The maximum employee contribution without regard to the match is 10% of her salary. She has been contributing 5% of her salary since she began working there in 1996. Her 401(k) has averaged an annual return of 7% over the past eight years. Her estate is currently designated as the beneficiary.

Karl has an individual retirement account (IRA) through his banker. He opened the account 10 years ago and has been contributing $3,000 each year since 2003. Before 2003, he contributed $2,000 annually. He has averaged a 6% annual return over the past 10 years. He always contributes on January 1 of the year in question. His estate is the beneficiary of the IRA.

Karl expects to collect $23,856 in Social Security benefits at age 67 or 70% of full retirement benefits at age 62 (in today's dollars). June expects to collect $22,840 in Social Security benefits at age 67 and 70% at age 62 (in today's dollars). They expect to begin receiving Social Security benefits as soon as they retire.

Gifts, Estates, Trusts, and Will Information

The Monroes have simple wills leaving all probate assets to each other.

STATEMENT OF ANNUAL CASH FLOWS
Karl and June Monroe
For the Year Ended December 31, 2008 (and projected for 2009)

INFLOWS

Karl's net income from the bar (Schedule C)	$64,000	
June's salary	57,200	
Dividend income	777	
Checking interest income	130	
Savings interest income	400	
Certificate of deposit	275	
Total inflows		$122,782

OUTFLOWS
Planned savings

401(k) 5% for June	$ 2,860	
IRA	3,000	
Total planned savings		$ 5,860

Ordinary living expenses

Mortgage (principal and interest)	$10,267	
Homeowners insurance premium	739	
Church donations—cash	5,200	
Lease on Honda	3,588	
Principal and interest on Cherokee	7,800	
Gas/oil/maintenance	2,000	
Auto insurance payments (both cars)	1,080	
Credit card payments	6,200	
Taxes on income	41,018	
Property taxes on residence	2,657	
Utilities	1,200	
Telephone	600	
Life insurance premiums (Karl)	2,361	
Accidental death and dismemberment	68	
Support for Gerdi and Maria	9,600	
Health	2,592	
Dental insurance	216	
Child care (paid to Alamo)	4,500	
Disability premium (both)	838	
Vacation expense	4,000	
Entertainment expense	3,250	
Food	3,250	
Clothing	3,000	
Total ordinary living expenses		$116,024
Total outflows		$121,884
Discretionary funds available		$ 898

NOTES REGARDING TAXES

FICA—Karl ($64,000 × .9235 × .153)	$9,043
FICA—June (7.65% × $57,200)	4,375
Estimated payments (Karl)	12,600
Federal withholding (June)	15,000
Total taxes	$41,018

STATEMENT OF FINANCIAL POSITION
Karl and June Monroe
January 1, 2009

Assets[1]			Liabilities and Net Worth[2]	
Cash/cash equivalents			**Current Liabilities**	
Checking account (2.5%)	CP	$ 5,200	Credit card balances (14.7%)	$ 8,200
Savings account (3.25%)[3]	CP	12,300	Car loan (Jeep Cherokee)	11,000
Total cash/cash equivalents		$ 17,500	**Total current liabilities**	19,200
Invested assets			**Long-term liabilities**	
Certificate of deposit	CP	$ 5,000	Home mortgage	$ 98,836
(5.5%, 2 year, mature 12/31/09)			(9.25% for 30 years)	
Saving bonds	CP	4,000	**Total long-term liabilities**	$ 98,836
(Zero-coupon EE bonds)	CP			
Mutual funds	CP	18,800		
Stocks	CP	13,600		
401(k) plan (June)	CP	31,331	**TOTAL LIABILITIES**	$118,036
IRA (Karl)	CP	27,942		
Proprietorship in bar	CP	138,000		
Rental property	W	84,000		
Cash value life insurance	CP	21,250		
Total investments		$343,923		
			NET WORTH	$402,787
Personal use assets				
House (land is $20,000)	CP	$125,000		
Jewelry (one diamond)	CP	8,000		
2006 Jeep Grand Cherokee	CP	20,000		
2000 Honda Civic	CP	4,000		
Baseball card collection	H	2,400		
Total personal use		$159,400		
TOTAL ASSETS		**$520,823**	**TOTAL LIABILITIES AND NET WORTH**	**$520,823**

Notes to financial statements

[1]Assets are stated at fair market value.

[2]Liabilities are stated at principal only and are all community obligations.

[3]The savings account is currently serving as their emergency fund.

General note: The numbers in parentheses reflect the interest that is being assessed.

Title designations

CP = Community property

H = Husband's separate property

W = Wife's separate property

Information Regarding Assets and Liabilities

Marlo's

Marlo's is located one block off the local college campus and has been in business for 32 years. Marlo had a taxable basis in the bar of $10,000 at his death. The fair market value at the time of Marlo's death was $40,000. Two years ago, Karl executed a legal document making Marlo's community property with June.

Karl completely refurbished the bar at a cost of $30,000. The building and property is currently valued at $78,000. Property taxes are high in this district; they are currently $2,278 (2.92 per hundred). The bar could be sold at a fair market value of $138,000 and is increasing at 3.5% per year. The bar's net income and cash flows for the last three years was $64,000, $59,600, and $57,500.

They also expect Karl's net income and cash flows from Marlo's to increase at 3.5% annually, both currently and over the long term.

Personal Residence

The Monroes purchased their home and financed the mortgage over 30 years at 9.25%. The house is a two-story, three-bedroom, brick house. It has a pool and a monitored burglar alarm.

Rental Property

The rental property, which is valued at $84,000, is located in Austin, Texas, and consists of a small strip shopping center. It is in a poor location and is currently a break-even proposition as income equals expenses. The property was acquired from June's Aunt Grace three years ago as a gift. Grace had a basis in the property of $20,000 ($5,000 for the land and $15,000 for the building) and paid gift tax on the transfer of $24,000. At the time of the gift, the property had a fair market value of $60,000. Grace died recently, and at the time of her death the property was valued at $84,000.

Prior to Grace's death, June and Karl would never dispose of the rental property for fear of offending Grace; however, they now want to buy a strip shopping center in San Antonio at a cost of $100,000 by using a small mortgage of $16,000. There is a tenant in the Austin property who would buy the rental property for the fair market value of $84,000.

Mutual Funds

	Fair Market Value	Beta	Expected Return
Balanced Fund	$ 5,600	0.65	8.5%
Growth Fund	2,400	1.24	12.4%
Bond Fund	10,800	0.55	6.5%
Total	**$18,800**		

QUESTIONS

1. List the Monroes' financial strengths and weaknesses.

2. After reading the case, what additional information would you request from the Monroes, and what actions would you take to complete your data-gathering phase?

3. Calculate the following financial ratios for the Monroes.

$$\frac{\text{Liquid Assets}}{\text{Monthly Expenses}}$$

$$\frac{\text{Liquid Assets}}{\text{Current Debt Payments}}$$

$$\frac{\text{Net Worth}}{\text{Total Assets}}$$

$$\frac{\text{Total Debt}}{\text{Total Assets}}$$

$$\frac{\text{Total Debt}}{\text{Annual Total Income*}}$$

$$\frac{\text{Housing and Monthly Debt Payments}}{\text{Monthly Gross Income}}$$

$$\frac{\text{Housing Costs}}{\text{Monthly Gross Income}}$$

$$\frac{\text{Investment Assets}}{\text{Annual Gross Income}}$$

$$\frac{\text{Monthly Savings}}{\text{Monthly Gross Income}}$$

*Annual Total Income is the same as Annual Gross Income.

4. Comment on any of the above ratios that you think are important.

5. Assuming the Monroes have always made their mortgage payments exactly as agreed, how much was their original mortgage?

6. Assuming the Monroes have always made their mortgage payments exactly as agreed, how many payments have the Monroes made on the mortgage loan?

7. Do the Monroes qualify to refinance their house?

8. If they refinance, how much will they save over the life of the loan for a 15-year or 30-year loan? Which loan should they select?

9. What other method might they consider to save on the repayment of the mortgage?

10. Is the health care insurance coverage adequate?

11. How much qualified residence interest can they deduct on their income tax return for last year?

12. Was Gerdi a dependent of the Monroes for income tax purposes last year? Explain why or why not.

13. Was Maria Rodriguez a dependent of the Monroes for income tax purposes last year? Explain why or why not.

14. How much of a dependent care credit, if any, can the Monroes take for last year?

15. For 2008, can Karl make a deductible contribution to an individual retirement account (IRA) as an alternative to or as an addition to any qualified plan he may implement?

16. Estimate the Monroes' federal adjusted gross income for last year.

17. Because Marlo's is a sole proprietorship, which types of retirement plans can Karl establish?

18. What type of qualified plan should Karl adopt if he wishes to maximize contributions and minimize his cash commitment?

19. What is the maximum contribution Karl can make to a qualified defined contribution plan in the current year?

20. What would be the impact on the Monroes' federal income tax liability for this year if Karl were to establish a Keogh and maximize his contributions? (Assume his Schedule C income is the same as last year.)

21. Discuss Karl's ability to have a loan provision if he establishes a Keogh plan.

22. What is the projected value of Marlo's at Karl's expected retirement date? (Use the current Statement of Financial Position valuation.)

23. Calculate the Monroes' capital needed at retirement. Assume an earnings rate of 11%.

24. Calculate the capital needed at retirement for the Monroes by using the annuity approach.

25. Calculate the capital needed at retirement for the Monroes by using the capital preservation approach. Assume an earnings rate of 11%.

26. Calculate the capital needed at retirement for the Monroes by using the purchasing power preservation approach.

27. Explain the differences between the capital preservation model and the purchasing power preservation model.

28. Can June make an in-service withdrawal from her 401(k) if Marlo's needs cash flow?

29. Can June's 401(k) plan have a loan provision?

30. Gerdi is considering going back to work and wants to know how much she can earn before she will lose any Social Security benefits. How much will she have to make to lose all benefits?

31. What are the income tax consequences of any disability benefits received by Karl and June?

32. Discuss the strengths and weaknesses of disability benefits for Karl and June.

33. Is the life insurance amount adequate for Karl and June?

34. Is the homeowners insurance coverage appropriate?

35. Analyze the Monroes' liability insurance coverage.

36. Should Karl replace his whole life policy? Use the Belth model.

37. What are the federal income tax consequences of a sale of the Austin rental property?

38. If, instead of a sale of the Austin property, June uses a tax-free exchange to acquire the San Antonio shopping center, what is her recognized gain or loss from the Austin property and her basis in the new property?

39. What is Karl and June's adjusted tax basis in Marlo's?

40. If Karl were to die today and June inherited and sold Marlo's for the current Statement of Financial Position value, what would be her income-adjusted basis at the time of the sale?

41. What is the expected return for the Monroes' mutual funds?

42. What is the weighted beta for the Monroes' mutual funds?

43. Consider the following modern portfolio theory statistics for the growth fund.

	1st Index	2nd Index	3rd Index
R^2	0.67	0.56	0.98
Beta	0.95	1.0	1.3
Alpha	1.2	3.25	0.05

Which of the indexes is the appropriate benchmark for the growth fund?

44. Assume that the Monroes want to invest $10,000. They decide to invest $7,000 in Portfolio A with the remainder in the S&P 500. Changes in the S&P 500 account for or explain 25% of the returns for Portfolio A. If Portfolio A has a standard deviation of 20% and the S&P 500 has a standard deviation of 11.5%, what is the standard deviation of the combined $10,000 portfolio?

ADDITIONAL QUESTIONS

1. What estate planning deficiencies do the Monroes have?

2. What is the total of all the assets that will be included in Karl's probate estate if he were to die today?

3. What could be done to reduce Karl's probate estate?

4. Calculate the value of Karl's gross estate assuming he died today.

12

Keith and Cindy Ross

Keith and Cindy Ross have come to you, a financial planner, for help in developing a plan to accomplish their financial goals. From your initial meeting, you have gathered the following information. Assume today is January 1, 2009.

Personal Information

Keith Ross (Age 65)

Keith is in excellent health. He owns Ross Big-N-Tall, Inc., a men's store focusing on men's attire for larger clients. Keith's salary is $250,000. Ross's employs 25 full-time and 10 part-time employees. The only debt that Keith is carrying on the business is a $230,000 short-term note.

Cindy Ross (Age 50)

Cindy is in excellent health. She is a certified public accountant and is employed by an international accounting firm, where she is currently a manager in the area of healthcare consulting. Her daughter from a former marriage, Beverly, is 30 years old and married with two children. Cindy's salary is $50,000.

The Rosses

They have been married for 25 years.

Children

Keith and Cindy have three children from their marriage in addition to Beverly.

Susie	Age 23
David	Age 21
Mary	Age 5
Beverly	Age 30 (Cindy's child from a previous marriage)

Helga Smatters

Cindy's mother, Helga, turned 71 on December 1, 2008, and is a widow with a substantial net worth. In addition to sizable holdings of real estate, stocks, and bonds, Helga has $450,000 in her individual retirement account (IRA) rollover account as of December 31, 2008 (her account grew by $25,000 during 2008). She has made no withdrawals from the IRA. Because she is in extremely poor health, she had an attorney draft a will leaving her entire estate to Cindy. Helga would like to give to her favorite charities but has not incorporated charitable giving into her financial or estate planning. Her will provides that if Cindy should disclaim any or all of the inheritance, the disclaimed portion will be left in trust for Cindy's four children.

Personal and Financial Objectives

1. Keith plans to sell his business and retire immediately. He believes the business can be sold this year. He expects to live 30 years.

2. Keith wants to continue to transfer some of his wealth to his children to avoid estate taxes. He will consider using the family limited partnership that is currently in place.

Economic Information

General

The Rosses expect inflation to average 3.5% annually both currently and for the long term.

US Treasury
Current Yield Curve

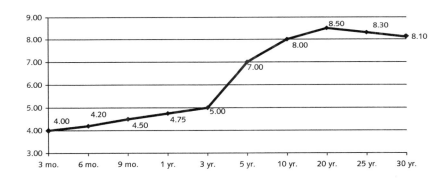

Economic Outlook—Investments

	Expected Returns (Pretax)		Expected Standard Deviation
Aggressive stocks	12%	±	15%
Growth stocks	10%	±	10%
S&P 500	11%	±	8%
Bonds	6%	±	4%
Insurance contracts	6%	±	2%
Money markets	4%	±	1%
T-bill	4%	±	1%

Banking

The Rosses have favorable banking relationships and are able to borrow money for any purpose at the following rates.

Type of Loan	Rates
Installment loan—secured	7.5%
Personal signature bank loans	9.0%
Mortgage loan—30-year fixed	7.5%
Mortgage loan—15-year fixed	7.0%

Investment Information

The Rosses consider $100,000 adequate for an emergency fund. They indicate a moderate level of risk tolerance in investments.

Income Tax Information

The Rosses are in a marginal tax bracket of 33% for federal and 6% for state. They pay on average 31% and 5% for federal and state tax, respectively. Capital gains are taxed at 15% for federal (no difference for state tax).

Insurance Information

Life Insurance	Policy 1	Policy 2
Insured	Keith Ross	Keith Ross
Face amount	$1,500,000	$250,000
Cash value	$175,000	$15,000
Type of policy	Whole Life	Whole life
Annual premium	$12,000	$3,500
Beneficiary	Beverly, Susie, David, Mary	Cindy Ross
Contingent beneficiary	Keith's estate	Ross Children's Insurance Trust
Policyowner	Ross Children's Insurance Trust*	Cindy Ross
Interpolated terminal reserve	$175,000	$15,000
Settlement options	N/A	Single life annuity (guaranteed for 10 years)

*The original owner of Policy 1 was Keith. It was transferred to the trust on June 30, 2007. William Bradley, a friend of Keith's since college, is the trustee for the Ross Children's Insurance Trust. The cash value and the interpolated terminal reserve at the date of transfer was $150,000. The policy was purchased January 1, 1999.

Cindy also has term insurance provided through her employer. She has selected $100,000 of coverage. Keith is the primary beneficiary on her term insurance.

Health Insurance

Keith: Currently has a good health insurance plan through Ross Big-N-Tall but will not be covered once any sale of the business has been finalized. Keith's health plan has the following features.

- $1,000 individual deductible
- $2,500 family deductible
- $3,500 stop-loss provision
- 80/20 coinsurance
- $5 million major medical limit

Cindy: Coverage is available through her employer, but she is currently covered under Keith's policy.

Disability Insurance

Keith does not have disability insurance coverage.

Cindy has disability coverage provided through her employer: 60% coverage, own occupation, 180-day elimination period.

Property and Liability Auto Insurance (both cars)

Type	Personal auto policy
Liability (bodily injury)	$100,000/$300,000
Property damage	$50,000
Medical payments	$1,000
Physical damage, own car	Actual cash value
Uninsured motorist	$100,000/$300,000
Collision deductible	$1,000
Comprehensive deductible	$500
Annual premium (two cars)	$1,800

Homeowners Insurance	
Type	HO-3
Dwelling	$700,000
Other structures	$70,000
Personal property	$350,000
Personal liability	$100,000
Medical payments	$1,000
Deductible	$100
Coinsurance	80%
Annual premium	$2,200

Personal Liability Umbrella Insurance

The policy has a face value of $3 million with a premium of $500 per year.

Retirement Information

Keith

- Keith has a profit sharing plan at Ross Big-N-Tall, Inc., with a balance of $1.35 million.

- Keith also has an IRA account with a balance of $30,000 (see details). The IRA plan was established in 1991.

- Cindy is the beneficiary of all of Keith's retirement accounts.

- The contingent beneficiaries on Keith's retirement accounts are Susie, David, and Mary.

Cindy

- Cindy has a 401(k) plan in which she is able to defer up to 16% of her salary. The accounting firm matches $0.25 for each $1.00 she defers, up to 6% of her salary. The firm's total match is 1.5% of compensation. Keith is the beneficiary of all of Cindy's retirement accounts.

Keith and Cindy are retiring today. Both Keith and Cindy expect to live until age 95.

Keith and Cindy have estimated that they need $250,000 per year in today's dollars for retirement. This amount would drop by 25% if only one was alive.

Asset Allocation

The Rosses plan to create a separate portfolio to provide for their retirement income. They expect to maintain a retirement portfolio with the following asset allocation.

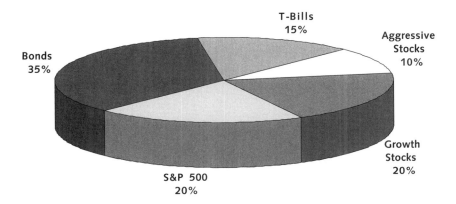

T-Bills
15%

Aggressive Stocks
10%

Bonds
35%

Growth Stocks
20%

S&P 500
20%

Education Information

Susie and David both attend Harvard University. The tuition is currently $40,000 annually for each child and is expected to increase by approximately 7% per year. This cost is being funded by Keith and Cindy from current earnings and savings. They are concerned about funding Mary's education because Keith and Cindy are retiring and will not be working while Mary is in school. Mary is extremely gifted and will likely attend an Ivy League school. They expect tuition to be $40,000 annually (today's cost) and to increase by 7% each year. They expect Mary, beginning at age 18, will attend four years of undergraduate and two years of graduate school. They are inclined to begin their college savings for Mary in a bond portfolio but are open to advice on a suitable allocation for Mary's college funding needs.

Information Regarding Wills, Trusts, and Estates

Wills

Both Keith and Cindy have wills. Each of the wills provides for all of the assets to be left in a qualified terminable interest property trust with the surviving spouse as the income beneficiary and the children as the remaindermen. The Rosses believe they need to have their wills updated.

The Ross Family Irrevocable Trust

The Ross Family Irrevocable Trust was established in 1993 to reduce the Rosses' estate tax. The primary beneficiaries of the trust are the four children with the contingent beneficiary being the American Cancer Society. If a child should die, that proportional interest would pass to that child's heirs. If no heir exists, then the interest would pass equally to the remaining children of the trust. If all children should die without heirs, then the American Cancer Society would immediately receive the entire corpus of the trust. Since the trust's inception, the Rosses have made a total of $1,775,000 in taxable gifts to the trust. The gift taxes owed on the total amount was $459,000 with $148,250 allocable to gifts made in the last three years. The gift tax from last year's contribution is $90,000 and is due April 15, 2009. The trust is currently valued at $3 million.

The Ross Children's Insurance Trust (All Four Children)

This irrevocable trust was set up in early 2006 to reduce the Rosses' estate tax liability. On June 30, 2007, Keith Ross transferred life insurance Policy 1 to the trust. There is a Crummey power provided in the trust document.

KECI Family Limited Partnership (KE = Keith; CI = Cindy; KECI = KE + CI)

Sid Johnson, one of the area's best estate planning attorneys, discussed the benefits of setting up a family limited partnership with the Rosses. With his help, the Rosses established KECI Family Limited Partnership (KECI FLP) in 2005. All of the assets transferred to the trust consisted of Keith's separate property. Keith currently owns 100% of the KECI FLP but intends to begin transferring some of the ownership to his children and possibly to Cindy. Sid has told Keith that transfers of limited partnership interests can carry a 35% overall discount for the minority interests and lack of marketability.

STATEMENT OF FINANCIAL POSITION
Keith and Cindy Ross
As of December 31, 2008

Assets[1]			Liabilities And Net Worth		
Cash/cash equivalents			**Liabilities[2]**		
W	Cash and checking[3]	$ 20,000	W	Credit card balances[4]	$ 15,000
H	Cash and checking[5]	250,000	H	Short-term note	230,000
H	Money market fund[6]	875,000		Auto note balances	0
	Total cash/equivalents	**$1,145,000**		Mortgage note	0
				Total liabilities	**$ 245,000**
Invested assets					
H	Profit sharing plan—Keith	$1,350,000			
H	IRA—Keith	30,000			
W	401(k)—Cindy	150,000			
H	Growth mutual fund	53,100			
H	Due from KECI	70,500			
	KECI Family Limited				
H	Partnership (capital)	1,193,600			
H	Common stock portfolio[7]	100,000			
	Ross Big-N-Tall, Inc.				
H	Common stock[8]	2,250,000			
	Total invested assets	**$5,197,200**		**Net worth**	**$7,539,200**
Use assets					
JT	Residence[9]	$1,000,000			
JT	Personal property	400,000			
JT	Autos	42,000			
	Total use assets	**$1,442,000**			
Total assets		**$7,784,200**		**Total liabilities and net worth**	**$7,784,200**

Notes to financial statements

[1]These are presented at fair market value.

[2]All liabilities are stated at principal only. All nonidentified liabilities are jointly owned.

[3]Cindy has a POD on this account naming Keith as her beneficiary.

[4]Credit card interest rate is 18%.

[5]Cash and checking earn 1.5% annually.

[6]The money market fund earns 4% annually.

[7]Publicly traded stock.

[8]The value is an approximation of the value of the business made by Mr. Ross. The company is a C corporation with an adjusted tax basis of $25,000.

[9]Adjusted tax basis of home is $200,000 (Purchase price contributions: Keith 75% and Cindy 25%).

Title designation: H = Husband only; W = Wife only; JT = Joint tenants with right of survivorship

STATEMENT OF CASH FLOWS
Keith and Cindy Ross
January 1, 2008 to December 31, 2008
(Expected to be similar in 2009)

INFLOWS—ANNUAL		
Keith's salary	$250,000	
Cindy's salary	50,000	
Dividend income	5,350	
Interest income	39,050	
Total inflows		$344,400
OUTFLOWS—ANNUAL		
Savings and investments	$ 56,600	$ 56,600
Fixed outflows—annual		
Property taxes	20,000	
Homeowners insurance	2,200	
Utilities	7,800	
Telephone	600	
Auto insurance	1,800	
Life insurance policy*	3,500	
Gas/oil/maintenance	1,800	
Credit card payments	8,500	
Umbrella insurance	500	$ 46,700
Variable outflows		
Taxes**	$121,030	
Food	7,800	
Medical/dental	2,000	
Clothing/personal care	6,000	
Child care	5,200	
Entertainment/vacation	10,000	
College	60,000	
Kindergarten	6,000	$218,030
Total Outflows		$321,330
Discretionary Cash Flow		$ 23,070

*Transfers to trust for life insurance Policy 1 are from discretionary cash flow.
**Notes on taxes

FICA—Keith	$ 9,949 [(102,000 × 0.062) + (250,000 × 0.0145)]
FICA—Cindy	3,825
Federal withholding—Keith	76,756
Federal withholding—Cindy	15,500
State—Keith	12,000
State—Cindy	3.000
	$121,030

Information Regarding Assets and Liabilities

Ross Big-N-Tall, Inc.	
	Cash Flow (NOI)
Year 1	$ 400,000
Year 2	$ 420,000
Year 3	$ 435,000
Year 4 (last year)	$ 440,000
Terminal Value	$3,000,000*

*The terminal value is calculated by dividing the forecasted net operating income (NOI) for Year 5 of $450,000 by an assumed discount rate of 15%.

Detailed Investment Portfolio (These are not in the Family Limited Partnership.)

Balanced Mutual Fund				
Account Name: IRA for Keith Ross			**Account No.:** IRA4340	
Date		**Amount**	**Price/Share**	**Shares**	**Cumulative Balance**
1/1/98	T	$16,000	$40.00	400	400
1/1/99	P	2,000	50.00	40	440
1/1/00	P	2,000	50.00	40	480
	T = Transfer		P = Purchase		
	Account Value as of 12/31/08		$30,000		

Note: The transfer in of $16,000 was the balance from a 401(k) plan with a previous employer.

Growth Mutual Fund				
Account Name: Keith Ross			**Account No.:** SLE123456	
Date	**Amount**	**Price/Share**	**Shares**	**Balance**
2/1/07				0
3/1/07	$7,500	$15.00	500	500
4/1/07	7,500	18.75	400	900
5/1/07	1,000	20.00	50	950
6/1/07	1,000	20.00	50	1,000
7/1/07	1,000	25.00	40	1,040
8/1/07	1,000	25.00	40	1,080
9/1/07	1,000	25.00	40	1,120
10/1/07	1,000	20.00	50	1,170
11/1/07	1,000	25.00	40	1,210
12/1/07	1,000	25.00	40	1,250
3/1/08	2,300	23.00	100	1,350
6/1/08	4,800	24.00	200	1,550
9/1/08	3,000	30.00	100	1,650
12/1/08	6,900*	27.60	250	1,900

*$2,700 was from a reinvested dividend.

Account Value as of 12/31/08: $53,100

Notes:
[1] The net asset value (NAV) of the fund on 12/31/07 was $26.00.
[2] No dividends were paid in 2007.
[3] Dividend of $1.50 per share was paid 12/1/08.
[4] The NAV of the fund on December 31, 2008 was $27.9474.

Common Stock Portfolio						
Account Name: Keith Ross						
Stock	**Avg./Exp. Return**	**Price/ Share**	**Total Shares**	**Cost Basis**	**Fair Market Value**	**Current Dividend**
A	15%	$25.55	1,250.00	$ 7,500	$ 31,937.50	3%
B	13%	$37.50	850.00	$10,000	$ 31,875.00	4%
C	5%	$87.00	175.00	$18,000	$ 15,225.00	0%
D	10%	$43.00	487.50	$16,000	$ 20,962.50	2.5%
	Total			$51,500	$100,000.00	

Notes:
[1] The standard deviation of the portfolio has been 10.9% in the past and is expected to be the same in the future.
[2] The stocks purchased are as follows.

Stock A	3/5/92
Stock B	4/7/97
Stock C	6/30/07
Stock D	6/30/07

KECI Family Limited Partnership Investments

Investment	Fair Market Value	Average Expected Return	Standard Deviation	Beta
Growth and income	$ 178,000	10.0%	9%	0.92
Balanced	246,500	8.5%	7%	0.72
Foreign	138,500	9.7%	15%	0.30
Brokerage account A	216,000	11.2%	13%	1.22
Brokerage account B	350,000	10.4%	10%	1.12
Total investments	$1,129,000			

STATEMENT OF FINANCIAL POSITION
KECI Family Limited Partnership
As of January 1, 2009

ASSETS[1]

Cash/cash equivalent

Cash	$ 45,000	
Money market	55,000	
Total cash/cash equivalent		$ 100,000

Invested assets

Growth and income mutual fund	$178,000	
Balanced mutual fund	246,500	
Foreign mutual fund	138,500	
Brokerage account A	216,000	
Brokerage account B	350,000	
Total invested assets		$1,129,000

Use assets[2]

Computer equipment	$ 4,000	
Luxury auto	37,500	
Depreciation[3]	(6,400)	
Total use assets		$ 35,100
Total assets		**$1,264,100**

LIABILITIES

Due to Keith Ross (on Ross Stmnt of Fin'l Position)	$ 70,500	
Total liabilities		$ 70,500
Partner's capital		$1,193,600
Total liabilities and partner's capital		$1,264,100

Notes to financial statements
[1]All assets, other than use assets, are stated at fair market value.
[2]Use assets are listed at historical cost.
[3]Depreciation (computer = $4,000 and automobile = $2,400)

QUESTIONS

1. List the Rosses' financial strengths and weaknesses.

2. After reading the case, what additional information would you request from the Rosses to complete your data-gathering phase?

3. Ross Big-N-Tall has been profitable for the past several years. Last year net income was $440,000. If you used a discount rate of 3% above the expected return for aggressive stocks, what would be the value of the business under the capitalized earnings approach?

4. The net income in the previous year was $440,000. The income from the company can be expected to grow in the future at least at the rate of inflation. How would these additional facts affect your valuation? What model would you use to value the company?

5. Because of her financial stability and sizable net worth, Helga Smatters intends to leave the funds in her IRA untouched. When she dies, she believes that these assets will get a step-up in basis for her heirs. Comment on her strategy and her beliefs and provide guidance to help her accomplish her objectives.

6. For the growth mutual fund (listed on the Statement of Financial Position), what is the time-weighted return from March 1, 2007, to December 31, 2007?

7. For the growth mutual fund (listed on the Statement of Financial Position), what is the dollar-weighted return from March 1, 2007, to December 31, 2007?

8. Explain the difference between time-weighted returns and dollar-weighted returns.

9. What is Keith's annualized dollar-weighted return for the growth mutual fund (listed on the Statement of Financial Position) as of December 31, 2008?

10. If Keith sold the shares of the growth mutual fund on January 1, 2009, what would be his after-tax annualized rate of return since he first purchased the shares?

11. If Keith needs additional cash, what would be the net proceeds from the sale of the balanced mutual fund IRA (listed on his personal Statement of Financial Position), including any taxes and penalties and assuming no basis?

12. What was the gift tax valuation of the life insurance policy transferred to the Ross Children's Insurance Trust?

13. Keith's estate is the contingent beneficiary of life insurance Policy 1. What are the implications?

14. What should Keith have done either before or at the time of the transfer of life insurance Policy 1 to the Ross Children's Insurance Trust?

15. What is the implication of Keith directly paying to the insurer the future premiums for Policy 1?

16. What are the consequences if, instead of directly paying the premiums, Keith simply adds $12,000 each January 1 to the trust to pay the premiums?

17. What if Cindy assigns her coverage of the term insurance policy of $100,000 to the Ross Children's Insurance Trust?

18. How much should the Rosses set aside today for Mary's education?

19. Assuming both Keith and Cindy plan to live to age 95, how much money do the Rosses need today to fund their retirement? (Assume a pre-tax portfolio. They will pay income taxes out of the gross retirement income.)

20. Do the Rosses have sufficient umbrella liability coverage?

21. If Keith were to die today, what assets would be included in his probate estate? Assume the Statement of Financial Position valuations.

22. Assuming Keith died today, calculate his gross estate. For purposes of this question, assume funeral and administrative costs total $100,000.

23. Assuming Keith died today, calculate his estate tax liability. For purposes of this question, assume funeral and administrative costs total $100,000.

24. If Cindy were to die today, what assets would be included in her probate estate?

25. Assuming Cindy died today, calculate her gross estate. For purposes of this question, assume funeral and administrative costs total $100,000.

26. Assuming Cindy died today, calculate her estate tax liability. For purposes of this question, assume funeral and administrative costs total $100,000.

27. If Keith died today and Cindy died three months later, what would be the total estate tax liability of both? Assume funeral and administrative costs are $100,000 each. Assume Cindy has retained her term insurance through her employer.

28. If Keith had an objective to leave his estate to his heirs but would like to make use of the CRAT or CRUT for retirement income and the charitable tax deduction, what device could he use to replace the assets given to the CRAT or CRUT that would replace the lost assets to his heirs?

29. What are the generation-skipping transfer tax implications if Cindy disclaims her interest in Helga's estate?

30. If, for some reason, the above disclaimer was not effective, what would be the consequences to Cindy?

31. Assume Keith is contemplating transferring some of his wealth by making an outright gift of an interest in the KECI Family Limited Partnership as follows.

Cindy	9%
Susie	9%
David	9%
Mary	9%
Beverly	9%
	45%

Determine the amount of additional federal gift tax Keith will have to pay if he completes such a transaction today (2009). Assume a minority discount of 35% and that the fair market value of KECI is $1,193,600.

32. What is the weighted-average rate of return of the common stock portfolio?

33. What is the probability that Keith's common stock portfolio (listed on the Statement of Financial Position) will have a return above 0.89%?

34. Assume Keith decides to purchase a new automobile in the KECI Family Limited Partnership. The cars in KECI are used 100% for business. The car he decides to buy costs $85,000. Keith trades in his old car (listed on the KECI Statement of Financial Position) and pays cash of $55,000 from the money market account.
    a. How much gain or loss does KECI realize?
    b. How much gain is ultimately reported (recognized) on Keith's Form 1040?
    c. What is the adjusted taxable basis to the partnership of the new car?

35. If Keith dies, would his gross estate include the Policy 1 life insurance proceeds?

36. Cindy's mother, Helga, has gifted all four of the children with stocks and bonds over the years. Mary has $3,500 in interest income in 2009. How much of this income will be taxable to Mary after allowing for her personal exemption and standard deduction?

37. Cindy's employer paid $.25 per $1,000 each month for her group term insurance last year. The federal table rate is $.23 per $1,000 per month. Cindy contributed $6.00 per month toward the premium. How much of the premium the employers paid annually for her group life insurance coverage was considered W-2 income for Cindy by her employer?

38. Keith plans to sell his business and retire immediately. What effect will this have on the group health coverage he currently has for himself, Cindy, Susie, David, and Mary?

39. Helga Smatters' poor health has made the Rosses think about planning for their own care. Keith and Cindy thought Medicare would provide long-term care coverage in the event they needed it. What coverage does Medicare provide?

40. The Rosses are reviewing their homeowners insurance coverage and have decided to have their home appraised. Their property was valued at $1.2 million of which the house was estimated to have a replacement cost of $1,050,000. Is the HO-3 coverage on the Rosses' home adequate to cover the home in case of a partial loss and, if not, what level of coverage do they need?

41. Assume that the return on Keith's common stock portfolio in 2009 is 15% and that the risk-free rate of return in 2009 is 4%. What is the Sharpe performance index for the portfolio?

42. How much must Helga withdraw from her IRA for the year 2008 to avoid a tax penalty? Use the appropriate divisor from the following table to calculate your answer. (Disregard the effects of the Worker, Retiree, and Employer Recovery Act of 2008.)

Age	Applicable Divisor
70	27.4
71	26.5
72	25.6

43. Describe any possible weaknesses you see in the coverage of the Rosses' personal property under their homeowners policy. What solutions are available that might address these weaknesses?

44. If Helga dies in 2009 and Cindy is the designated beneficiary of her IRA, what options are available to Cindy for taking distributions from the IRA? (Disregard the effects of the Worker, Retiree, and Employer Recovery Act of 2008.)

45. What is the beta of Keith's common stock portfolio? Assume that the standard deviation of the market is 8% and the correlation coefficient between the portfolio and the market is 0.75.

13

Peter and Patricia Morgan

Today is January 1, 2009. Peter and Patricia Morgan have come to you, a financial planner, for help in developing a plan to accomplish their financial goals. From your initial meeting together, you have gathered the following information.

Personal Background and Information

Peter Morgan (Age 62)

Peter has been employed 25 years as a vice president for an oil field services company. He participates in a defined-benefit plan. Peter's first wife is deceased.

Patricia Morgan (Age 29)

Patricia owns Publications, Inc., and Patricia Advertising, Inc.

The Morgans

They met July 4, 2005, at a Fourth of July picnic. Peter was rollerblading and had a nasty fall. Patricia saw him fall and ran to his rescue. She drove him to the emergency room, and they fell in love. They have been together since the accident and married in November of the same year. They have no children together.

Peter's Children

Peter has four children from his first marriage.

Martin	Age 34
Julius	Age 33
Brad	Age 32
Laena	Age 31

All of the children are healthy, employed, married, and none are living with Peter and Patricia. Peter has several grandchildren.

Patricia's Family

Patricia's parents are deceased but before her marriage to Peter she had been living with her grandmother, Natalie Fortune, a recent widow, who is 81 years old. Patricia's grandfather, Robert, died April 19, 2007, after a long illness during which Patricia helped with his care. Natalie is in good health for her age but no longer drives and has been relying on Patricia for transportation for shopping, doctor's appointments and visiting friends. Because Peter and Patricia want to travel now that he is retiring, Patricia and Natalie are looking for alternatives so Natalie's lifestyle is not negatively impacted by the Morgan's plans. Natalie lives in the same home she has lived in for 50 years and she and her husband raised their two children there. Her other child, Penny is a married mother of one child and does not live in the same state as Natalie.

Personal and Financial Objectives

1. Patricia plans to sell her businesses. At this time, Patricia has no plans to continue working.

2. Peter plans to retire in 2009 (January 1, 2009) (his life expectancy is 25.75 years).

3. Patricia's life expectancy is 57.75 years, and that is also their joint life expectancy.

4. They plan to sell their primary residence and will purchase a new home conducive to a retirement lifestyle.

5. They plan to refinance their vacation home.

6. They plan to travel extensively before deciding where to permanently relocate.

Economic Information

- They expect inflation to average 3% (consumer price index) annually over both the short and long term.

- They expect stock market returns of 11% annually on the S&P 500 Index.

- T-bills are currently yielding 2%.

- Current mortgage rates are 6.75% for a fixed 15-year mortgage and 7.25% for a fixed 30-year mortgage.

- Mortgage closing costs are expected to be 3% of any mortgage.

Insurance Information

Life Insurance

	Policy 1	Policy 2
Insured	Peter	Patricia
Owner	Peter	Patricia
Beneficiary	Children	Peter
Face amount	$450,000	$450,000
Cash value	$0	$0
Type of policy	Term	Term
Settlement options	Lump sum	Lump sum
Premium (annual)	$2,000	$450

Note: These are not employer provided.

Health Insurance

Peter's employer currently provides health insurance for both Peter and Patricia. The employer will continue to provide the health insurance during retirement as a retirement benefit.

The health insurance has the following provisions:
- 80/20 major medical
- $2,000 family stop-loss provision
- $250 per person deductible
- $1 million maximum lifetime benefit

Disability Insurance

Neither Peter nor Patricia has disability insurance.

Homeowners Insurance

They have HO-3 policies on both the primary residence and the vacation home.

	Residence	Vacation Home
Dwelling	$600,000	$450,000
Coinsurance clause	80%	80%
Deductible	$ 1,000	$ 500

Umbrella Policy

They have a $5 million personal umbrella liability policy.

Automobile Insurance

They carry the maximum liability coverage but have no comprehensive or collision coverage.

Investment Information

■ They believe a $60,000 emergency fund is adequate.

■ They can accept moderate risk.

■ Peter's individual retirement account (IRA) investment portfolio is $600,000 of which $300,000 is invested in low-to-medium-risk equity mutual funds. Patricia is the beneficiary of the IRA and Peter's children are named as contingent beneficiaries.

■ The other $300,000 of the IRA is invested in staggered maturity, short-term Treasury notes.

■ Peter expects to use the income and some of the principal from the $300,000 in Treasury notes in his IRA to make up any shortfall between his retirement needs and his defined benefit plan annuity, for the period of time until Social Security benefits are received.

■ Peter is currently earning 4.5% on the $300,000 invested in Treasury notes and expects the earnings rate to continue until the notes mature.

Income Tax Information

Peter and Patricia file a joint federal tax return and are both average and marginal 28% federal income taxpayers, but pay no state income tax. (See also Assets)

Retirement Information

Peter (Date of birth December 31, 1946)

■ Has an employer-provided defined benefit plan that will pay him a joint and survivor annuity equal to 80% of a single life annuity at any retirement age of 60 or older. There is no reduction or increase for retirement after age 60.

■ The defined benefit formula is 1.25% times the number of years of service times the final salary with no offset for Social Security. (Peter's salary for 2008 was $200,000.)

■ The present value of Peter's projected annual Social Security benefits beginning at age 66 is $25,500 per year or approximately 75% (rounded) of that amount if begun at age 62. Social Security benefits are expected to increase proportionally with the general inflation rate.

— Peter is expected to retire immediately, January 1, 2009. He has three options to elect regarding his defined benefit plan assets.

— Take a lump sum distribution of $1,200,000.

— Take a single life annuity with monthly payments beginning January 1, 2009.

— Take a joint and survivor annuity with monthly payments beginning January 1, 2009.

Gifts, Estates, Trusts, and Will Information

Gifts

The following are all of the lifetime taxable gifts made.

1. In 1995, Peter gifted $800,000 to each of his four children. The $3,200,000 was put into an irrevocable trust. During the same year he gave $10,000 to each child (total $40,000) to use the 1995 annual exclusion. He paid gift tax of $75,000 at the time. He inherited the $3,315,000 ($3,200,000 + $40,000 + $75,000) as the primary legatee of his mother in 1995. The successor legatees were the four grandchildren (children of Peter).

2. In February, 2006, just after his marriage to Patricia, Peter gave each of his four children $211,000 ($200,000 taxable and $11,000 annual exclusion) and paid gift tax of $59,500 at that time.

3. Patricia has made no taxable gifts during her lifetime.

Estates

For purposes of estimating the estate tax liability (of either spouse) last illness and funeral expenses are estimated to be $5,000 and estate administration expenses are estimated to be $85,000.

Wills

Peter and Patricia have simple wills leaving all probate assets to the other. The debts and taxes are to be paid from the inheritance of the surviving spouse. They had the wills drafted shortly after their marriage and just prior to a vacation they took abroad. No other estate planning documents exist.

STATEMENT OF FINANCIAL POSITION
Peter and Patricia Morgan
As of January 1, 2009

Assets[1]			Liabilities and Net Worth[2]		
Cash/Cash Equivalents			**Liabilities**		
JT	Cash (money market)	$ 120,000		**Current:**	
			H	Credit card 1	$ 15,000
			W	Credit card 2	21,000
	Total Cash/Cash Equivalents	$ 120,000	W	Credit card 3	24,000
			H	Auto 1 balance	30,000
			W	Auto 2 balance	30,000
Invested Assets				Current liabilities	$ 120,000
W	Publications, Inc.	$ 900,000			
W	Patricia's Advertising, Inc.	300,000			
W	Patricia's investment portfolio (see detail)	270,000		**Long-term:**	
H	Single premium deferred annuity (SPDA)	332,403		Mortgage—primary	$ 450,000
H	Peter's investment portfolio (IRA)	600,000		Mortgage—vacation	360,000
H	Defined benefit plan (vested)	1,200,000		Long-term liabilities	$ 810,000
	Total investments	$3,602,403			
Personal Use Assets				Total liabilities	930,000
JT	Primary residence[3]	900,000			
JT	Vacation home[4]	540,000			
JT	Personal property and furniture	300,000		**Net Worth**	$4,658,403
H	Auto 1	60,000			
W	Auto 2	66,000			
	Total Personal Use	$1,866,000			
	Total Assets	**$5,588,403**	**Total Liabilities and Net Worth**		**$5,588,403**

Notes to financial statements

[1] All assets are stated at fair market value.

[2] Liabilities are stated at principal only.

[3] Fair market value of $100,000 for the lot is included.

[4] Fair market value of $80,000 for the lot is included.

Titles and Ownership Information

H = Husband separate property

W = Wife separate property

JT = Joint husband and wife (with survivorship rights)

Information Regarding Assets and Liabilities

Publications, Inc. (Patricia 100% shareholder of C Corporation)

- The fair market value is $900,000.

- The original and present adjusted taxable basis is $225,000 (acquired by purchase January 1, 2002).

- Patricia has agreed to sell Publications, Inc., for $900,000 on April 1, 2009. The terms are 20% down on April 1, and the balance paid in equal monthly installments over 10 years at 11% interest beginning on May 1, 2009.

Patricia's Advertising, Inc. (Patricia 100% shareholder of C Corporation—Section 1244 stock)

- She started the business January 1, 1999, and her adjusted taxable basis is $750,000.

Peter's SPDA

- The SPDA was acquired December 31, 1981, for $79,602. The current fair market value is $332,403.

- Contract had back-end surrender charges of 4.5% for the first seven years.

- Currently the earnings rate is 6% compounded quarterly.

- The annuity start date is October 1, 2009, and will consist of quarterly payments over Peter's life (Peter's life expectancy is 25 years as of October 1, 2009).

- Patricia is the named beneficiary if Peter dies before the annuity start date.

Defined Benefit Plan

- The vested benefits are valued at $1,200,000.

- In the event of Peter's death before retirement benefits begin, the entire balance ($1,200,000) is paid directly to Patricia as his named beneficiary. The contingent beneficiaries are Peter's children.

Primary Residence

- The house was originally owned by Peter, but one-half was given to Patricia when they were married in 2006.

■ The fair market value of the residence is $900,000 with an adjusted taxable basis of $420,000.

■ They expect to pay 6% real estate commission on any sale of the personal residence.

Vacation Home

■ The fair market value is $540,000.

■ The original mortgage was for 15 years at 9% with a 30% down payment.

■ The original and current payment is $4,560 per month (principal and interest).

■ The current mortgage balance is $360,000, with a remaining term of 120 months.

Patricia's Detailed Investment Portfolio

Description	Quantity	Fair Market Value	Beta	Maturity	Coupon	Yearly Returns				
						08	07	06	05	04
Stock A	600	$ 18,000.00	1.15			10%	15%	12%	6%	(5%)
Stock B	1,500	$ 30,000.00	0.90			5%	6%	3%	7%	(6%)
Stock C	3,750	$ 30,000.00	0.85			5%	9%	8%	8%	(1%)
Stock D	1,200	$ 60,000.00	1.20			11%	15%	12%	10%	3%
Growth Fund	4,200	$ 63,000.00	1.15			5%	11%	14%	9%	2%
Treasury A (1 bond)	3	$ 2,788.92		2	3.75%					
Treasury B (2 bonds)	6	$ 6,151.86		3	4.25%					
Treasury C (2 bonds)	6	$ 6,816.84		5	4.5%					
Cash		$ 53,242.38								
Total		$ 270,000.00								

Note: The correlation coefficient between Patricia's portfolio and the market is 0.9. All bonds have a par value of $1,000. The duration of each Treasury A bond is 1.96 years; the duration of each Treasury B bond is 2.88 years; and the duration of each Treasury C bond is 4.62 years.

QUESTIONS

1. List the Morgans' financial strengths and weaknesses.

2. After reading the case, what additional information would you request from the Morgans to complete your data-gathering phase?

3. Calculate the following financial ratios for the Morgans.

$$\frac{\text{Net Worth}}{\text{Total Assets}}$$

$$\frac{\text{Total Debt}}{\text{Total Assets}}$$

4. Comment on any of the above ratios that you think are important.

5. Rounding to the nearest dollar and excluding the down payment, what is the total of the expected installment payments to be received in 2009 by Patricia from the sale of Publications, Inc.?

6. Calculate the first annuity payment from the SPDA for Peter, assuming he starts the annuity as scheduled (October 1, 2009).

7. Peter and Patricia have decided to refinance their vacation home over the remaining life of their existing current mortgage. If closing costs are paid separately, what will be the monthly principal and interest payment required for such a refinance?

8. Assuming Peter and Patricia sell their primary residence for the fair market value today, what are the 2009 tax consequences?

9. Peter is contemplating gifting his life insurance policy to his children, who are the current beneficiaries. What is the value of the policy for gift tax purposes?

10. In the event of a $25,000 loss due to fire on the personal residence, how much will the homeowners insurance company pay?

11. You review the insurance coverage on Patricia and Peter for catastrophic coverage and estate planning. Discuss any deficiencies in their insurance coverage and estate planning.

12. What are the weighted beta and the weighted geometric average return of Patricia's investment portfolio over the last five years based on current market values (excluding bonds and cash)?

13. With what risks should Patricia be concerned with regard to her investment portfolio?

14. Considering Patricia's current bond portfolio, what types of risks is she *not* subject to?

15. Determine which of the following bonds Patricia should purchase if she wants to increase the duration of her bond portfolio.

    ■ Bond 1: Three-year, zero-coupon bond selling for $772.18 (Duration = 3 years)
    ■ Bond 2: Four-year bond selling for $1,923.32 with an annual coupon of $375 (Duration = 2.985 years)
    ■ Bond 3: Four-year bond selling for $983.80 with an annual coupon of $85 (Duration = 3.55 years)

    Note: All bonds have a maturity of $1,000.

16. Is Patricia's portfolio of common stocks (including the mutual fund) subject to unsystematic risk?

17. By using the capital asset pricing model and assuming that the market yielded an annual compound return of 7.4% over the past five years, has Patricia's stock portfolio, including the mutual fund, outperformed its expected return?

18. Using the Treynor ratio and the geometric average return over the five-year period, which of the common stocks (including the mutual fund) has the best risk-adjusted return?

19. Assuming that Patricia treats the sale of Publications, Inc., as an installment sale, what is the tax treatment for 2009 of the down payment made on April 1, 2009?

20. Rounding to the nearest dollar, calculate the amount of ordinary income and capital gain that Patricia will have in 2009 from the sale of Publications, Inc.

21. Assume that Patricia immediately sells Patricia's Advertising, Inc., for the current fair market value. What is the impact of such a transaction on the joint federal income tax return for the Morgans for 2009?

22. Assume Peter decides to withdraw $45,000 from his SPDA today, January 1, 2009. The insurance company has informed him that his quarterly annuity (ordinary) payment will be reduced to $5,735.43 per quarter. What is the income tax effect of Peter's proposed withdrawal?

23. Assume that Peter begins his SPDA annuity as scheduled. What is the portion of that annuity that is includable in taxable income in 2009?

24. Calculate Peter's expected defined benefit monthly annuity payment, assuming he elects the single life annuity.

25. If Peter elects to take a lump sum distribution instead of electing an annuity, what options are available to him?

26. Calculate the annual implicit earnings rate for the single and joint life annuity payments for the defined benefit plan.

27. Peter elects to execute a trustee-to-trustee direct transfer of the lump sum benefit of his defined benefit plan into a rollover IRA. He believes he can earn 10% annually on the IRA rollover account and that inflation will equal the projected consumer price index. What single life monthly annuity in today's dollars could he create assuming the payments were made at the beginning of each month starting today? What would be the nominal payment at 10%? Should he take one of the defined benefit plan annuity payouts or the lump sum?

28. Assuming Peter decides to take Social Security retirement benefits beginning January 1, 2009, calculate his expected annual Social Security benefits for 2009.

29. If Peter died today, what would be the total of his probate estate?

30. If Peter died today, what would be the total of his gross estate?

31. What would be Peter's tentative estate tax base?

32. Assuming no state estate taxes, what would Peter's estate tax liability be?

33. What could Peter have done back in 1995 to avoid the current estate situation and still have accomplished the same property transfers?

34. Are the current levels of homeowners coverage adequate on the personal residence and the vacation home?

35. A person receiving Social Security benefits under normal retirement age can receive income up to a maximum threshold without reducing Social Security benefits. However, there are certain types of income that do not count against the threshold. What types of income do not count against the threshold?

36. Patricia pays premiums for workers' compensation insurance for her employees at Patricia's Advertising, Inc. What are the benefits?

37. Peter and Patricia have been notified by the bank that the provisions of their loan documents require they must provide proof of comprehensive and collision coverage on their financed automobiles. Describe this coverage.

38. Peter is very fit for his age and likely to live a long time, but he has realized that Patricia is younger than his youngest child and it is unlikely much of his estate would ultimately pass to any of his children upon Patricia's death. Peter is considering an irrevocable life insurance trust (ILIT) to provide for his children. How does an ILIT work, and why is it a good choice for Peter in his estate planning?

39. What basic will documents are missing from the Morgans' estate plan?

40. If Peter dies today, what would Patricia's options be for taking distributions from his IRA?

41. Peter and Patricia have received an unexpected offer for the vacation home of $600,000 on August 30, 2009. How much is the gain or loss on the sale of the vacation home at this price, and what are the tax implications? The house was never used as a rental by the Morgans.

42. In 1958, Natalie and Robert Fortune, Patricia's grandparents, paid $30,000 for their home that included three acres of land. It has been lovingly maintained and doubled in size over the years with $100,000 in improvements. The area has become very desirable and in Robert's estate, the fair market value was a staggering $675,000. They owned the home as joint tenants with rights of survivorship. Natalie is seriously considering an offer of $750,000 for the property she received from a developer February 1, 2009. She wants to move to an assisted living complex that will offer escalated levels of care if she needs it. Several of her friends live there, and it provides transportation for the residents that will take Natalie wherever she wants to go. What will be Natalie's taxable gain on the sale of the residence to the developer if she sells the home in February, 2009?

43. Natalie wants to establish a trust for Penny and Patricia. She had not yet used any of her GSTT lifetime exemption amount but has made gifts of $500,000 in recent years and used half of her $1 million gift tax exclusion amount. The trust will be irrevocable, and the beneficiaries will be Penny and Patricia. Each beneficiary is to receive $100,000 annually beginning with the year of the gift, and the trustee may invade corpus to make up any income shortfalls. In the event of either of their deaths, their children are named as contingent beneficiaries. If there is no child (Patricia's intention of having children seems remote at this time), Robert's alma mater, Louisiana State University, is named as contingent beneficiary for that primary beneficiary's share. Natalie will be funding the trust with $4,000,000. Calculate the generation-skipping transfer tax and the gift tax Natalie will have to pay on the gift to the trust.

Mary and Robert Trenticosta

Today is January 1, 2009. Mary and Robert Trenticosta have come to you, a financial planner, for help in developing a plan to accomplish their financial goals. From your initial meeting together, you have gathered the following information.

Personal Background and Information

Mary Trenticosta (Age 45)

Mary owns an 80% interest in a closely held company, Crescent City Publications. She has recently been diagnosed with cancer and is considering selling the business or transferring some or all of the business to her son Dominic.

Robert Trenticosta (Age 24)

Robert is a nurse who works for an orthopedist in the building where Mary has her office.

The Trenticostas

Mary and Robert met when Mary sought treatment at the orthopedic clinic after she hurt her back. Mary and Robert have been married for two years. They live in a community property state but have a prenuptial agreement declaring that all property owned is separate property.

The Children

Mary and Robert have no children together. Mary has two children from a former marriage: Valerie, age 18, who is a college student, and Dominic, age 27, who works in the publications business with Mary. The children's father is deceased.

Personal and Financial Objectives

1. They plan to retire when Mary reaches age 65.

2. They need adequate retirement income.

3. They want to avoid or minimize death taxes at the death of the first spouse.

4. They want to minimize death taxes at the death of the second spouse.

5. They want to provide adequate estate liquidity.

Economic Information

■ They expect inflation to average 4.0% annually, both currently and for the long term.

■ They each expect salaries and net income to increase at 4.0% annually, both currently and long term.

■ They believe the S&P 500 is a good measure of the market's performance. It has a historical rate of return of 12%, which is expected to continue.

Assumed Treasury Yield Curve

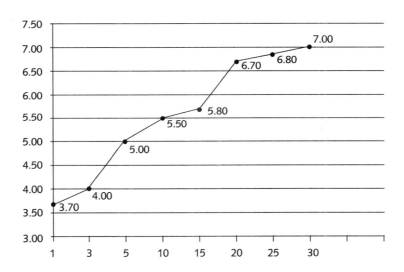

Economic Outlook—Investments

	Return	Standard Deviation
Small company stocks	13%	15%
Large company stocks	11%	12%
S&P 500	12%	12%
Corporate bonds	8.5%	6%
Long-term treasury bonds	7.0%	5%
T-bills	3.7%	2%

Insurance Information

Life Insurance

	Policy 1	Policy 2	Policy 3[1]
Insured	Mary Trenticosta	Mary Trenticosta	Robert Trenticosta
Face amount	$1 million	$300,000	$56,000
Type	Universal life	Term	Term
Cash surrender value	$10,000	$0	$0
Annual premium	$3,000	$300	$56
Beneficiary	Robert Trenticosta	Robert Trenticosta	Mary Trenticosta
Owner	Mary Trenticosta	Mary Trenticosta	Robert Trenticosta
Contingent beneficiary	Estate of Mary Trenticosta[2]	Estate of Mary Trenticosta[2]	Dominic and Valerie

[1]Robert's term policy is employer provided. The current year premium has not been paid.
[2]Mary listed her estate as the contingent beneficiary because she was concerned about her husband's ability to pay off their debt obligations in the event that she should have an untimely death.

Health Insurance

Robert currently has a health plan provided through his employer. Robert and Mary are both covered by his plan. Robert's plan has the following characteristics.

- $1,000 individual deductible
- $2,500 family deductible
- $4,000 stop-loss provision
- 80/20 coinsurance provision
- $3 million major medical limit

Note: Valerie is also covered under this plan and is eligible to remain covered until age 25.

Crescent City Publications does not have a health insurance plan. Dominic is currently covered under Dominic's wife's health insurance policy.

Disability Insurance

Robert has disability coverage provided through his employer (60% of gross pay coverage, own occupation, 90-day elimination period). Crescent City Publications does not provide disability insurance to its employees. Mary has purchased a disability policy on her own. The policy is own occupation and provides 65% of gross pay coverage and a 180-day elimination period. The premium for this policy is $2,400 per year, and the policy provides benefits to age 65.

Property and Liability Auto Insurance

	Mary and Robert's Cars	Valerie's Car
Type	Personal auto policy	Personal auto policy
Liability (bodily injury)	$250,000/$500,000	$100,000/$200,000
Property damage	$100,000	$50,000
Medical payments	$2,000	$2,000
Physical damage, own car	Actual Cash Value	Actual cash value
Uninsured motorist	$250,000/$500,000	N/A
Collision deductible	$1,000	N/A
Comprehensive deductible	$1000	N/A
Annual premium	$3,600 (two cars)	$2,700

Homeowners Insurance

	Personal Residence	Ski Condo
Type	HO-3	HO-6
Dwelling	$300,000	$0*
Other structures	$ 30,000	$0
Personal property	$150,000	$150,000
Personal liability	$200,000	$200,000
Medical payments	$ 2,000	$ 2,000
Deductible	$ 500	$ 1,000
Coinsurance clause	80%	80%
Annual premium	$ 3,000	$ 2,200
*1,000 on owner's additions and alterations		

Umbrella Liability Insurance

The policy coverage is for $4 million, and their premium is $600 per year.

Investment Information

The Trenticostas have a required rate of return of 9%. They consider themselves to be moderate to moderate-aggressive investors, and they consider $100,000 an adequate amount for an emergency fund.

Income Tax Information

The Trenticostas are in the 28% marginal tax bracket for federal income tax purposes. Capital gains are taxed at 15%. There is no state income tax.

Retirement Information

Robert is eligible to participate in his employer's 401(k) plan, but he has chosen not to participate. His employer provides a dollar-for-dollar match of up to 3% of his gross salary.

Mary does not have a retirement plan at Crescent City Publications, but she usually makes individual retirement account (IRA) contributions for Robert and herself. Mary has several other retirement accounts from previous employers, all of which are qualified plan assets.

Mary and Robert would both like to retire when Mary reaches age 65. They believe that together they would need about $150,000 (in today's dollars) annual pre-tax income during their retirement. This amount would decrease by one-third at the death of the first spouse.

Although Mary is battling cancer, they believe that her condition is not terminal and expect her to live to age 95. Robert also expects to live to age 95.

Gifts, Estates, Trusts, and Will Information

Gifts

Neither Mary nor Robert has made any previous taxable gifts.

Estates

Mary and Robert estimate that funeral expenses will be $50,000 and administrative expenses will be $80,000 for each of them.

Wills

Mary has a will that leaves $1 million to each child with the remainder of the estate going to the surviving spouse. Robert has a will that leaves everything to Mary. Mary is interested in other estate planning techniques that would maximize the actual transfer to the children but still protect Robert for his life.

STATEMENT OF CASH FLOWS
Mary and Robert Trenticosta
Expected For the Year 2009

CASH INFLOWS

Salary—Mary	$120,000	
Salary—Robert	56,000	
Investment income	31,417	
Rental income	4,200	
TOTAL CASH INFLOWS		$211,617

CASH OUTFLOWS

Ordinary living expenses

Savings—IRA contributions	$ 10,000	
Savings—bond mutual fund income reinvestment	12,000	
Food	9,600	
Clothing	5,000	
Travel	7,000	
Entertainment at home	3,000	
Utilities	6,000	
Telephone	7,200	
Auto maintenance	4,800	
Pool service	1,400	
Lawn service	1,680	
Church	2,400	
Total ordinary living expenses		$70,080

Other payments

Automobile payment	$ 14,400	
Mortgage payment (principal residence)	23,494	
Mortgage payment (ski condo)	25,886	
Total other payments		$63,780

Insurance premiums

Automobile	$ 6,300	
Disability	2,400	
Homeowners	5,200	
Life	3,300	
Umbrella	600	
Total insurance premiums		$ 17,800

(Continued on next page)

STATEMENT OF CASH FLOWS
Mary and Robert Trenticosta
Expected For the Year 2009 *(continued)*

Taxes

Federal income tax	$32,000
FICA—Robert ($56,000 × 7.65%)	4,284
FICA—Mary ($120,000 × 1.45% + $106,800 × 6.2%)	8,362
Property tax (principal residence)	1,000
Property tax (ski condo)	600

Total taxes	**$ 46,246**
TOTAL EXPENSES AND PLANNED SAVINGS	**$ 197,906**
BALANCE AVAILABLE FOR DISCRETIONARY INVESTMENT	**$ 13,711**

Notes:

Investment income:		
	Checking	$ 0
	Savings	1,528
	Money market account	401 **
	Equity brokerage account	3,188
	Bond mutual fund	12,000 *
	Bond portfolio	12,500
	High-Tech Stock	1,600
	Brown Foreman Stock	200
	TOTAL	$31,417

*All income is automatically reinvested in the bond mutual fund.
**Current interest paid on money market account is 2%.

STATEMENT OF NET WORTH
Mary and Robert Trenticosta
As of January 1, 2009

Assets[1]			Liabilities[2, 3] and Net Worth	
Cash and cash equivalents			**Current liabilities**	
JT Checking[4]	$ 16,000	W	Automobile notes payable	$ 38,000
H Checking[5]	10,000			
JT Savings[6,7]	50,950	H	Credit cards	7,000
Total cash and equivalents	$ 76,950		Current liabilities	$ 45,000
Invested assets				
W Stock in Crescent City Publications[8]	$ 320,000		Long-term liabilities	
W Equity brokerage account	116,242	JT	Mortgage on residence	$ 278,300
W Bond mutual fund	272,000	W	Mortgage on ski condo	215,254
W Bond brokerage account	200,000		Long-term liabilities	$ 493,554
W High-Tech Stock[9]	40,000			
H Brown Foreman Stock[10]	10,000		Total liabilities	$ 538,554
W Pension plan #1[11]	569,188			
W Pension plan #2[11]	697,352			
W IRA rollover[11]	130,156			
W IRA	29,300			
H IRA	34,700			
W Cash surrender value life insurance	10,000			
Total invested assets	$ 2,428,938		Net worth	$ 2,941,334
Use assets				
JT Personal residence[5]	$ 360,000			
W Ski condo	240,000			
JT Personal property[5]	200,000			
W Automobiles (3)	174,000			
Total use assets	$ 974,000			
Total assets	**$3,479,888**		**Total liabilities and net worth**	**$3,479,888**

Notes

[1] Assets are stated at fair market value with exception of Crescent City Publications stock.

[2] Liabilities are stated at principal only.

[3] All liabilities go with the associated asset for title purposes.

[4] This is joint tenancy with right of survivorship with son, Dominic. Checking account does not earn interest. Mary contributed 100%.

[5] Robert has a POD on the checking account naming Mary as the beneficiary.

[6] Joint tenancy with right of survivorship rights with spouse.

[7] The current interest rate for savings accounts is 3%.

[8] This is Mary's guess at what Crescent City Publications is worth. Her basis is $50,000.

[9] 2,000 shares at $20 per share. The current dividend is $0.80 per share and is expected to grow at 3% per year.

[10] 200 shares.

[11] All pension plans have the spouse of participant as named beneficiary.

Title Designations

H = Husband (sole owner)
W = Wife (sole owner)
JT = Joint tenancy with right of survivorship

Information Regarding Assets and Liabilities

High-Tech Stock

This stock was given to Mary as a Christmas present after being purchased October 15, 2004, by Mary's brother Brian. Brian's basis in the stock was $17,000, and the value at the date of the gift was $50,000. The current value of the stock is $40,000. The stock currently pays a dividend of $0.80. See Footnote on Statement of Financial Position.

Bond Mutual Fund

The bond mutual fund was inherited from Mary's uncle, Gary, who died December 10, 2006, at which time the bond fund was valued at $296,000. Uncle Gary had just bought the bond fund on November 1, 2006, and paid $290,000 for it. All earnings are automatically reinvested in the fund, and Mary has had no distributions since inheriting it. The fund reinvested income of $12,000 in 2008, but unfortunately is only valued at $272,000 today due to changes in interest rates.

Bond Brokerage Account

Description	Maturity (Years)	Coupon[1]	Duration	Cost Basis	Fair Market Value
20,000 US T-bills	1	N/A	1.00	$ 19,280.00	$ 19,286.40
40,000 US T-bonds	30	8%	13.00	40,000.00	44,988.94
20,000 US T-bonds	20	0%	20.00	2,626.00	5,250.60
40,000 Big Company bonds[2]	20	9%	10.81	40,000.00	48,542.02
30,000 Weak Company bonds[3]	25	9%	3.23	30,000.00	6,000.94
50,000 Texas municipal bonds	15	6%	10.54	50,000.00	55,232.58
				$181,906.00	$179,301.48
Money market account					$ 20,698.52
TOTAL					$200,000.00

Account Value as of 12/31/08: $200,000.00

Notes
[1] Assume all coupon payments are made once a year.
[2] Bonds are investment quality.
[3] Bonds are non investment quality.

Equity Brokerage Account

Stock[1]	Shares	Beta	Standard Deviation	Dividend Yield[2]	Average Return	Cost	Fair Market Value
Big Company	2,000	0.88	12.5%	4.0%[3]	12.5%	$16,092.94	$ 29,000.00
Small Company	2,000	1.24	18.0%	0.0%	15.0%	21,448.70	24,666.00
Oil Company	2,000	1.00	10.0%	3.5%[3]	8.0%	22,271.40	30,300.00
Auto Company	2,000	1.12	10.0%	3.0%[4]	10.0%	24,249.44	32,276.00
					Total	$84,062.48	$116,242.00

Notes
[1] The stock portfolio has a correlation coefficient with the market of 0.80.
[2] The dividend yield is the current yield.
[3] The growth of the dividend is expected to remain at 3%.
[4] The expected growth of the dividend is zero.

Brown Foreman Stock

Robert inherited the Brown Foreman stock from his great-aunt Sarah, who had bought the stock when the price was $42.00 per share. When Sarah died, she left Robert 100 shares of Brown Foreman stock. Robert knows that on the date of Sarah's death Brown Foreman stock closed at $35.00 per share with a high price of $38.00 and low price of $34.00. The stock has since split two-for-one and has a current dividend yield of 2%.

Personal Residence

The Trenticostas purchased their personal residence for $350,000 nine months ago. They put down 20% from the sale of their previous home. They were able to get a mortgage rate of 7.5% financed over 30 years. Their monthly payment is $1,957.80 with a balance of $278,300.78 and 352 payments remaining.

Ski Condo

Mary purchased the ski condo three years ago for $300,000 and put 20% down. The balance was financed over 15 years at 7%. The monthly payment is $2,157.18, and they have made 30 payments. The balance on the loan is $215,254.14. Since the purchase of the condo, Mary has incurred the following restoration costs.

Wood floors	$4,000
Furniture	7,000
Ceiling fans	600
Carpet	2,400
Kitchen appliances	4,400
Total	$18,400

The Trenticostas use the condo quite often in the winter and summer, but they are usually able to rent it to friends for 14 days per year at $300.00 per day.

QUESTIONS

1. List the Trenticostas' financial strengths and weaknesses.

2. After reading the case, what additional information would you request from the Trenticostas to complete your data-gathering phase?

3. If Mary were to die today, what would be the value of her gross estate?

4. If Mary were to die today, what would be the value of her probate assets?

5. Mary is concerned about having a high estate tax liability in the instance that her assets rapidly increased in value by the time of her death. What estate planning techniques could be used to alleviate this concern?

6. Evaluate Mary's current estate plan.

7. If Robert were to die today, what would be the value of his gross estate?

8. What would be the value of Robert's probate estate if he died today?

9. What would be Robert's estate tax liability if he died today, assuming Robert's last medical, funeral, and administrative expenses were $130,000?

10. Assume Robert died on January 1, 2009, and Mary died within a month of Robert. Calculate the second-to-die estate tax liability for Mary's estate. Use the fair market value (FMV) of Mary's assets and assume that her funeral and administrative expenses are $130,000.

11. Mary is considering liquidating the bond mutual fund and expects to receive net proceeds of $272,000 from the sale. What are the tax consequences of such a sale, assuming that it takes place on April 15, 2009?

12. Mary is considering disposing of her stock in Crescent City Publications by one or more of the following methods: grantor retained annuity trust (GRAT), private annuity, charitable remainder annuity trust (CRAT), or self-canceling installment note (SCIN). Which method or methods are reasonable under the circumstances? Any sale contemplates getting the value of the stock out of her gross estate.

13. Which of Mary's assets would be the best choice to gift to her children if the objective is estate minimization?

14. Mary is considering making a gift of 40% of her ownership share in Crescent City Publications to her son, Dominic. She discusses this transaction with a valuation expert who tells her that her share in the company is probably worth $350,000. The valuation expert also says that with the transfer of the 40% share she could apply a valuation discount of 50%. Answer the following questions, assuming that Mary makes the gift with the above appraisal information.

    a. What is the value of the gift that would be reported on Form 709?
    b. If Mary and Robert split the gift, what amount would be reported on Mary's Form 709?
    c. What are the requirements for making the split-gift election?
    d. How much of Robert's applicable credit will remain, assuming this is his first gift?

15. To improve Mary's estate plan, you are considering how to structure the estate. Based on the facts in the case, what is the best disposition arrangement for Mary with regard to assets? (Outright bequest? A power of appointment trust? A bypass trust? A qualified terminable interest property trust? A charitable remainder unitrust?)

16. If Mary and Robert can earn their required rate of return, how much would they need when Mary is age 65 to provide for both of them in retirement? (Round to the nearest thousand and assume they are both expected to live to age 95.)

17. Describe the Trenticostas' situation regarding planning for the federal generation-skipping transfer tax (GSTT).

18. Which bonds in the bond portfolio are subject to:

    a. Default risk?
    b. Reinvestment risk?
    c. Foreign currency risk?
    d. Interest rate risk?
    e. Liquidity risk?

19. How would Mary protect her gain in Big Company stock without selling the stock?

20. Determine the yield to maturity for each bond by using the current fair market value.

21. Excluding the money market funds, what is the duration of the bond portfolio in the bond brokerage account?

22. On the basis of value of the bonds in the bond brokerage account, what have interest rates been doing during the holding period?

23. How much cash and cash equivalents do the Trenticostas actually have?

24. By using the capital asset pricing model, determine the expected return for each of the stocks in the portfolio.

25. By using the Jensen performance measure, determine alpha for each of the stocks in the brokerage account. Assume that the actual returns are as follows:

	Actual Return
Big Company	13.0%
Small Company	13.5%
Oil Company	9.0%
Auto Company	10.5%

26. What is the expected return of the entire stock portfolio in terms of dollars? In percentage terms?

27. What is the weighted alpha of the entire stock portfolio?

28. Assuming an income tax rate of 30%, what is the after-tax equivalent yield to maturity for the Texas municipal bonds?

29. How does the return on the municipal bond compare with other interest rates?

30. On the basis of other prevailing interest rates, does the pre-tax return for the Texas municipal bond seem reasonable? Why?

31. Determine the holding period return for each of the stocks in the equity brokerage account. Ignore dividends for this purpose.

32. What percentage of the change in the value of the equity brokerage account can be explained by changes in the stock market?

33. On the basis of the constant growth dividend model, what must the Trenticostas' required rate of return be for the high tech stock to be priced fairly? What are the implications of buying, selling, or holding the stock?

34. Mary only recently made Dominic the co-owner of her checking account. What are the consequences to Mary? When does this become a taxable gift from Mary to Dominic?

35. Crescent City Publications used a cross-purchase life insurance program to protect themselves from early and untimely death of a principal shareholder. Mary owns 80%; two other individuals (A and C) own 10% each. Assume that Crescent City Publications is worth $437,500. How many policies did they have and for what amounts?

36. Determine the basis in Robert's Brown Foreman stock.

37. If Robert were to sell the Brown Foreman stock today, what would be the income tax consequences?

38. How much qualified residence interest can the Trenticostas deduct for income tax in 2009?

39. By using the dividend growth model, determine the price per share for each of the following stocks.
    a. Big Company
    b. Oil Company
    c. Auto Company

40. Since Mary was diagnosed with cancer, she has been distracted by her health concerns and forgot to make her IRA contribution for 2008. Can she still make a 2008 contribution in 2009?

41. Mary wants your help in determining the probability of achieving certain returns within her portfolio.
    a. Determine the probability of getting a positive return for the Big Company.
    b. Determine the probability of getting a return above 30% from Auto Company.
    c. Determine the probability of earning a return between 15% and 33% for Small Company.

42. Mary is considering rebalancing her equity brokerage account portfolio by selling the Oil Company stock and the Auto Company stock. She wants to invest the entire portfolio as follows:

    ■ 60% in Small Company
    ■ 40% in Big Company

    The two stocks have a tendency to not move together since the correlation between them is only 0.3. If Mary pays 15% tax for capital gains out of this portfolio, how much will be invested in the Big Company and Small Company?

43. What is the expected return for this new portfolio? Assume the same facts as in the previous question.

44. What will be the standard deviation of her new portfolio? Use the same facts as in the previous questions.

45. Mary and Robert have the following income and expenses from the rental of the condo during 2008.

Rental Income (14 days at $300 per day)	$4,200
Interest Expense	$14,714
Property Tax	$600
Depreciation	$9,600
Utilities	$2,000

    How should they treat the above items on their 2008 federal income tax return?

46. Mary has surgery in January 2009 to remove a small tumor from her arm as an outpatient. She incurs $3,200 in expenses. How much will she have to pay (i.e., how much is not covered by the health insurance policy)?

47. Crescent City Publications had earnings of $54,000 last year. How does the capitalized earnings approach method of valuation compare with Mary's guess of what Crescent City is worth? Use the Trenticostas' required rate of return.

48. Based on the earnings of $54,000, how does Mary's guess of the value of Crescent City compare with using the P/E ratio of similar companies to determine the value of Crescent City? Assume the P/E ratio for similar companies is 12:1.

49. If Mary sold the ski condo and all the contents in 2009 for $320,000, how much tax would she pay from this sale? Assume a real estate commission of 6%.

Use the following information for questions 50 through 55.

Mary is concerned about the price of Big Company. During July 2009, she decides to buy a put option to protect her position in the stock. The price of the stock has dropped to $14.00 per share. The put option has an expiration of January 2010, an exercise price of $13.00, and a premium of $2.00.

50. How many option contracts should she buy to fully hedge her long position in Big Company stock?

51. Mary fully hedges her position with the above option. On December 31, 2009, the price of the stock has dropped $10.

   a. What is her gain or loss on the option contracts?
   b. How much gain or loss does she have to recognize for this put on her 2009 Form 1040?
   c. How much is the gain or loss on her long position in Big Company for the time she has held this option?
   d. Based on your analysis, has Mary done an effective job of hedging Big Company stock? If not, why? What alternative strategy might you suggest? Describe the pros and cons of the put and your suggestions, if applicable.

52. In January 2010, the option expires unexercised. The price of Big Company has increased to $15.00 per share. How should Mary treat this on her 2010 individual tax return (Form 1040)?

53. Because the price of Big Company stock has rebounded and the entire market is doing well, Mary believes that the price of Big Company will continue to increase above the $14.50 level (current price). How do you advise her as her financial planner?

54. After your discussion with her, Mary decides to enter into a futures contract on the S&P 500 to take advantage of the rising market. The contract expires January 2011.

   a. Should she buy or sell the contract?
   b. The S&P 500 contract has had the following prices:

Upon entering into contract	$100
At 12/31/09	$110
Expiration	$125

   How much gain or loss should Mary report for tax purposes in 2009 and 2010? What is the nature of this gain or loss?

55. What are two methods Mary could use to value her option against the market values?

56. If Mary and Robert died, how should their beneficiaries treat the inherited IRAs?

57. The Trenticostas are concerned about future estate taxes. Mary has been reading about strategies to reduce estate taxes and learns the proceeds of her life insurance will be received tax free by the beneficiary but will be included in her estate because she is the owner of the policies. She plans on leaving $1 million each to her children, Valerie and Dominic. She determines she can accomplish two goals at once and changes the beneficiary of her $1 million life insurance policy to her daughter, Valerie, and makes Robert the owner of the policy to remove the proceeds from her gross estate. What are the tax consequences of Mary's idea?

58. While working in the orthopedic office, Robert slips and falls, severely fracturing his arm. The fracture requires surgery and a cast, as well as several weeks of rehabilitation. Robert is unable to perform his nursing duties for four months, but he does try to help out at the office whenever possible. Robert receives a $5,000 workers' compensation payment for medical expenses, as well as any benefits due from his disability insurance coverage. Additionally, for the hours Robert helped out at the office over the four month period, Robert was paid a total of $5,000. Assuming Robert is in a 28% marginal tax bracket, how much money, after taxes, has he received over the four month period?

59. Mary is pleased that Valerie is attending college and studying business, as she hopes Valerie will become interested in one day working at Crescent City Publications. As a reward and incentive to stay in college, Mary gives Valerie her brokerage account to help pay for college, and, hopefully, graduate school. As the brokerage account was Mary's prior to meeting Robert, she did not consult Robert in the education funding arrangement. Assuming the brokerage account continues its current yield and that all of the stocks produce qualified dividends, what are the tax consequences of the education funding plan?

60. Mary's will bequeaths $1 million each to Valerie and Dominic. Mary worries that leaving $1 million in a lump sum will lead to money management problems and mistakes for Valerie and Dominic, as neither is a savvy investor. She has decided to amend her will and create a testamentary trust, into which $2 million of her assets will be placed. The trust assets will be professionally managed with a distribution schedule of the assets to Valerie and Dominic over a period of years. Calculate Mary's gross estate and probate estate to reflect the testamentary trust.

61. Assume at the time of Mary's death Pension Plan #1, Pension Plan #2, and the ski condo have each grown in value to a FMV of $1 million. What would be the tax consequences if Robert immediately liquidated Pension Plan #1 and the ski condo for the date of death FMV to obtain the capital needed to start his own business?

62. On November 10, 2009, Mary purchased stock with a FMV of $50,000 and added it to her equity brokerage account. On December 12, 2011, Mary gifts the stock to Valerie. What would Valerie's basis, holding period, and gain or loss be if she then sold the securities one month later for:
    a. $38,000
    b. $55,000
    c. $45,000

63. Assume Mary makes a gift of property with a fair market value of $100,000 and an adjusted basis of $40,000 to Dominic. What would Dominic's basis in the property be if Mary paid gift taxes of $20,440 (assume that at time of this gift, she has previously used all of her lifetime exemption amount) and applied an annual exclusion to the transfer.

64. Assume Big Company stock is currently paying a dividend of $.58 per share. Rather than the dividend payout growing at a steady 3%, assume the dividend is expected to grow for three years at 6% and then 7% annually thereafter. Furthermore, assume that the Trenticostas' required rate of return is 9%. What is the intrinsic value of Big Company based on the multistage (variable) growth dividend model?

Appendix

List of Exhibits

Exhibit 1: The Financial Planning Process

1. Meet with Client—Identify Financial Goals.
   Goals generally include some or all of the following:

   a. Purchase of residence.
   b. Vacation.
   c. Education of children.
   d. Investment review.
   e. Adequate retirement.
   f. Efficient and effective transfer of estate.

2. Collect and Analyze Client Information.
   a. Personal information about client and family.
   b. Current personal financial statements, which include cash flow statement and statement of financial position.
   c. Personal and business tax returns (5 years).
   d. All insurance policies (health, life, disability, auto, homeowners, and umbrella).
   e. Employee benefits booklets and reports.
   f. Descriptions in detail regarding:
      1.) Indebtedness—Original amount of loan, date, principal amount, interest rate, monthly payment, current loan balance remaining, and number of payments.
      2.) Each investment—When purchased, what is the adjusted taxable basis, number of shares, and so forth.
   g. Wills, trusts, and so forth.

3. Develop Strategies for Meeting Goals.

4. Select and Recommend a Comprehensive Plan.
   a. Should include cash flow projections.
   b. Should include a description of each goal and how and when it is to be accomplished.

5. Implement Plan.

6. Monitor and Evaluate.

Exhibit 2: Personal Financial Statements

1. Statement of Financial Position (Balance Sheet).
   a. Assets and liabilities should be presented at fair market value.
   b. Statement needs to be appropriately dated.
   c. Net worth should be indicated.
   d. Footnotes should be utilized to describe details of both assets and liabilities.
   e. Property should be identified with owner (e.g., JTWROS, H for husband, or W for wife.).
   f. Categories of assets—Depends on interest of client.
      1.) Cash and cash equivalents.
      2.) Invested assets (investment portfolio).
      3.) Use assets (residence, furniture, and autos).
   g. Liabilities should be categorized according to maturity date.
      1.) Current liabilities—due within one year.
      2.) Long-term liabilities—generally mortgages and notes.
   h. Net worth = assets − liabilities.

2. Statement of Cash Flows for Past Year and Pro Forma for Next Year.
   a. Indicate period covered.
   b. Inflows:
      1.) Gross salaries.
      2.) Interest income.
      3.) Dividend income.
      4.) Rental income.
      5.) Refunds due (tax).
      6.) Other incoming cash flows.
      7.) Alimony received.
   c. Outflows:
      1.) Savings and investment—by item.
      2.) Fixed outflows—nondiscretionary.
         a.) House payments.
         b.) Auto payments.
         c.) Taxes.
      3.) Fixed outflows—discretionary. (club dues).
      4.) Variable outflows—nondiscretionary.
         a.) Food.
         b.) Utilities.
      5.) Variable outflows—discretionary.
         a.) Vacations.
         b.) Entertainment.
   d. Net discretionary cash flow = inflows − outflows.
   e. Footnotes should be used to explain.

Exhibit 3: Housing Costs and Debt Repayment

Indicators of Financial Strength and Weakness
As a Percentage of Gross Income

Type of Cost	Weak			Strong	
	Extreme	Moderate	Neutral	Moderate	Extreme
Housing Costs	≥40%	≥35%	≤30%	≤28%	≤20%
Housing Costs Plus Other Debt Repayments	≥48%	≥43%	≤38%	≤36%	≤28%

- Housing costs include principal payments, interest, taxes, insurance, and any association dues or costs.

- The total of all housing costs as a percentage of monthly gross income generally must be ≤28% to qualify for a mortgage.

- Other debt repayments include credit card payments, automobile loan payments, student loan payments, and the like.

- The combination of housing costs and other monthly debt repayments generally must be ≤36% of monthly gross income to qualify for a home mortgage.

Exhibit 4: Annual Savings

As a Percentage of Annual Gross Income, by Age

Age, Years	Weak			Strong	
	Extreme	Moderate	Neutral	Moderate	Extreme
25	≤0%	≤2%	5%	≥7%	≥10%
30	≤0%	≤4%	7%	≥10%	≥13%
35	≤3%	≤7%	10%	≥13%	≥16%
40	≤6%	≤10%	13%	≥16%	≥19%
45	≤9%	≤13%	16%	≥19%	≥22%

This table assumes that the person is beginning a savings plan at the indicated age. Modification to the table will have to be made to accommodate analysis for a person who previously had some savings. This table is just a guide to wage replacement at about 80% of preretirement income, assuming a normal portfolio of 60% stocks and 40% fixed instruments.

Exhibit 5: Progress to Retirement, by Age and Income

An indicator of progress toward adequate retirement.
Assumes an 80% wage replacement ratio.

TARGET WEALTH LEVEL		
Investment assets as a percentage of current income		

INCOME LEVEL	$25,000 ▼
WAGE REPLACEMENT RATIO	80%
DISCOUNT RATE	9%

Inadequate Progress

Age, Years	VERY WEAK			WEAK		
	No SS	Single	WSAS	No SS	Single	WSAS
25	0.14	0.08	0.05	0.21	0.12	0.07
30	0.22	0.12	0.07	0.33	0.18	0.11
35	0.33	0.18	0.11	0.50	0.28	0.16
40	0.52	0.28	0.17	0.77	0.43	0.25
45	0.79	0.44	0.26	1.19	0.65	0.39
50	1.22	0.67	0.40	1.83	1.01	0.59
55	1.88	1.03	0.61	2.82	1.55	0.92
60	2.89	1.59	0.94	4.33	2.38	1.41
65	4.44	2.44	1.44	6.67	3.67	2.17

Adequate Progress

Age, Years	AVERAGE			GOOD		
	No SS	Single	WSAS	No SS	Single	WSAS
25	0.28	0.16	0.09	0.42	0.23	0.14
30	0.44	0.24	0.14	0.65	0.36	0.21
35	0.67	0.37	0.22	1.00	0.55	0.33
40	1.03	0.57	0.34	1.55	0.85	0.50
45	1.59	0.87	0.52	2.38	1.31	0.77
50	2.44	1.34	0.79	3.66	2.01	1.19
55	3.75	2.07	1.22	5.63	3.10	1.83
60	5.78	3.18	1.88	8.67	4.77	2.82
65	8.89	4.89	2.89	13.33	7.33	4.33

Strong Progress

Age, Years	STRONG			EXTRA STRONG		
	No SS	Single	WSAS	No SS	Single	WSAS
25	0.71	0.39	0.23	0.99	0.54	0.32
30	1.09	0.60	0.35	1.52	0.84	0.50
35	1.67	0.92	0.54	2.34	1.29	0.76
40	2.58	1.42	0.84	3.61	1.98	1.17
45	3.97	2.18	1.29	5.55	3.05	1.80
50	6.10	3.36	1.98	8.54	4.70	2.78
55	9.39	5.16	3.05	13.14	7.23	4.27
60	14.44	7.94	4.69	20.22	11.12	6.57
65	22.22	12.22	7.22	31.11	17.11	10.11

No SS = No Social Security   Single = Social Security benefits for a single person
WSAS = Social Security benefits for a married individual whose spouse is not working and is the same age

TARGET WEALTH LEVEL
Investment assets as a percentage of current income

INCOME LEVEL	$40,000 ▼
WAGE REPLACEMENT RATIO	80%
DISCOUNT RATE	9%

Inadequate Progress

Age, Years	VERY WEAK			VERY WEAK		
	No SS	Single	WSAS	No SS	Single	WSAS
25	0.14	0.09	0.06	0.21	0.13	0.09
30	0.22	0.14	0.10	0.33	0.20	0.14
35	0.33	0.21	0.15	0.50	0.31	0.22
40	0.52	0.32	0.23	0.77	0.48	0.34
45	0.79	0.50	0.35	1.19	0.74	0.52
50	1.22	0.76	0.53	1.83	1.14	0.80
55	1.88	1.17	0.82	2.82	1.76	1.23
60	2.89	1.81	1.26	4.33	2.71	1.90
65	4.44	2.78	1.94	6.67	4.17	2.92

Adequate Progress

Age, Years	AVERAGE			GOOD		
	No SS	Single	WSAS	No SS	Single	WSAS
25	0.28	0.18	0.12	0.42	0.27	0.19
30	0.44	0.27	0.19	0.65	0.41	0.29
35	0.67	0.42	0.29	1.00	0.63	0.44
40	1.03	0.64	0.45	1.55	0.97	0.68
45	1.59	0.99	0.69	2.38	1.49	1.04
50	2.44	1.53	1.07	3.66	2.29	1.60
55	3.75	2.35	1.64	5.63	3.52	2.46
60	5.78	3.61	2.53	8.67	5.42	3.79
65	8.89	5.56	3.89	13.33	8.33	5.83

Strong Progress

Age, Years	STRONG			EXTRA STRONG		
	No SS	Single	WSAS	No SS	Single	WSAS
25	0.71	0.44	0.31	0.99	0.62	0.43
30	1.09	0.68	0.48	1.52	0.95	0.67
35	1.67	1.05	0.73	2.34	1.47	1.03
40	2.58	1.61	1.13	3.61	2.25	1.58
45	3.97	2.48	1.73	5.55	3.47	2.43
50	6.10	3.81	2.67	8.54	5.34	3.74
55	9.39	5.87	4.11	13.14	8.21	5.75
60	14.44	9.03	6.32	20.22	12.64	8.85
65	22.22	13.89	9.72	31.11	19.44	13.61

TARGET WEALTH LEVEL
Investment assets as a percentage of current income

INCOME LEVEL	$55,000 ▼
WAGE REPLACEMENT RATIO	80%
DISCOUNT RATE	9%

Inadequate Progress

Age, Years	VERY WEAK			WEAK		
	No SS	Single	WSAS	No SS	Single	WSAS
25	0.14	0.10	0.08	0.21	0.15	0.11
30	0.22	0.15	0.12	0.33	0.23	0.18
35	0.33	0.23	0.18	0.50	0.35	0.27
40	0.52	0.36	0.28	0.77	0.54	0.42
45	0.79	0.55	0.43	1.19	0.82	0.64
50	1.22	0.85	0.66	1.83	1.27	0.99
55	1.88	1.30	1.01	2.82	1.95	1.52
60	2.89	2.00	1.56	4.33	3.00	2.34
65	4.44	3.08	2.40	6.67	4.62	3.60

Adequate Progress

Age, Years	AVERAGE			GOOD		
	No SS	Single	WSAS	No SS	Single	WSAS
25	0.28	0.20	0.15	0.42	0.29	0.23
30	0.44	0.30	0.24	0.65	0.45	0.35
35	0.67	0.46	0.36	1.00	0.70	0.54
40	1.03	0.71	0.56	1.55	1.07	0.83
45	1.59	1.10	0.86	2.38	1.65	1.28
50	2.44	1.69	1.32	3.66	2.54	1.98
55	3.75	2.60	2.03	5.63	3.90	3.04
60	5.78	4.00	3.12	8.67	6.01	4.68
65	8.89	6.16	4.80	13.33	9.24	7.20

Strong Progress

Age, Years	STRONG			EXTRA STRONG		
	No SS	Single	WSAS	No SS	Single	WSAS
25	0.71	0.49	0.38	0.99	0.69	0.53
30	1.09	0.75	0.59	1.52	1.06	0.82
35	1.67	1.16	0.90	2.34	1.63	1.27
40	2.58	1.79	1.39	3.61	2.50	1.95
45	3.97	2.75	2.14	5.55	3.85	3.00
50	6.10	4.23	3.29	8.54	5.92	4.61
55	9.39	6.51	5.07	13.14	9.11	7.09
60	14.44	10.01	7.80	20.22	14.02	10.91
65	22.22	15.40	11.99	31.11	21.57	16.79

TARGET WEALTH LEVEL
Investment assets as a percentage of current income

INCOME LEVEL	$70,000 ▼
WAGE REPLACEMENT RATIO	80%
DISCOUNT RATE	9%

Inadequate Progress

Age, Years	VERY WEAK			WEAK		
	No SS	Single	WSAS	No SS	Single	WSAS
25	0.14	0.11	0.09	0.21	0.16	0.13
30	0.22	0.16	0.14	0.33	0.24	0.20
35	0.33	0.25	0.21	0.50	0.38	0.31
40	0.52	0.39	0.32	0.77	0.58	0.48
45	0.79	0.59	0.50	1.19	0.89	0.74
50	1.22	0.92	0.76	1.83	1.37	1.14
55	1.88	1.41	1.17	2.82	2.11	1.76
60	2.89	2.17	1.81	4.33	3.25	2.71
65	4.44	3.33	2.78	6.67	5.00	4.17

Adequate Progress

Age, Years	AVERAGE			GOOD		
	No SS	Single	WSAS	No SS	Single	WSAS
25	0.28	0.21	0.18	0.42	0.32	0.27
30	0.44	0.33	0.27	0.65	0.49	0.41
35	0.67	0.50	0.42	1.00	0.75	0.63
40	1.03	0.77	0.64	1.55	1.16	0.97
45	1.59	1.19	0.99	2.38	1.78	1.49
50	2.44	1.83	1.53	3.66	2.75	2.29
55	3.75	2.82	2.35	5.63	4.22	3.52
60	5.78	4.33	3.61	8.67	6.50	5.42
65	8.89	6.67	5.56	13.33	10.00	8.33

Strong Progress

Age, Years	STRONG			EXTRA STRONG		
	No SS	Single	WSAS	No SS	Single	WSAS
25	0.71	0.53	0.44	0.99	0.74	0.62
30	1.09	0.82	0.68	1.52	1.14	0.95
35	1.67	1.26	1.05	2.34	1.76	1.47
40	2.58	1.93	1.61	3.61	2.71	2.25
45	3.97	2.97	2.48	5.55	4.16	3.47
50	6.10	4.58	3.81	8.54	6.41	5.34
55	9.39	7.04	5.87	13.14	9.86	8.21
60	14.44	10.83	9.03	20.22	15.17	12.64
65	22.22	16.67	13.89	31.11	23.33	19.44

TARGET WEALTH LEVEL
Investment assets as a percentage of current income

INCOME LEVEL	$85,000 ▼	
WAGE REPLACEMENT RATIO	80%	
DISCOUNT RATE	9%	

Inadequate Progress

Age, Years	VERY WEAK			WEAK		
	No SS	Single	WSAS	No SS	Single	WSAS
25	0.14	0.11	0.10	0.21	0.17	0.15
30	0.22	0.17	0.15	0.33	0.26	0.23
35	0.33	0.27	0.23	0.50	0.40	0.35
40	0.52	0.41	0.36	0.77	0.61	0.53
45	0.79	0.63	0.55	1.19	0.94	0.82
50	1.22	0.97	0.84	1.83	1.45	1.27
55	1.88	1.49	1.30	2.82	2.24	1.95
60	2.89	2.29	2.00	4.33	3.44	2.99
65	4.44	3.53	3.07	6.67	5.29	4.61

Adequate Progress

Age, Years	AVERAGE			GOOD		
	No SS	Single	WSAS	No SS	Single	WSAS
25	0.28	0.22	0.20	0.42	0.34	0.29
30	0.44	0.35	0.30	0.65	0.52	0.45
35	0.67	0.53	0.46	1.00	0.80	0.69
40	1.03	0.82	0.71	1.55	1.23	1.07
45	1.59	1.26	1.10	2.38	1.89	1.64
50	2.44	1.94	1.69	3.66	2.91	2.53
55	3.75	2.98	2.60	5.63	4.47	3.89
60	5.78	4.59	3.99	8.67	6.88	5.99
65	8.89	7.06	6.14	13.33	10.59	9.22

Strong Progress

Age, Years	STRONG			EXTRA STRONG		
	No SS	Single	WSAS	No SS	Single	WSAS
25	0.71	0.56	0.49	0.99	0.79	0.68
30	1.09	0.86	0.75	1.52	1.21	1.05
35	1.67	1.33	1.16	2.34	1.86	1.62
40	2.58	2.05	1.78	3.61	2.87	2.49
45	3.97	3.15	2.74	5.55	4.41	3.84
50	6.10	4.84	4.22	8.54	6.78	5.90
55	9.39	7.45	6.49	13.14	10.44	9.08
60	14.44	11.47	9.98	20.22	16.06	13.98
65	22.22	17.65	15.36	31.11	24.71	21.50

TARGET WEALTH LEVEL
Investment assets as a percentage of current income

INCOME LEVEL	$100,000 ▼
WAGE REPLACEMENT RATIO	80%
DISCOUNT RATE	9%

Inadequate Progress

Age, Years	VERY WEAK			WEAK		
	No SS	Single	WSAS	No SS	Single	WSAS
25	0.14	0.12	0.10	0.21	0.18	0.16
30	0.22	0.18	0.16	0.33	0.27	0.24
35	0.33	0.28	0.25	0.50	0.41	0.37
40	0.52	0.43	0.38	0.77	0.64	0.57
45	0.79	0.65	0.58	1.19	0.98	0.88
50	1.22	1.01	0.90	1.83	1.51	1.35
55	1.88	1.55	1.38	2.82	2.32	2.08
60	2.89	2.38	2.13	4.33	3.57	3.20
65	4.44	3.67	3.28	6.67	5.50	4.92

Adequate Progress

Age, Years	AVERAGE			GOOD		
	No SS	Single	WSAS	No SS	Single	WSAS
25	0.28	0.23	0.21	0.42	0.35	0.31
30	0.44	0.36	0.32	0.65	0.54	0.48
35	0.67	0.55	0.49	1.00	0.83	0.74
40	1.03	0.85	0.76	1.55	1.28	1.14
45	1.59	1.31	1.17	2.38	1.96	1.75
50	2.44	2.01	1.80	3.66	3.02	2.70
55	3.75	3.10	2.77	5.63	4.65	4.15
60	5.78	4.77	4.26	8.67	7.15	6.39
65	8.89	7.33	6.56	13.33	11.00	9.83

Strong Progress

Age, Years	STRONG			EXTRA STRONG		
	No SS	Single	WSAS	No SS	Single	WSAS
25	0.71	0.58	0.52	0.99	0.82	0.73
30	1.09	0.90	0.80	1.52	1.26	1.12
35	1.67	1.38	1.24	2.34	1.93	1.73
40	2.58	2.13	1.90	3.61	2.98	2.66
45	3.97	3.27	2.92	5.55	4.58	4.09
50	6.10	5.03	4.50	8.54	7.05	6.30
55	9.39	7.74	6.92	13.14	10.84	9.69
60	14.44	11.92	10.65	20.22	16.68	14.91
65	22.22	18.33	16.39	31.11	25.67	22.94

Exhibit 6: Typical Strengths and Weaknesses

Strengths	Weaknesses
Adequate savings	Inadequate savings
Appropriate financial ratios	Ratios indicate poor management
Appropriate use of debt	Inappropriate debt use
Appropriate investments	Inappropriate investments
Appropriate risk coverage	Uncovered catastrophic risks: life, health, disability, property, liability, umbrella
Appropriate net worth	Inadequate net worth
Appropriate emergency fund	Inadequate emergency fund
Valid and appropriate will and transfer plan	No will or invalid will
Well-articulated goals	Inadequately defined financial goals
Excellent cash flow management	Poor budget—improper use of cash flow
Knowledgeable about investments	Lacks knowledge about investments

Exhibit 7: Summary of Various Company Ratings

Rank	AM Best	Best's Description	Fitch	Moody's	S&P	Weiss	Weiss's Description
1	A+ +	Superior	AAA	Aaa	AAA	A+	Excellent
2	A+	Superior	AA+	Aa1	AA+	A	Excellent
3	A	Excellent	AA	Aa2	AA	A–	Excellent
4	A–	Excellent	AA–	Aa3	AA–	B+	Good
5	B+ +	Very Good	A+	A1	A+	B	Good
6	B+	Very Good	A	A2	A	B–	Good
7	B	Good	A–	A3	A–	C+	Fair
8	B–	Good	BBB+	Baa1	BBB+	C	Fair
9	C+ +	Fair	BBB	Baa2	BBB	C–	Fair
10	C+	Fair	BBB–	Baa3	BBB–	D+	Weak
11	C	Marginal	BB+	Ba1	BB+	D	Weak
12	C–	Marginal	BB	Ba2	BB	D–	Weak
13	D	Below Minimum Standards	BB–	Ba3	BB–	E+	Very Weak
14	E	Under State Supervision	B+	B1	B+	E	Very Weak
15	F	In Liquidation	B	B2	B	E–	Very Weak
16						F	Under Supervision

Rating Companies

- AM Best Company—Ratings are based on public information and interviews with management.

- Fitch Ratings—Uses public information and management interviews. Public information alone may be used to assign ratings.

- Moody's Investors Service—May assign ratings based on public information alone.

- Standard & Poor's Corporation—Rates companies only upon request.

- Weiss Research—Ratings are based on public information and proprietary methods of evaluation and are available only on a company-by-company basis.

Exhibit 8: Life Insurance Policy Replacement—The Basics

The decision to replace one policy with another should be made cautiously. The methodology for such a decision includes fact gathering, calculations, and benchmark comparisons.

The Belth price of protection model formula is as follows:

$$CPT = \frac{(P + CV_0)(1 + i) - (CV_1 + D)}{(DB - CV_1)(0.001)}, \text{ where}$$

CPT   =   cost,

P   =   annual premium,

CV_0 =   cash value at beginning of year,

i   =   net after tax earning rate,

CV_1 =   cash value at year-end,

D   =   current dividend, and

DB   =   death benefit.

Compare to benchmark table:

■ If cost is less than the benchmark price, then retain the policy.

■ If cost is greater than the benchmark but less than 2 times the benchmark, then retain the policy.

■ If cost is greater than 2 times the benchmark, consider replacement.

Table (Joseph M. Belth, author)

Age, Years	Benchmark Price of Insurance per $1,000
<30	$1.50
30–34	$2.00
35–39	$3.00
40–44	$4.00
45–49	$6.50
50–54	$10.00
55–59	$15.00
60–64	$25.00
65–69	$35.00
70–74	$50.00
75–79	$80.00
80–84	$125.00

Exhibit 9: Summary of Homeowners Insurance Policies

There are six standard homeowners policy forms.

HO-2:   broad form, residential. This named-peril form policy insures the dwelling, other structures, and personal property for specifically named perils.

HO-3:   special form, residential. This special form insures the dwelling and other property against losses to the property for open perils (all except those specifically excluded). Personal property is subject to the same named-peril coverage as HO-2 (unless an endorsement is added).

HO-4:   contents broad form, residential, and tenant. HO-4 provides protection from named perils (same as HO-2) for a tenant's personal property.

HO-5:   the HO-5 is similar to HO-3 except the coverage for personal property. HO-3 covers personal property on a broad perils basis. HO-5, however, covers personal property on an open-perils basis.

HO-6:   unit-owners form, condominium. HO-6 insures the personal property of the insured (condominium owner) for named perils (same perils as HO-2).

HO-8:   modified coverage form, residential. This modified coverage provides protection for dwellings that have a fair market value (FMV) that is less than the replacement value of the dwelling (for example: a home, actual cash value of $150,000 with a replacement value of $400,000).

Exhibit 10: List of Covered Perils

BASIC NAMED PERILS		
1. Fire	5. Riot or civil commotion	9. Vandalism or malicious mischief
2. Lightning	6. Aircraft	10. Explosion
3. Windstorm	7. Vehicles	11. Theft
4. Hail	8. Smoke	12. Volcanic eruption

BROAD NAMED PERILS

Basic Named Perils 1–12, plus 13–18

13. Falling objects

14. Weight of ice, snow, or sleet

15. Accidental discharge or overflow of water or stream

16. Sudden and accidental tearing apart, cracking, burning, or bulging of a steam, hot water, air conditioning, or automatic fire protective sprinkler system, or from within a household appliance

17. Freezing of a plumbing, heating, air conditioning, or automatic fire sprinkler system, or of a household appliance

18. Sudden and accidental damage from artificially generated electrical current

	HO-1*	HO-2	HO-3**	HO-4	HO-5	HO-6	HO-8
Coverage A—Dwelling	Basic	Broad	Open	N/A	Open	Limited	Basic
Coverage B—Other Structures	Basic	Broad	Open	N/A	Open	N/A	Basic
Coverage C—Personal Property	Basic	Broad	Open	Broad	Open	Broad	Basic
Coverage D—Loss of Use	Basic	Broad	Broad	Broad	Open	Broad	Basic

*HO-1 is no longer offered in most states.

**Can be endorsed with HO-15 endorsement to provide coverage for personal property on an open perils basis and can be endorsed to provide loss settlement for personal property on a replacement cost basis.

Exhibit 11: Eight General Exclusions for Homeowners

- Ordinance or Law
- Earth Movement
- Water Damage
- Power Failure

- Neglect
- War
- Nuclear Hazard
- Intentional Loss

Exhibit 12: Wage Replacement % and Social Security Benefits

Real Wages (2008)	% of Wage Replaced by Social Security Benefits (Married with Same Age Non-Working Spouse)	Private Pension and Personal Savings Required	Replacement Target %
$ 20,000	79%	1%	80%
$ 35,000	64%	16%	80%
$ 50,000	58%	22%	80%
$ 65,000	51%	29%	80%
$ 80,000	45%	35%	80%
$102,000	39%	41%	80%
$200,000	20%	60%	80%

Exhibit 13: Group Term Life Insurance Cost Per $1,000 of Protection for One Month (IRC §79)

Age, Years	Monthly Cost per $1,000
<25	$0.05
25–29	$0.06
30–34	$0.08
35–39	$0.09
40–44	$0.10
45–49	$0.15
50–54	$0.23
55–59	$0.43
60–64	$0.66
65–69	$1.27
≥70	$2.06

Exhibit 14: Total Risk

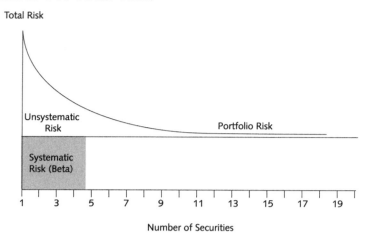

Exhibit 15: Systematic and Unsystematic Risks

Systematic Risks	Unsystematic Risks
Purchasing Power Risk	Business Risk
Reinvestment Risk	Financial Risk
Interest Rate Risk	Default Risk
Market Risk	Country Risk
Foreign Currency Risk	Regulation Risk
	Investment Management Risk

Exhibit 16: Risk Pyramid

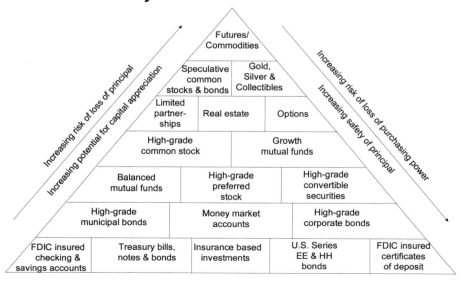

Exhibit 17: Summary of Rates of Return for Various Securities

Type of Security	Rate of Return	Standard Deviation (σ)
Small Cap. Stocks	12%	35%
Large Cap. Stocks	10%	21%
Corporate Bonds	5%	9%
Intermediate Govt. Bonds	5%	9%
Long-Term Govt. Bonds	5%	9%
Treasury Bills	4%	3%
Inflation	3%	5%

The table above depicts the approximate performance and risk level of various securities over a 50-year time period. Notice that the bonds have hardly outpaced the rate of inflation over this long period of time. Stocks have performed substantially better than bonds over the same period of time; however, stocks have sustained substantially more volatility than bonds. The investors who have long-term perspectives and are willing to sustain higher levels of volatility are more suited to equity-type investments.

Exhibit 18: The Call Option

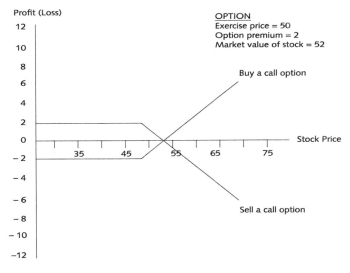

The exhibit above depicts the profit (loss) for both a buyer and a seller of a call option. Notice that the buyer has unlimited profit potential, whereas the seller has unlimited loss potential. Likewise, the buyer's loss and the seller's gain are limited to the premium paid.

Exhibit 19: The Put Option

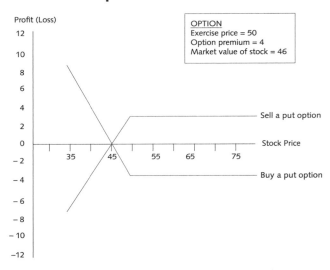

The exhibit above depicts the profit (loss) for both a buyer and a seller of a put option. Notice that the buyer has a large profit potential, whereas the seller has a large loss potential. Likewise, the buyer's loss and the seller's gain are limited to the premium paid.

Exhibit 20: Area Under the Curve

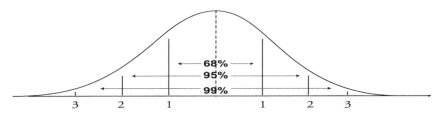

■ The curve represents 100% of possible outcomes. These outcomes tend to cluster around the mean; however, some occurrences will fall away from the mean (i.e., in the tails of the bell-shaped curve).

■ Approximately 68% of outcomes will fall within one standard deviation (both above and below) of the mean. **Note:** One standard deviation will be different for each individual security and may have a wide range.

■ Approximately 95% of outcomes will fall within two standard deviations (both above and below) of the mean.

■ Approximately 99% of outcomes will fall within three standard deviations (both above and below) of the mean.

■ This information about the normal curve allows investors to determine the probability of specific outcomes.

Exhibit 21: Standard Deviation of Two Securities

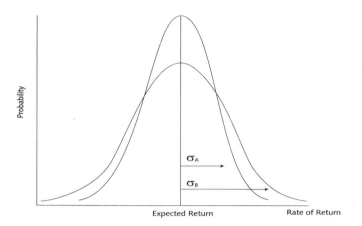

The exhibit above illustrates that two securities can have the same expected return with different levels of risk. Security B is more risky than Security A because its standard deviation is greater.

Exhibit 22: Explanation of Standard Deviation and Expected Return

Standard deviation is calculated by taking the square root of the sum of the squared differences between the average return, which will remain constant, and the individual observations (or returns) divided by the number of observations minus one. This calculation can be done in five steps.

1. For each observation, take the difference between the average return and the individual observations.

2. Square each difference.

3. Sum the squared differences.

4. Divide this sum by one less than the number of observations (if there are 10 observations, divide by 9).

5. Take the square root of this division.

Note 1:   Certain requirements must be met to use this technique with accuracy.

Note 2:   The standard deviation equals the square root of the variance. Thus, step 4 is equal to the variance, and step 5 is equal to the standard deviation.

Expected return is calculated by summing the product of the probability of an occurrence and the occurrence. For example, the following observations: 9, 11, 13, with the following probabilities: 0.25, 0.50, 0.25, will yield an expected return of 11. This figure is calculated as follows: $(0.25 \times 9) + (0.50 \times 11) + (0.25 \times 13) = 11$.

Note: The standard deviation for a set of investment returns can be calculated very efficiently using a financial calculator, such as the HP 10BII. Using the information in the first column of the table below as the historical returns over a 12-year period for a given investment, the keystrokes would be:

Keystrokes	Display
[■] [C] [ALL}	0.0000
13.5 [Σ+]	1.0000
12.0 [Σ+]	2.0000
5.0 [Σ+]	3.0000
± 2.0 [Σ+]	4.0000
7.0 [Σ+]	5.0000
23.0 [Σ+]	6.0000
6.0 [Σ+]	7.0000
10.0 [Σ+]	8.0000
45.0 [Σ+]	9.0000
10.0 [Σ+]	10.0000
0.5 [Σ+]	11.0000
14.0 [Σ+]	12.0000
[■][SxSy]	**12.2938**

The result will be the same as calculating the standard deviation by longhand but acomplished much faster on the calculator.

Exhibit 23: Performance Measurements

1. **Single-Period Rate of Return.**

   a. The single-period return (also known as the holding period return) is the basic method used to evaluate the speed at which an investment grows or declines. The single-period return is determined by dividing the change in wealth by the initial investment.

   b. The formula for the single-period rate of return is as follows:

   $$\frac{(SP - PP + CF)}{PP}, \text{ where}$$

   SP = the current sales price for the asset,
   PP = the initial purchase price of the asset, and
   CF = any cash flows that occurred during the holding period, such as dividends, interest, or other income.

   c. The holding period return (single-period rate of return) refers to the overall percentage gain the investor has received. The holding period return is not often used as a measure of performance because it ignores the time value of money, and it does not address the time over which the investment has grown.

2. **Arithmetic Average Return.**

   a. The arithmetic average return, which is the same as a normal average or mean, is equal to the sum of the returns per interval divided by the number of observations. For example, the average return for the following set of data would be approximately 12.41%.

2001	2002	2003	2004	2005	2006	2007	2008
12.1%	10.0%	11.3%	15.2%	9.1%	6.5%	18.3%	16.8%

   b. The arithmetic average return is an approximation of the earnings rate for an investment over time; however, large fluctuations in returns from year to year, especially negative returns, will have a tendency to cause the arithmetic return to be incorrect.

3. **Geometric Average Return.**

   a. Geometric average return is the average compounded return, or the internal rate of return (annualized return). This return is calculated by subtracting 1 from the $1/n$th root of the product of each interval return plus 1. Therefore, the geometric average return for the data above is equal to $[(1 + 0.121) \times (1 + 0.100) \times (1 + 0.113) \times (1 + 0.152) \times (1 + 0.091) \times (1 + 0.065) \times (1 + 0.183) \times (1 + 0.168)]^{1/8} - 1$. Thus, the compound annual return is equal to 12.35%.

b. The arithmetic and geometric average returns are different because the arithmetic return does not take into consideration the compounding effect of the returns.

c. The geometric return is the same as the IRR, or annual compound return.

4. **Real Return (inflation adjusted).**

a. The loss of purchasing power is one of the risks that investors face in achieving their financial goals. Real returns reflect the excess earnings from an investment that are above the inflation rate. Simply subtracting the rate of inflation from the investment rate of return, however, will not yield the real return.

b. The real return can be calculated using the following formula:

$$\left[\frac{(1 + \text{nominal return})}{(1 + \text{inflation rate})} - 1 \right] \times 100, \text{ where}$$

nominal rate = the absolute return (in the example above, it was 10%).

5. **Total Return.**

a. The total return for any investment can be thought of as the sum of the appreciation and the earnings from that investment. For stocks, this would be the appreciation in stock price plus dividends received. Similarly, the total return for bonds includes appreciation and interest payments. These two components are taken into consideration in the basic present value model discussed earlier.

6. **Internal Rate of Return (IRR).**

a. The IRR is the earnings rate at which the present value of a series of cash flows will equal its cost. Recall the basic model, or determining the present value of a series of cash flows.

b. The basic model is as follows:

$$P_0 = \frac{CF_1}{(1 + k)^1} + \frac{CF_2}{(1 + k)^2} + \cdots + \frac{CF_t}{(1 + k)^t}, \text{ where}$$

P_0 = the value of the security today,
CF_t = the cash flow for period t,
k = the discount rate or internal rate of return, and
t = the number of cash flows to be evaluated.

c. The underlying assumption of this equation is that the cash flows that occur during the life of the investment will be reinvested at the investment's internal rate of return. This is the same assumption found in computing the yield to maturity.

7. **Time Weighted versus Dollar Weighted.**

   The internal rate of return is a dollar-weighted return because it takes into consideration the different cash flows of the investor. A time-weighted return is determined without regard to the cash flows of the investor. It is a measure of the performance of an investment over time, without regard to specific cash flows. It can be used to determine how well an investment has done over time. For example, most returns reported on mutual funds are time-weighted returns.

8. **Tax-Adjusted Returns.**

   A tax-adjusted return is the realized return multiplied by (1 − tax rate). It is important to factor in taxes when comparing one investment alternative to another. For example, the after-tax yield on a municipal bond may be higher than for a corporate bond, even though the corporate bond carries a higher stated rate of return or has a higher yield to maturity.

   The after-tax return should reflect both federal and local taxes.

   Nontaxable Income.

   a. Federal—The interest from municipal bonds is not taxable by the federal government. In addition, unrealized appreciation is not taxable by the federal government.

   b. Municipalities—The interest from Treasury bills, bonds, and notes, as well as from savings bonds, is not taxable by states and municipalities. Additionally, most municipalities do not tax interest from municipal bonds issued by their own government.

9. **Risk-Adjusted Returns.**

   It is important to compare or benchmark returns with some standard, such as the S&P 500 Index. As mentioned above, it is also important to compare after-tax returns of different investments. Another equally important comparison is the risk-adjusted return. It is important to know that the return from an investment is not only better than a more conservative investment but is also better on a risk-adjusted basis. This permits the investor to determine whether the return was worth the risk that was undertaken.

   Treynor, Sharpe, and Jensen ratios are possible methods of comparing risk-adjusted returns.

10. **Weighted Average Return.**

   The weighted average return represents the return for a set of securities, such as a portfolio, where each return is weighted by the proportion of the security to the entire group or portfolio.

Exhibit 24: Investment Formulas

*Denotes a formula that will likely be provided on the CFP® exam.
(See the next exhibit for actual formulas provided on the CFP® exam.)

Capital Asset Pricing Model (CAPM)

*Capital Market Line (CML)

$$R_p = R_f + \left(\frac{R_m - R_f}{\sigma_m} \right) \sigma_p, \text{where}$$

R_p = the return of the portfolio,
R_f = the risk-free rate of return,
R_m = the return on the market,
$(R_m - R_f)$ = the return from the market that exceeds the risk-free rate of return,
σ_m = the standard deviation of the market, and
σ_p = the standard deviation of the portfolio.

* Security Market Line (SML)

$$R_s = R_f + \beta (R_m - R_f), \text{where}$$

R_s = the return for a stock,
R_f = the risk-free rate of return,
β = beta, which is a measure of the systematic risk associated with a particular stock, and
$(R_m - R_f)$ = the risk premium, which is the additional return of the market over the risk-free rate of return.

Arbitrage Pricing Theory (APT)

Arbitrage Pricing Theory (APT)

$$R = a_0 + b_1F_1 + b_2F_2 + \ldots + b_nF_n + e, \text{where}$$

R = the return from the security,
a_0 = the return that is expected for all securities when the value of all factors is zero. (in some cases, this is called the expected return),
b_n = the sensitivity of the security to factor F_n,
F_n = the factor that affects the security, such as GDP of 3%, and
e = the return that is unique to the security (it is also called an error term in some cases).

Note: This error term should drop out if all relevant factors are captured by the equation.

Measures of Risk

*Beta

$$\beta_p = \left(\frac{\sigma_p}{\sigma_m}\right)(R_{pm}), \text{ where}$$

β_p = beta,
σ_p = standard deviation of the portfolio,
σ_m = standard deviation of the market, and
R_{pm} = correlation coefficient between the portfolio and the market.

Weighted Average Beta

$$\bar{\beta}_w = \sum_{i=1}^{N}(\beta_i \times \%_i), \text{ where}$$

β_w = weighted average,
β_i = return for security i,
$\%_i$ = portion of security i to total portfolio, and
N = number of securities.

Expected Rate of Return

$$E_r = P_1(R_1) + P_2(R_2) + \ldots + P_t(R_t), \text{ where}$$

E_r = the expected return,
P_1 = the probability assigned to the first rate or return,
R_1 = the rate of return for period one, and
t = the number of events that are being examined.

Standard Deviation of Forecasted Returns

$$\sigma = Var_r^{1/2} = [P_1(r_1 - E_r)^2 + P_2(r_2 - E_r)^2 + \ldots + P_t(r_t - E_r)^2]^{1/2}, \text{ where}$$

E_r = expected return (calculated),
r_t = forecasted return for outcome t,
P_t = probability of outcome t, and
σ = standard deviation.

Standard Deviation of Historical Returns

$$s = \sqrt{\frac{\sum_{i=1}^{n}(r_i - \bar{r})^2}{(n-1)}}$$

s = standard deviation,
n = number of observations,
r_i = actual return for period i, and
$\bar{r}$ = average return.

Standard Deviation of a Two-Security Portfolio

$$\sigma = \sqrt{W_A^2\sigma_A^2 + W_B^2\sigma_B^2 + 2W_A W_B(\sigma_A\sigma_B R_{AB})}, \text{ where}$$

σ^2 = variance,
σ = standard deviation,
W_A = the percentage of the portfolio invested in security A,
W_B = the percentage of the portfolio invested in security B,
$(\sigma_A\sigma_B R_{AB})$ = covariance between security A and B, and
R_{AB} = correlation coefficient.

Note: W_A plus W_B must sum to 100%.

Duration (Example)

Bond:

PV = $974.23
n = 3
i = 8%
PMT = 70
FV = $1,000.00

Duration Calculation

Year	Cash Flow	Year × Cash Flow	PV at 8%
1	70	70	$64.81
2	70	140	$120.03
3	1,070	3,210	$2,548.20
	1,210	N/A	$2,733.04

Duration = 2,733.04 ÷ 974.23 = 2.8 years

Change in Price Using Duration

$$\frac{\Delta P}{P} = \frac{-D}{1 + y} \times \Delta(1 + y), \text{ where}$$

$\dfrac{\Delta P}{P}$ = percentage change in price of a bond,

D = duration, and

y = yield to maturity,

or

$$\frac{\Delta P}{P} = -D \left[\frac{\Delta(1 + y)}{1 + y} \right], \text{ where}$$

D = duration, and

y = yield to maturity.

Performance Measures

* **The Sharpe Ratio**

$$S_p = \frac{(R_p - R_f)}{\sigma}, \text{ where}$$

S_p = Sharpe ratio for portfolio p,

R_p = the average rate of return for a given time period,

R_f = the risk-free rate of return during the same time period, and

σ = the standard deviation of the rate of return for portfolio p during the same time interval.

* **The Treynor Ratio**

$$T_p = \frac{R_p - R_f}{B_p}, \text{ where}$$

T_p = Treynor ratio for portfolio p,

R_p = the average rate of return for a given time period,

R_p = the risk-free rate of return during the same time period, and

B_p = Beta for the same period or the slope of the portfolio's characteristic line during the period.

* The Jensen Performance Measure

$$\alpha_p = R_p - [R_f + \beta_p(R_m - R_f)], \text{ where}$$

α_p = alpha, which represents the return that is able to be earned above or below an unmanaged portfolio with identical market risk,

R_p = the average rate of return for a given period,

R_f = the risk-free rate of return,

β_p = beta, which is a measure of the systematic or market risk, and

$(R_m - R_f)$ = the risk premium, which is the additional return of the market over the risk-free rate of return.

Rates of Return

Holding Period Return (HPR)

$$HPR = \frac{\text{Ending Value of Investment} - \text{Beginning Value of Investment} +/- \text{Cash Flows}}{\text{Beginning Value of Investment}}$$

Internal Rate of Return (IRR)

$$P_0 = \frac{CF_1}{(1 + k)^1} + \frac{CF_2}{(1 + k)^2} + \cdots + \frac{CF_t}{(1 + k)^t}, \text{ where}$$

P_0 = the value of the security today,

CF_t = the cash flow for period t,

k = the discount rate based on the security type, and

t = the number of cash flows to be evaluated.

Yield to Maturity (YTM)

$$P_0 = \frac{CF_1}{(1 + k)^1} + \frac{CF_2}{(1 + k)^2} + \cdots + \frac{Par}{(1 + k)^t}, \text{ where}$$

P_0 = the value of the security today,

CF_t = the cash flow for period t,

k = the discount rate based on the security type, and

t = the number of cash flows to be evaluated.

Yield to Call (YTC)

$$P_0 = \frac{CF_1}{(1+k)^1} + \frac{CF_2}{(1+k)^2} + \ldots + \frac{\text{Call Price}}{(1+k)^t} \text{, where}$$

P_0 = the value of the security today,
CF_t = the cash flow for period t,
k = the discount rate based on the security type, and
t = the number of cash flows to be evaluated.

Arithmetic Mean

$$AM = \frac{\sum_{t=1}^{n} HPR_t}{n}$$

Time-Weighted Return

$$P_0 = \frac{CF_1}{(1+k)^1} + \frac{CF_2}{(1+k)^2} + \ldots + \frac{CF_t}{(1+k)^t} \text{, where}$$

P_0 = the value of the security today,
CF_t = the cash flow for period t,
k = the discount rate based on the security type, and
t = the number of cash flows to be evaluated.

Note: Time-weighted return considers cash flows of investment only. It does not consider cash flows of the investor. Same as the internal rate of return (IRR).

Geometric Mean

$$GM = \sqrt[n]{(1+R_1)(1+R_2)\ldots(1+R_n)} - 1 \text{, where}$$

R_n = return for each period, and
n = number of periods.

After-Tax Rate of Return

$$\text{Tax-adjusted return} = R(1 - TR), \text{ where}$$

R = before-tax return or earnings rate, and
TR = tax rate.

Inflation-Adjusted Rate of Return

$$R_i = \left[\frac{(1 + R)}{(1 + IR)} - 1 \right] \times (100), \text{ where}$$

R_i = inflation-adjusted return,
R = earnings rate, and
IR = inflation rate.

Weighted-Average Return

$$\overline{x}_w = \sum_{i=1}^{N} \left[(R_i)(\%_i) \right], \text{ where}$$

$\overline{x}_w$ = weighted average,
R_i = return for security i,
$\%_i$ = portion of security i to total portfolio, and
n = number of securities.

Valuation Models

The Basic Present Value (Valuation) Model

$$P_0 = \frac{CF_1}{(1 + k)^1} + \frac{CF_2}{(1 + k)^2} + \cdots + \frac{CF_t}{(1 + k)^t}, \text{ where}$$

P_0 = the value of the security today,
CF_t = the cash flow for period t,
k = the discount rate based on the type of security and risk level of
        the investment, and
t = the number of cash flows to be evaluated.

Note: Same as the internal rate of return (IRR).

*Constant Dividend Growth Model

$$P_0 = \frac{D_1}{k - g}, \text{ where}$$

P_0 = price for the security,
D_1 = the dividend paid at period 1,
k = the investor's required rate of return, and
g = the growth rate of the dividends. The growth rate can be negative, positive, or zero. See perpetuities for a zero growth rate.

Capitalized Earnings

$$V = \frac{E}{R_d}, \text{ where}$$

V = the value of the company or firm,
E = the earnings used to value the firm, and
R_d = the discount rate.

Perpetuity

$$P_0 = \frac{D}{k}, \text{ where}$$

P_0 = price for the security,
D = the dividend paid per period, and
k = investor's required rate of return.

*Conversion Value

$$CV = \left(\frac{\text{Par}}{\text{CP}}\right)(P_s), \text{ where}$$

CV = conversion value,
CP = conversion price of stock, and
P_s = current price of stock.

Note: Par = $1,000.

Exhibit 25: Formula Page Provided on CFP® Certification Exam

CERTIFIED FINANCIAL PLANNER
      BOARD OF STANDARDS, INC.

Provided Formulas

These formulas are provided with the exam booklets when taking the CFP® Certification Examination:

$$V = \frac{D_1}{r-g}$$

$$r_i = r_f + (r_m - r_f)\beta_i$$

$$r = \frac{D_1}{P} + g$$

$$r_p = r_f + \sigma_p \left(\frac{r_m - r_f}{\sigma_m} \right)$$

$$COV_{ij} = \rho_{ij}\sigma_i\sigma_j$$

$$S_p = \frac{\overline{r}_p - \overline{r}_f}{\sigma_p}$$

$$\sigma_p = \sqrt{W_i^2\sigma_i^2 + W_j^2\sigma_j^2 + 2W_iW_j COV_{ij}}$$

$$\alpha_p = \overline{r}_p - \left[\overline{r}_f + \left(\overline{r}_m - \overline{r}_f \right)\beta_p \right]$$

$$\beta_i = \frac{COV_{im}}{\sigma_m^2} = \frac{\rho_{im}\sigma_i}{\sigma_m}$$

$$T_p = \frac{\overline{r}_p - \overline{r}_f}{\beta_p}$$

$$\sigma_r = \sqrt{\frac{\sum\limits_{t=1}^{n}(r_t - \overline{r})^2}{n}}$$

$$D = \frac{\sum\limits_{t=1}^{n}\frac{c_t(t)}{(1+i)^t}}{\sum\limits_{t=1}^{n}\frac{c_t}{(1+i)^t}}$$

$$S_r = \sqrt{\frac{\sum\limits_{t=1}^{n}(r_t - \overline{r})^2}{n-1}}$$

$$D = \frac{1+y}{y} - \frac{(1+y)+t(c-y)}{c\left[(1+y)^t - 1\right]+y}$$

$$CV = \frac{Par}{CP} \times P_s$$

$$\frac{\Delta P}{P} = -D\left[\frac{\Delta y}{1+y}\right]$$

$$IR = \frac{R_P - R_B}{\sigma_A}$$

Reprinted, with permission, from the CFP Board's *Guide to CFP® Certification*.

Exhibit 26: Tax-Rate Schedules (2009)

Single—Schedule X

If taxable income is: Over	But not over	The tax is	Of the amount over
$0	$8,350	10%	$0
8,350	33,950	$835.00 + 15%	8,350
33,950	82,250	4,675.00 + 25%	33,950
82,250	171,550	16,750.00 + 28%	82,250
171,550	372,950	41,754.00 + 33%	171,550
372,950	—	108,216.00 + 35%	372,950

Head of Household—Schedule Z

If taxable income is: Over	But not over	The tax is	Of the amount over
$0	$11,950	10%	$0
11,950	45,500	$1,195.00 + 15%	11,950
45,500	117,450	6,227.50 + 25%	45,500
117,450	190,200	24,215.00 + 28%	117,450
190,200	372,950	44,585.00 + 33%	190,200
372,950	—	104,892.50 + 35%	372,950

Married Filing Jointly or Qualifying Widow(er)—Schedule Y-1

If taxable income is: Over	But not over	The tax is	Of the amount over
$0	$16,700	10%	$0
16,700	67,900	$1,670.00 + 15%	16,700
67,900	137,050	9,350.00 + 25%	67,900
137,050	208,850	26,637.50 + 28%	137,050
208,850	372,950	46,741.50 + 33%	208,850
372,950	—	100,894.50 + 35%	372,950

Married Filing Separately—Schedule Y-2

If taxable income is: Over	But not over	The tax is	Of the amount over
$0	$8,350	10%	$0
8,350	33,950	$835.00 + 15%	8,350
33,950	68,525	4,675.00 + 25%	33,950
68,525	104,425	13,318.75 + 28%	68,525
104,425	186,475	23,370.75 + 33%	104,425
186,475	—	50,447.25 + 35%	186,475

Exhibit 27: Standard Deduction Amount and Additional Deduction

Standard Deduction		
Filing Status	**2008**	**2009**
Single	$5,450	$5,700
Married, filing jointly/SS	$10,900	$11,400
Head of household	$8,000	$8,350
Married, filing separately	$5,450	$5,700

SS—Surviving Spouse

Additional Standard Deduction*		
Filing Status	**2008**	**2009**
Single	$1,350	$1,400
Married, filing jointly/SS	$1,050	$1,100
Head of household	$1,350	$1,400
Married, filing separately	$1,050	$1,100

*Over 64 or blind.

Standard deduction for an individual claimed as a dependent by another taxpayer may not exceed the regular standard deduction and is limited to the greater of $900 (2008)/$950 (2009), or the sum of $300 (2008/2009) plus the individual's earned income.

Exhibit 28: Tax Formula for Individuals

Income (broadly conceived)	$xx,xxx
Less: Exclusions from Gross Income	(x,xxx)
Gross Income	$xx,xxx
Less: Deductions for Adjusted Gross Income	(x,xxx)
Adjusted Gross Income (AGI)	$xx,xxx
Less: The Greater of:	
Total Itemized Deductions or Standard Deduction	(x,xxx)
Less: Personal and Dependency Exemptions	(x,xxx)
Taxable Income	$xx,xxx

Exhibit 29: Dependency Exemption

Overview of the Rules for Claiming an Exemption for a Dependent
Caution. This table is only an overview of the rules. For details, see IRS Publication 17.

- You cannot claim any dependents if you, or your spouse if filing jointly, could be claimed as a dependent by another taxpayer.

- You cannot claim a married person who files a joint return as a dependent unless that joint return is only a claim for refund and there would be no tax liability for either spouse on separate returns.

- You cannot claim a person as a dependent unless that person is a U.S. citizen, U.S. resident alien, U.S. national, or a resident of Canada or Mexico, for some part of the year.[1]

- You cannot claim a person as a dependent unless that person is your **qualifying child** or **qualifying relative.**

Tests To Be a Qualifying Child	Tests To Be a Qualifying Relative
1. The child must be your son, daughter, stepchild, foster child, brother, sister, half brother, half sister, stepbrother, stepsister, or a descendant of any of them.	1. The person cannot be your qualifying child or the qualifying child of any other taxpayer.
2. The child must be (a) under age 19 at the end of the year, (b) under age 24 at the end of the year and a full-time student, or (c) any age if permanently and totally disabled.	2. The person either (a) must be related to you in one of the ways listed under *Relatives who do not have to live with you,* or (b) must live with you all year as a member of your household[2] (and your relationship must not violate local law).
3. The child must have lived with you for more than half of the year.[2]	3. The person's gross income for the year must be less than $3,400.[3]
4. The child must not have provided more than half of his or her own support for the year.	4. You must provide more than half of the person's total support for the year.[4]
5. If the child meets the rules to be a qualifying child of more than one person, you must be the person entitled to claim the child as a qualifying child.	

[1]There is an exception for certain adopted children.
[2]There are exceptions for temporary absences, children who were born or died during the year, children of divorced or separated parents, and kidnapped children.
[3]There is an exception if the person is disabled and has income from a sheltered workshop.
[4]There are exceptions for multiple support agreements, children of divorced or separated parents, and kidnapped children.

IRS Publication 17

NOTE: TO BE A QUALIFYING RELATIVE IN 2009, THE PERSON'S GROSS INCOME FOR THE YEAR MUST BE LESS THAN $3,650.

Exhibit 30: Deductible Travel Expenses

Expense	Description
Transportation	The cost of travel by airplane, train, or bus between your home and your business destination. If you were provided with a ticket or if you are riding free as the result of a frequent traveler or similar program, your cost is zero.
Taxi, Commuter Bus, and Limousine	Fares for these and other types of transportation between the airport or station and your hotel, or between the hotel and your work location away from home.
Baggage and Shipping	The cost of sending baggage and sample or display material between your regular and temporary work location.
Car	The costs of operating and maintaining your car when traveling away from home or business. You may deduct actual expenses or the standard mileage rate, including business-related tolls and parking. If you lease a car while away from home or business, you can deduct business-related expenses only.
Lodging	The cost of lodging if your business trip is overnight or long enough to require you to get substantial sleep or rest to properly perform your duties.
Meals	The cost of meals only if your business trip is overnight or long enough to require you to stop to get substantial sleep or rest. Includes amounts spent for food, beverages, taxes, and related tips. Only 50% of meal expenses are allowed as a deduction.
Cleaning	Cleaning and laundry expenses while away from home overnight.
Telephone	The cost of business calls while on your business trip, including business communication by fax machine or other communication devices.
Tips	Tips you pay for any expenses in this chart.
Other	Other similar ordinary and necessary expenses related to your business travel, such as public stenographer's fees and computer rental fees.

IRS Publication 334

Exhibit 31: Deductible Educational Expenses

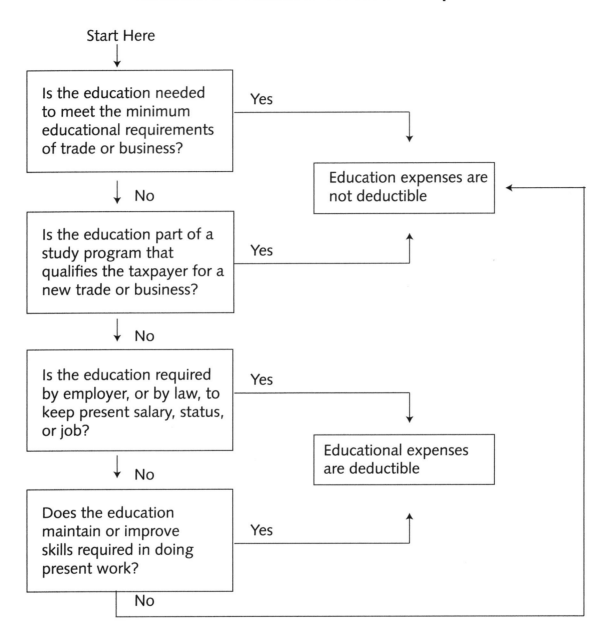

Exhibit 32: Travel, Entertainment, Gift Expenses, and Reimbursements

Type of Reimbursement (or Other Expense Allowance) Arrangement	Employer Reports on Form W-2	Employee Shows on Form 2106
Accountable		
Actual expense reimbursement. Adequate accounting and excess returned.	Not reported.	Not shown if expenses do not exceed reimbursement.
Actual expense reimbursement. Adequate accounting and return of excess both required but excess not returned.	Excess reported as wages in box 1. Amount adequately accounted for is reported only in box 13—it is not reported in box 1.	All expenses (and reimbursements reported on Form W-2, box 13) only if some or all of the excess expenses are claimed. Otherwise, the form is not filed.
Per diem or mileage allowance (up to federal rate). Adequate accounting and excess returned.	Not reported.	All expenses and reimbursements only if excess expenses are claimed. Otherwise, form is not filed.
Per diem or mileage allowance (exceeds federal rate). Adequate accounting up to the federal rate only and excess not returned.	Excess reported as wages in box 1. Amount up to the federal rate is reported only in box 13—it is not reported in box 1.	All expenses (and reimbursements equal to the federal rate) only if expenses in excess of the federal rate are claimed. Otherwise, form is not filed.
Non-accountable		
Either adequate accounting or return of excess, or both, not required by plan.	Entire amount is reported as wages in box 1.	All expenses.
No Reimbursement		
	Normal reporting of wages, etc.	All expenses.

Exhibit 33: Child and Dependent Care Credit

Adjusted Gross Income		Applicable Percentage
More than	**But less than**	
$0	$15,000	35%
15,000	17,000	34%
17,000	19,000	33%
19,000	21,000	32%
21,000	23,000	31%
23,000	25,000	30%
25,000	27,000	29%
27,000	29,000	28%
29,000	31,000	27%
31,000	33,000	26%
33,000	35,000	25%
35,000	37,000	24%
37,000	39,000	23%
39,000	41,000	22%
41,000	43,000	21%
43,000	No Limit	20%

Exhibit 34: Section 79 Costs for Group Term Insurance

Age	Cost
Under 25	$0.05
25 through 29	$0.06
30 through 34	$0.08
35 through 39	$0.09
40 through 44	$0.10
45 through 49	$0.15
50 through 54	$0.23
55 through 59	$0.43
60 through 64	$0.66
65 through 69	$1.27
70 or older	$2.06

Exhibit 35: Section 179 Maximum Writeoffs

Tax Year Beginning In	Maximum Section 179
2007	$125,000
2008	$250,000
2009	$133,000

Exhibit 36: Retirement Plans

Qualified Plans[A]		Other Tax-Advantaged Plans	Nonqualified Plans
Pension Plans[B]	**Profit Sharing Plans[C]**		
Defined benefit plans[D]	Profit sharing plans	SEPs	Deferred compensation plans
Cash balance plans	Stock bonus plans	SARSEPs	Nonqualified stock option plans
Money purchase pension plans	ESOPs	Traditional IRA	Incentive stock option plans
Target benefit plans[D]	401(k) plans[E]	Roth IRA	Phantom stock plans
	Thrift plans	SIMPLE (IRA)	Split-dollar life insurance
	SIMPLE 401(k)	403(b) plans	457 plans
	Age-based profit sharing plans[D]	ESPPs	
	New comparability plans[D]		

[A] Distribution from qualified plans may qualify for 10-year forward averaging. Other plans and nonqualified plans do not.

[B] Pension plans promise either a benefit or contributions; therefore, mandatory annual funding and no in-service withdrawals are allowed.

[C] Profit sharing plans promise tax deferral; therefore, no mandatory annual funding and in-service withdrawals are allowed if the plan so provides.

[D] Tested for discrimination based on benefits as opposed to contributions.

[E] Tested for discrimination regarding employee elective deferrals and employer matching contributions.

Exhibit 37: Comparison of Defined Benefit, Defined Contribution, and Cash Balance Plans

	Typical Defined Benefit Plan DB	Typical Defined Contribution Plan DC	Cash Balance Plan CB
Contribution	Actuarially determined	Percentage of salary (could be age weighted)	Percentage of salary (actuarially determined)
Investment Risk	Employer	Employee	Employer
Size of Work Force	Any size	Any size	Large
Investment Earnings	Employer responsible	Variable	Guaranteed
Social Security Integration	Yes	Yes*	Yes
Pension Benefit Guarantee Corporation Insurance	Yes	No	Yes
401(k) Feature	No	Available in profit sharing plan	No
Favors Older Entrants	Yes	No	No
Administrative Cost	Generally higher than DC Plans due to actuary and insurance	Generally lower than DB Plans	Generally higher than DC Plans due to actuary and insurance

*ESOPs are not eligible for integration.

Exhibit 38: ACP/ADP General Rules (Simplified)

If ADP for NHC:	Maximum ADP for HC is:
$\leq 2\%$	2 × ADP of NHC
$\geq 2\%$, but $\leq 8\%$	2% + ADP of NHC
$> 8\%$	1.25 × ADP of NHC

NHC = Non-highly compensated
HC = Highly compensated

Exhibit 39: Target Benefit Illustration

Assume that a business owner is age 49, earns $170,000 per year, and selects a benefit formula equal to 137.26% of compensation reduced by 1/25th for each year of participation less than 25 years. The plan will also benefit one employee age 25 earning $18,000 per year. The first year deposit is determined as follows, assuming a normal retirement age of 65 and 8.5% interest.

	Business Owner	Employee
Age	49	25
Compensation	$170,000	$18,000
Target Benefit	$138,210*	$2,927**
Factor (age)	2.338	0.304
PV of Benefit	$323,135	$890
Factor	0.1075	0.0812
Theoretical Contribution	$34,737	$72
415 Limit (100% or $49,000 in 2009)	$49,000	$4,500
Top-heavy Minimum (3% of compensation)	$0	$540
Actual Contribution	$34,737	$540
Contribution Rate	20%	3%
Percent of Contribution	98.5%	1.5%

*The benefit for the business owner is 135.5% × $170,000 × (15 ÷ 25) = $138,210.

**Benefit for employee is 137.26% × $18,000 × (3 ÷ 25) = $2,927.

Exhibit 40: Age-based Profit Sharing Plan Illustration

Assume that a business owner is age 49, earns $230,000 per year, and elects to make a maximum contribution to a discretionary age-based profit sharing plan. The plan will also benefit one employee, age 25, earning $18,000 per year.

	Business Owner	Employee	Total
Age	49	25	
Compensation	$230,000	$18,000	$248,000
Adjustment factor	0.294139	0.038265	
Age-adjusted compensation	$67,652	$689	$68,341
Allocation	$49,041	$499	$49,540
Annual allocation limit (100% or $49,000)	$49,000	$18,000	
Top-heavy minimum (3% of Compensation)	$0	$540	
Actual allocation	$49,000	$540	$49,540
Contribution rate	21%	3%	
Percent of contribution	98.90%	1.10%	

Although the maximum deductible limit for a profit sharing plan is 25% of eligible compensation (25% × $248,000 = $62,000) the employer would only fund the plan so that he reached the $49,000 limit in 2009.

$$\frac{\$67,652}{\$68,341} \times \$49,540 = \$49,041$$

$$\frac{\$689}{\$68,341} \times \$49,540 = \$499$$

Exhibit 41: Fringe Benefits by Entity Type

Benefit	Proprietorship	Partnership	S Corp	LLC	C Corp
Qualified plan	Yes	Yes	Yes	Yes	Yes
Group life	No	No	No	No	Yes
Group health*	Yes	Yes	Yes	Yes	Yes
Group disability	No	No	No	No	Yes
Medical reimbursement plans	No	No	No	No	Yes
Accidental death	No	No	No	No	Yes
Disability income plan	No	No	No	No	Yes
Employee death benefit					
–Employer provided	No	No	No	No	Yes
–Qualified plan	Yes	Yes	Yes	Yes	Yes
Cafeteria plan	No	No	No	No	Yes
Deferred compensation	No	No	No	No	Yes

LLC = Limited Liability Company
*Self-employed taxpayers and wage earners who are more than 2% shareholders of an S corporation can take a 100% deduction (not to exceed net earnings from self-employment) for amounts paid for health insurance for taxpayers, spouses, and dependents.

Exhibit 42: Keogh Worksheet for a Single Profit Sharing Plan or a Single Money Purchase Pension Plan

Line 1	Net business profits (from Schedule C)	$100,000
Line 2	Deduction for self-employment tax (From IRS Form 1040) (given)	$7,065
Line 3	Adjusted net business profits (subtract Line 2 from line 1)	$92,935
Line 4	Contribution percentage	0.25
Line 5	Contribution factor (add 1.00 to line 4)	1.25
Line 6	Adjusted earned income (divide line 3 by line 5)	$74,348
Line 7	Maximum earned income on which contributions can be based (enter $245,000)	$245,000
Line 8	Final earned income (the lesser of line 6 and line 7)	$74,348
Line 9	Preliminary contribution amount (multiply line 4 by line 8, round down to closest dollar)	$18,587
Line 10	Maximum dollar contribution amount (enter $49,000)	$49,000
Line 11	Contribution amount (the lesser of line 9 and line 10)	$18,587

Exhibit 43: Keogh Worksheet for a Tandem Profit Sharing and Money Purchase Pension Plan*

Line 1	Net business profits (from Schedule C)	$160,000
Line 2	Deduction for self-employment tax (from IRS Form 1040) (given)	$8,764
Line 3	Adjusted net business profits (Subtract Line 2 from Line 1)	$151,236
Line 4	Money purchase plan contribution percentage (expressed as a decimal) (fixed percentage, plan established 3–25)	0.10
Line 5	Profit sharing plan contribution percentage (expressed as decimal) (percentage which can vary every year, 0–15%)	0.15
Line 6	Total contribution percentage (expressed as decimal (between 3–25%)	0.25
Line 7	Contribution factor (add 1.00 to line 4)	1.25
Line 8	Adjusted earned income (divide line 3 by line 7)	$120,989
Line 9	Maximum earned income on which contributions can be based (enter $245,000 in 2009)	$245,000
Line 10	Final earned income (lesser of line 8 and line 9)	$120,989
Line 11	Preliminary money purchase plan contribution amount (multiply line 10 by line 4, round down to closest dollar) (10%)	$12,099
Line 12	Maximum money purchase plan dollar contribution amount (enter $49,000 for 2009)	$49,000
Line 13	Money purchase plan contribution amount (lesser of line 11 and line 12)	$12,099
Line 14	Preliminary profit sharing plan contribution amount (multiply line 10 x line 5) (15%)	$18,148
Line 15	Maximum profit sharing plan dollar contribution amount (subtract line 13 from line 12)	$30,247
Line 16	Profit sharing contribution amount (Lesser of line 14 and line 15)	$18,148
Line 17	Total tandem plan contribution amount (the sum of line 13 and line 16) (limit to $40,000)	$30,247

*New money purchase plans are uncommon due to the Economic Growth and Tax Relief Reconciliation Act of 2001.

Exhibit 44: IRA Current Phaseout Limits

Traditional IRAs

| | Taxpayer Filing Status | |
| | | |
Tax Year	Phaseout Range Single	Phaseout Range Married Filing Jointly
2008	$53,000–63,000	$85,000–105,000
2009	$55,000–65,000	$89,000–109,000

An individual will no longer be considered an active participant in an employer-sponsored retirement plan solely because his spouse is an active participant. However, when only one spouse is an active participant, the nonparticipant spouse will have his deduction phased out at AGI levels between $166,000 and $176,000.

ROTH IRAs

| Taxpayer Filing Status | | | |
| Modified AGI Phaseout Ranges | | | |
Tax Year	Single	Married Filing Jointly	Married Filing Separately
2008	$101,000–116,000	$159,000–169,000	$0–10,000
2009	$105,000–120,000	$166,000–176,000	$0–10,000

Exhibit 45: Table V—Ordinary Life Annuities One Life—Expected Return Multiples (Reg. Section 1.72-9)

Age	Multiple	Age	Multiple	Age	Multiple
5	77.7	42	41.7	79	10.8
6	76.7	43	40.7	80	10.2
7	75.8	44	39.8	81	9.7
8	74.8	45	38.8	82	9.1
9	73.8	46	37.9	83	8.6
10	72.8	47	37.0	84	8.1
11	71.8	48	36.0	85	7.6
12	70.8	49	35.1	86	7.1
13	69.9	50	34.2	87	6.7
14	68.9	51	33.3	88	6.3
15	67.9	52	32.3	89	5.9
16	66.9	53	31.4	90	5.5
17	66.0	54	30.5	91	5.2
18	65.0	55	29.6	92	4.9
19	64.0	56	28.7	93	4.6
20	63.0	57	27.9	94	4.3
21	62.1	58	27.0	95	4.1
22	61.1	59	26.1	96	3.8
23	60.1	60	25.2	97	3.6
24	59.1	61	24.4	98	3.4
25	58.2	62	23.5	99	3.1
26	57.2	63	22.7	100	2.9
27	56.2	64	21.8	101	2.7
28	55.3	65	21.0	102	2.5
29	54.3	66	20.2	103	2.3
30	53.3	67	19.4	104	2.1
31	52.4	68	18.6	105	1.9
32	51.4	69	17.8	106	1.7
33	50.4	70	17.0	107	1.5
34	49.4	71	16.3	108	1.4
35	48.5	72	15.5	109	1.2
36	47.5	73	14.8	110	1.1
37	46.5	74	14.1	111	0.9
38	45.6	75	13.4	112	0.8
39	44.6	76	12.7	113	0.7
40	43.6	77	12.1	114	0.6
41	42.7	78	11.4	115	0.5

Exhibit 46: Table VI—Ordinary Joint Life and Last Survivor Annuities Two Lives—Expected Return Multiples (Reg. Section 1.72-9)

Ages	65	66	67	68	69	70	71	72	73	74
65	26.2	25.8	25.4	25.0	24.6	24.3	23.9	23.7	23.4	23.1
66	25.8	25.3	24.9	24.5	24.1	23.7	23.4	23.1	22.8	22.5
67	25.4	24.9	24.4	24.0	23.6	23.2	22.8	22.5	22.2	21.9
68	25.0	24.5	24.0	23.5	23.1	22.7	22.3	22.0	21.6	21.3
69	24.6	24.1	23.6	23.1	22.6	22.2	21.8	21.4	21.1	20.8
70	24.3	23.7	23.2	22.7	22.2	21.8	21.3	20.9	20.6	20.2
71	23.9	23.4	22.8	22.3	21.8	21.3	20.9	20.5	20.1	19.7
72	23.7	23.1	22.5	22.0	21.4	20.9	20.5	20.0	19.6	19.3
73	23.4	22.8	22.2	21.6	21.1	20.6	20.1	19.6	19.2	18.8
74	23.1	22.5	21.9	21.3	20.8	20.2	19.7	19.3	18.8	18.4
75	22.9	22.3	21.6	21.0	20.5	19.9	19.4	18.9	18.4	18.0
76	22.7	22.0	21.4	20.8	20.2	19.6	19.1	18.6	18.1	17.6
77	22.5	21.8	21.2	20.6	19.9	19.4	18.8	18.3	17.8	17.3
78	22.4	21.7	21.0	20.3	19.7	19.1	18.5	18.0	17.5	17.0
79	22.2	21.5	20.8	20.1	19.5	18.9	18.3	17.7	17.2	16.7
80	22.1	21.3	20.6	20.0	19.3	18.7	18.1	17.5	16.9	16.4
81	21.9	21.2	20.5	19.8	19.1	18.5	17.9	17.3	16.7	16.2
82	21.8	21.1	20.4	19.7	19.0	18.3	17.7	17.1	16.5	15.9
83	21.7	21.0	20.2	19.5	18.8	18.2	17.5	16.9	16.3	15.7
84	21.6	20.9	20.1	19.4	18.7	18.0	17.4	16.7	16.1	15.5
85	21.6	20.8	20.1	19.3	18.6	17.9	17.3	16.6	16.0	15.4
86	21.5	20.7	20.0	19.2	18.5	17.8	17.1	16.5	15.8	15.2
87	21.4	20.7	19.9	19.2	18.4	17.7	17.0	16.4	15.7	15.1
88	21.4	20.6	19.8	19.1	18.3	17.6	16.9	16.3	15.6	15.0
89	21.3	20.5	19.8	19.0	18.3	17.6	16.9	16.2	15.5	14.9
90	21.3	20.5	19.7	19.0	18.2	17.5	16.8	16.1	15.4	14.8
91	21.3	20.5	19.7	18.9	18.2	17.4	16.7	16.0	15.4	14.7
92	21.2	20.4	19.6	18.9	18.1	17.4	16.7	16.0	15.3	14.6
93	21.2	20.4	19.6	18.8	18.1	17.3	16.6	15.9	15.2	14.6
94	21.2	20.4	19.6	18.8	18.0	17.3	16.6	15.9	15.2	14.5
95	21.1	20.3	19.6	18.8	18.0	17.3	16.5	15.8	15.1	14.5
96	21.1	20.3	19.5	18.8	18.0	17.2	16.5	15.8	15.1	14.4
97	21.1	20.3	19.5	18.7	18.0	17.2	16.5	15.8	15.1	14.4
98	21.1	20.3	19.5	18.7	17.9	17.2	16.4	15.7	15.0	14.3
99	21.1	20.3	19.5	18.7	17.9	17.2	16.4	15.7	15.0	14.3

Ages	65	66	67	68	69	70	71	72	73	74
100	21.1	20.3	19.5	18.7	17.9	17.1	16.4	15.7	15.0	14.3
101	21.1	20.2	19.4	18.7	17.9	17.1	16.4	15.6	14.9	14.2
102	21.1	20.2	19.4	18.6	17.9	17.1	16.4	15.6	14.9	14.2
103	21.0	20.2	19.4	18.6	17.9	17.1	16.3	15.6	14.9	14.2
104	21.0	20.2	19.4	18.6	17.8	17.1	16.3	15.6	14.9	14.2
105	21.0	20.2	19.4	18.6	17.8	17.1	16.3	15.6	14.9	14.2
106	21.0	20.2	19.4	18.6	17.8	17.1	16.3	15.6	14.8	14.1
107	21.0	20.2	19.4	18.6	17.8	17.0	16.3	15.6	14.8	14.1
108	21.0	20.2	19.4	18.6	17.8	17.0	16.3	15.5	14.8	14.1
109	21.0	20.2	19.4	18.6	17.8	17.0	16.3	15.5	14.8	14.1
110	21.0	20.2	19.4	18.6	17.8	17.0	16.3	15.5	14.8	14.1
111	21.0	20.2	19.4	18.6	17.8	17.0	16.3	15.5	14.8	14.1
112	21.0	20.2	19.4	18.6	17.8	17.0	16.3	15.5	14.8	14.1
113	21.0	20.2	19.4	18.6	17.8	17.0	16.3	15.5	14.8	14.1
114	21.0	20.2	19.4	18.6	17.8	17.0	16.3	15.5	14.8	14.1
115	21.0	20.2	19.4	18.6	17.8	17.0	16.3	15.5	14.8	14.1

Exhibit 47: Indexed Limits for Pension and Other Plans

Type of Limit	2008	2009
Defined benefit maximum limit	$185,000	$195,000
Defined contribution plan maximum limit	$46,000	$49,000
401(k) deferral limit	$15,500	$16,500
HC Employee—414(q)		
– 5% owner	Any	Any
– compensation	$105,000	$110,000
SIMPLE deferral	$10,500	$11,500
SEP plans		
– minimum earnings	$500	$550
– maximum earnings	$230,000	$245,000
457 plans	15,500	$16,500
Max. compensation	$230,000	$245,000
S.S. Integration		
– rate	5.70	5.70
– wage base	$102,000	$106,800
Medicare		
– wage base	Unlimited	Unlimited
S.S. earnings limitation		
Under full retirement age	$13,560	$14,160
Full retirement age or older	Not applicable	Not applicable
PBGC Limit (monthly)	$4,312.50	Not yet available

Exhibit 48: Table III—Uniform Lifetime, IRS Publication 590*

Age	Applicable Divisor	Age	Applicable Divisor
70	27.4	93	9.6
71	26.5	94	9.1
72	25.6	95	8.6
73	24.7	96	8.1
74	23.8	97	7.6
75	22.9	98	7.1
76	22.0	99	6.7
77	21.2	100	6.3
78	20.3	101	5.9
79	19.5	102	5.5
80	18.7	103	5.2
81	17.9	104	4.9
82	17.1	105	4.5
83	16.3	106	4.2
84	15.5	107	3.9
85	14.8	108	3.7
86	14.1	109	3.4
87	13.4	110	3.1
88	12.7	111	2.9
89	12.0	112	2.6
90	11.4	113	2.4
91	10.8	114	2.1
92	10.2	115	1.9

*Use this table if the beneficiary is someone other than a spouse who is more than 10 years younger than the beneficiary.

Exhibit 49: Self-Employed Person's Rate Table

Column A If the plan contribution rate is: (shown as a percentage)	Column B The self-employed person's rate is: (shown as a decimal)
1	0.009901
2	0.019608
3	0.029126
4	0.038462
5	0.047619
6	0.056604
7	0.065421
8	0.074074
9	0.082569
10	0.090909
11	0.099099
12	0.107143
13	0.115044
14	0.122807
15	0.130435
16	0.137931
17	0.145299
18	0.152542
19	0.159664
20	0.166667
21	0.173554
22	0.180328
23	0.186992
24	0.193548
25*	0.200000*

*The deduction for annual employer contributions to a SEP cannot exceed 25% of the common-law employee participant's compensation or 20% of the self-employed compensation (figured without deducting contributions) from the business that has the plan. The factor is calculated as follows: 0.25 ÷ 1.25 = 0.20

Note: The deduction for annual employer contributions to a profit sharing or money-purchase plan is also limited to 25% of the employee's compensation, or 20% of the self-employed compensation.

Exhibit 50: Summary of Retirement Plans

	Money Purchase Plan	Profit Sharing Plan	Stock Bonus Plan	Savings or Thrift Plan	401(k) Plan	ESOP	SEP/ SARSEP	Cash Balance Pension Plan	Target Benefit Plans (not profit sharing)
Employer Contributions									
Fixed	✔				✔	✔		✔	✔
Discretionary		✔	✔	✔	✔	✔			
Employee Contributions									
Pretax		✔			✔				
After Tax	✔	✔		✔ (usually)					
Investment in Company Stock									
Restricted	✔						✔	✔	✔
Not Restricted		✔	✔	✔	✔	✔			
Guaranteed Investment Return								✔	
Right to Vote	N/A	No	Yes	No	N/A	On some matters	N/A	N/A	N/A
Leverage Borrowing to Purchase Company Stock	N/A	N/A	N/A	N/A	N/A	✔	N/A	N/A	N/A
In-Service Withdrawals, Timing, and Form of Distribution Before Retirement	No	Yes	Yes	Yes	Yes	Yes	Yes	No	No
At Retirement in Cash	✔	✔	Perhaps	✔	✔	Perhaps	✔	Possible	Possible
Company Stock	N/A	Possible	✔	N/A	N/A	✔	Perhaps	Possible	Possible
Integration	Yes	Yes	Yes	Yes	Yes*	No	Yes/No	Yes	Yes
Forfeitures Reduce Plan Coverage	Can	Can	Can	Can	Can	Can	N/A	Must	Must
Loans	Can	Can	Can	Can	Can	Can	No	Can	Can

(Continued on next page)

Summary of Retirement Plans (*continued*)

	Money Purchase Plan	Profit Sharing Plan	Stock Bonus Plan	Savings or Thrift Plan	401(k) Plan	ESOP	SEP/ SARSEP	Cash Balance Pension Plan	Target Benefit Plans (not profit sharing)
10-Year Forward Averaging	Yes	Yes	Yes	Yes	Yes	Yes	No	Yes	Yes
Investment Risk									
Employee	✔	✔	✔	✔	✔	✔	✔		✔
Employer								✔	
PBGC Insurance	No	No	No	No	No	No	No	Yes	No
Actuarial Costs	No	No	No	No	No	No	No	Yes	Yes
Vesting									
Immediate (100%)	No	No	No	No	No	No	Yes	No	No
5-Year Cliff or 3–7 Graduated	Yes	No	No	No	No	No	No	Yes	Yes
3-Year Cliff or 2–6 Graduated**	If top heavy	Yes	Yes	Yes	Yes	Yes	No	If top heavy	If top heavy
Favors Older (O) or Younger (Y) Employees	Y	Y	Y	Y	Y	Y	Y	Y	O

*Only the profit sharing portion of a 401(k) plan can be integrated.

** Beginning after December 31, 2006, defined contribution plans must use this accelerated schedule for all employer contributions (except corrective contributions which vest immediately at 100%).

Exhibit 51: Determining Full Retirement Age

Full Retirement Age for Retired Worker and Spouse Benefits	Year of Birth	Full Retirement Age for Surviving Spouse Benefits
	Before 1938	65
65 and 2 months	1938	65
65 and 4 months	1939	65
65 and 6 months	1940	65 and 2 months
65 and 8 months	1941	65 and 4 months
65 and 10 months	1942	65 and 6 months
66	1943	65 and 8 months
66	1944	65 and 10 months
66	1945–54	66
66 and 2 months	1955	66
66 and 4 months	1956	66
66 and 6 months	1957	66 and 2 months
66 and 8 months	1958	66 and 4 months
66 and 10 months	1959	66 and 6 months
67	1960	66 and 8 months
67	1961	66 and 10 months
67	1962 and after	67

Exhibit 52: Reduced Retirement Benefits for Workers

Year of Birth	You will receive this percentage of your PIA if you retire at age:				
	62	63	64	65	66
Before 1938	80.0%	86.6%	93.3%	100.0%	—
1938	79.1%	85.5%	92.2%	98.8%	—
1939	78.3%	84.4%	91.1%	97.7%	—
1940	77.5%	83.3%	90.0%	96.6%	—
1941	76.6%	82.2%	88.8%	95.5%	—
1942	75.8%	81.1%	87.7%	94.4%	—
1943–1954	75.0%	80.0%	86.6%	93.3%	100.0%
1955	74.1%	79.1%	85.5%	92.2%	98.8%
1956	73.3%	78.3%	84.4%	91.1%	97.7%
1957	72.5%	77.5%	83.3%	90.0%	96.6%
1958	71.6%	76.6%	82.2%	88.8%	95.5%
1959	70.8%	75.8%	81.1%	87.7%	94.4%
1960 and later	70.0%	75.0%	80.0%	86.6%	93.3%

Note: Decimals are rounded down.

You may retire at ages between the ones shown. The reduction factor applied to the PIA is 5/9 of 1% for each of the first 36 months that entitlement is before the FRA, plus 5/12 of 1% for each such month in excess of 36. These reduction factors are for workers only. Different reduction factors are used for spouses.

Exhibit 53: Assets Passing Through and Around the Probate Process

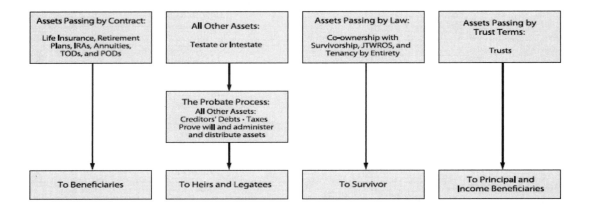

Exhibit 54: Unified Tax Rate Schedule (for Gifts and Estates 2007–2009)

Over $0 but not over $10,000	18% of such amount
Over $10,000 but not over $20,000	$1,800 plus 20% of the excess of such amount over $10,000
Over $20,000 but not over $40,000	$3,800 plus 22% of the excess of such amount over $20,000
Over $40,000 but not over $60,000	$8,200 plus 24% of the excess of such amount over $40,000
Over $60,000 but not over $80,000	$13,000 plus 26% of the excess of such amount over $60,000
Over $80,000 but not over $100,000	$18,200 plus 28% of the excess of such amount over $80,000
Over $100,000 but not over $150,000	$23,800 plus 30% of the excess of such amount over $100,000
Over $150,000 but not over $250,000	$38,800 plus 32% of the excess of such amount over $150,000
Over $250,000 but not over $500,000	$70,800 plus 34% of the excess of such amount over $250,000
Over $500,000 but not over $750,000	$155,800 plus 37% of the excess of such amount over $500,000
Over $750,000 but not over $1,000,000	$248,300 plus 39% of the excess of such amount over $750,000
Over $1 million but not over $1.25 million	$345,800 plus 41% of the excess of such amount over $1,000,000
Over $1.25 million but not over $1.5 million	$448,300 plus 43% of the excess of such amount over $1,250,000
Over $1.5 million but not over $2 million	$555,800 plus 45% of the excess of such amount over $1,500,000
Over $2 million but not over $3.5 million	$780,800 plus 45% of the excess of such amount over $2,000,000
Over $3.5 million	$1,455,800 plus 45% of the excess of such amount over $3,500,000

Lifetime gifts	2007–2008	2009
Annual exclusion	$12,000	$13,000
Applicable credit	$345,800	$345,800
Estates		
Applicable credit	$780,000	$1,455,800

Exhibit 55: GSTT Rates and Exemptions

Year	GSTT Rate	GSTT Exemption
2007–2008	45%	$2 million
2009	45%	$3.5 million
2010	Repealed	Repealed

Exhibit 56: Gift Tax Formula

(1) Total gifts in current year (fair market value of all gifts) $ _____

(2) Less:

    (a) One-half of value of gifts split with spouse   _____

    (b) Annual exclusions ($13,000 per donee for present interests)   _____

    (c) Marital deduction (can be unlimited if spouse is a US citizen)   _____

    (d) Charitable deduction (can be unlimited)   _____

    (e) Total subtractions   _____

(3) Equals: Taxable gifts in current year $ _____

(4) Add: Post-1976 taxable gifts made in previous years   _____

(5) Equals: Total taxable gifts to date (tax base)   _____

(6) Tentative tax on total taxable gifts to date   _____

(7) Less: Tax paid or deemed paid on prior taxable gifts   (_____)

(8) Equals: Gift tax on current year taxable gifts before applicable credit   _____

(9) Less: Applicable credit   (_____)

(10) Equals: Gift tax due on current year taxable gifts $ _____

Exhibit 57: Estate Tax Formula

(1)   Total gross estate $ _____

(2)   Less: Expenses, debts, and losses:

    (a)   Funeral and administrative expenses   _____

    (b)   Debts of decedent, mortgages, losses   _____

(3)   Equals: Adjusted gross estate (AGE)*   _____

(4)   Less: Total allowable deductions:

    (a)   Charitable deduction   _____

    (b)   Marital deduction   _____

    (c)   State death taxes paid   _____

    Total allowable deductions   (____)

(5)   Equals: Taxable estate $ _____

(6)   Add: Adjusted taxable gifts (post-1976)   _____

(7)   Compute: Tentative tax base   _____

(8)   Compute: Tentative tax   _____

(9)   Less: Tax paid or deemed paid on prior taxable gifts   (____)

(10) Equals: Estate tax before reduction for allowable credits   _____

(11) Less:

    Applicable credit amount   _____

    Other credits   _____

(12) Equals: Estate Tax Liability $ _____

*The term *adjusted gross estate* is not on Form 706; however, this concept applies to Section 6166. Section 303 and Section 2032A and may be tested on the exam.

Exhibit 58: Charitable Remainder Trusts

	CRAT	CRUT	Pooled Income Fund
Income tax deduction	Total value of property—PV of retained interest income	Total value of property—PV of retained interest income	Total value of property—PV of retained interest income
Income recipient	Noncharitable beneficiary (usually donor)	Noncharitable beneficiary (usually donor)	Noncharitable beneficiary (usually donor)
Payment	At least 5% of initial FMV of assets paid at least annually for life or term ≤20 years (similar to fixed annuity); cannot exceed 50% of value of trust	At least 5% of current FMV of assets (revalued annually) paid at least annually for life or term ≤20 years (similar to variable annuity); cannot exceed 50% of value of trust	Trust rate of return for year
Remainderman	Charity	Charity	Charity
Additional contributions	No	Yes	Yes
Sprinkling	Yes	Yes	No
When income is insufficient for payout	Must invade corpus	Can pay up to income and make up deficiency in subsequent year	N/A
Can hold tax-exempt securities	Yes	Yes	No

Exhibit 59: Structure of a Trust

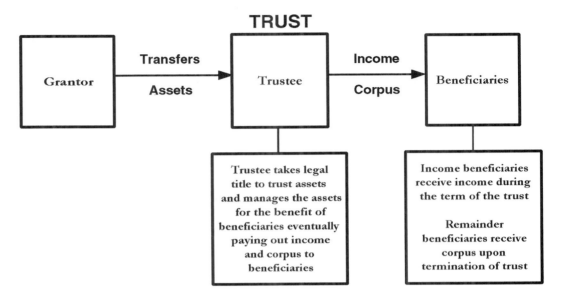

Exhibit 60: Parties to a Trust

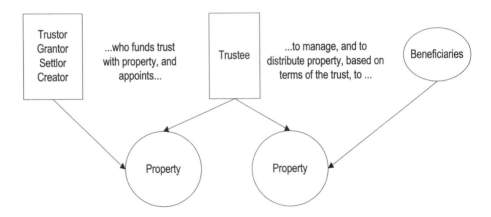

Reasons for creating trusts:
1. To provide for multiple beneficiaries.
2. To manage property if grantor becomes incapacitated.
3. To protect beneficiaries from themselves and others.
4. To avoid or reduce taxes.

Trust characteristics:
1. Revocable or irrevocable.
2. Intervivos or testamentary.
3. Funded or unfunded.

Exhibit 61: Estate Tax Reduction Techniques

1. Do not overqualify the estate. Use the applicable exclusion amount.

2. Do not underqualify the estate. Use the appropriate amount for the marital deduction, generally, to reduce the estate tax to zero.

3. Generally, remove life insurance from the estate of the client.

4. Change the ownership of life insurance or use irrevocable life insurance trust (must remove all incidents of ownership).

5. Use lifetime gifts. Make use of annual exclusions with gift splitting.

6. Use basic trusts.

7. Use charitable contributions, transfers, and trusts.

Exhibit 62: Common Estate Planning Mistakes

1. Invalid, Out-of-Date, or Poorly Drafted Will.

   - Will does not meet statutory requirements.

   - Will does not contemplate changes in tax laws.

   - Decedent has moved to another state of residence and domicile.

   - Will has no residuary clause or lacks drafting specificities.

2. Simple Wills (Sweetheart or I Love You Wills).

   - Leaving everything to a spouse may cause an overqualification of the estate.

   - Mismanagement of assets may occur.

3. Improperly Arranged or Inadequate Life Insurance.

   - Failure to remove proceeds from estate.

   - Leaving proceeds directly to beneficiary.

   - Inadequate life insurance coverage.

4. Possible Adverse Consequences of Jointly Held Property.

   - Joint title may result in state and federal gift and estate tax. If joint title results in a completed gift, consequences may be federal and state gift tax liability.

   - Double estate taxation. For jointly owned property (not by spouses), property value may be included in first decedent's estate and then included in survivor's estate (recall credit for tax on prior transfer).

- Property passed by law, not by will (JTWROS), can thwart the intentions of decedent because property will pass automatically by law.

- Jointly held property allows survivor to name ultimate remainderman. Decedent may not be able to direct property to person or entity wishes.

5. Estate Liquidity Problems.

   - Insufficient cash assets.

   - Inadequate planning.

6. Wrong Executor/Trustee/Manager.

   - Poor estate management always makes costs increase.

   - Potential conflicts of interest.

   - Proximity problems/family conflict.

   - Named executor/trustee is incapable of administering estate efficiently and effectively.

Exhibit 63: CFP Board's 89 Topics List (page 1 of 8)

CERTIFIED FINANCIAL PLANNER
BOARD OF STANDARDS, INC.

TOPIC LIST FOR CFP® CERTIFICATION EXAMINATION

The following topics, based on the 2004 Job Analysis Study, are the basis for the CFP® Certification Examinations. Each exam question will be linked to one of the following topics, in the approximate percentages indicated following the general headings. Questions will pertain to all levels in Bloom's taxonomy with an emphasis on the higher cognitive levels. Questions often will be asked in the context of the financial planning process and presented in an integrative format.

In addition to being used for the CFP® Certification Examination, this list indicates topic coverage requirements to fulfill the pre-certification educational requirement. Continuing education (CE) programs and materials that address these topics will be eligible for CFP Board CE credit.

(References to sections (§) in this list refer to sections of the Internal Revenue Code)

First Test Date: November 2006

GENERAL PRINCIPLES OF FINANCIAL PLANNING (11%)

1. Financial planning process
   A. Purpose, benefits, and components
   B. Steps
      1) Establishing client-planner relationships
      2) Gathering client data and determining goals and expectations
      3) Determining the client's financial status by analyzing and evaluating general financial status, special needs, insurance and risk management, investments, taxation, employee benefits, retirement, and/or estate planning
      4) Developing and presenting the financial plan
      5) Implementing the financial plan
      6) Monitoring the financial plan
   C. Responsibilities
      1) Financial planner
      2) Client
      3) Other advisors

2. CFP Board's *Code of Ethics and Professional Responsibility* and *Disciplinary Rules and Procedures*
   A. *Code of Ethics and Professional Responsibility*
      1) Preamble and applicability
      2) Composition and scope
      3) Compliance
      4) Terminology
      5) Principles
         a) Principle 1 – Integrity
         b) Principle 2 – Objectivity
         c) Principle 3 – Competence
         d) Principle 4 – Fairness
         e) Principle 5 – Confidentiality
         f) Principle 6 – Professionalism
         g) Principle 7 – Diligence
      6) Rules
   B) *Disciplinary Rules and Procedures*

3. CFP Board's *Financial Planning Practice Standards*
   A) Purpose and applicability
   B) Content of each series (use most current *Practice Standards*, as posted on CFP Board's Web site at www.CFP.net)
   C. Enforcement through *Disciplinary Rules and Procedures*

4. Financial statements
   A. Personal
      1) Statement of financial position
      2) Statement of cash flow
   B. Business
      1) Balance sheet
      2) Income statement
      3) Statement of cash flows
      4) *Pro forma* statements

5. Cash flow management
   A. Budgeting
   B. Emergency fund planning
   C. Debt management ratios
      1) Consumer debt
      2) Housing costs
      3) Total debt
   D. Savings strategies

6. Financing strategies
   A. Long-term vs. short-term debt
   B. Secured vs. unsecured debt
   C. Buy vs. lease/rent
   D. Mortgage financing
      1) Conventional vs. adjustable-rate mortgage (ARM)
      2) Home equity loan and line of credit
      3) Refinancing cost-benefit analysis
      4) Reverse mortgage

7. Function, purpose, and regulation of financial institutions
   A. Banks
   B. Credit unions
   C. Brokerage companies
   D. Insurance companies
   E. Mutual fund companies
   F. Trust companies

8. Education planning
   A. Funding
      1) Needs analysis
      2) Tax credits/adjustments/deductions
      3) Funding strategies
      4) Ownership of assets
      5) Vehicles
         a) Qualified tuition programs (§529 plans)
         b) Coverdell Education Savings Accounts
         c) Uniform Transfers to Minors Act (UTMA) and Uniform Gifts to Minors Act (UGMA) accounts
         d) Savings bonds
   B. Financial aid

Exhibit 63: CFP Board's 89 Topics List (page 2 of 8)

9. Financial planning for special circumstances
   A. Divorce
   B. Disability
   C. Terminal illness
   D. Non-traditional families
   E. Job change and job loss
   F. Dependents with special needs
   G. Monetary windfalls

10. Economic concepts
    A. Supply and demand
    B. Fiscal policy
    C. Monetary policy
    D. Economic indicators
    E. Business cycles
    F. Inflation, deflation, and stagflation
    G. Yield curve

11. Time value of money concepts and calculations
    A. Present value
    B. Future value
    C. Ordinary annuity and annuity due
    D. Net present value (NPV)
    E. Internal rate of return (IRR)
    F. Uneven cash flows
    G. Serial payments

12. Financial services regulations and requirements
    A. Registration and licensing
    B. Reporting
    C. Compliance
    D. State securities and insurance laws

13. Business law
    A. Contracts
    B. Agency
    C. Fiduciary liability

14. Consumer protection laws
    A. Bankruptcy
    B. Fair credit reporting laws
    C. Privacy policies
    D. Identity theft protection

INSURANCE PLANNING AND RISK MANAGEMENT (14%)

15. Principles of risk and insurance
    A. Definitions
    B. Concepts
       1) Peril
       2) Hazard
       3) Law of large numbers
       4) Adverse selection
       5) Insurable risks
       6) Self-insurance
    C. Risk management process

    D. Response to risk
       1) Risk control
          a) Risk avoidance
          b) Risk diversification
          c) Risk reduction
       2) Risk financing
          a) Risk retention
          b) Risk transfer
    E. Legal aspects of insurance
       1) Principle of indemnity
       2) Insurable interest
       3) Contract requirements
       4) Contract characteristics
       5) Policy ownership
       6) Designation of beneficiary

16. Analysis and evaluation of risk exposures
    A. Personal
       1) Death
       2) Disability
       3) Poor health
       4) Unemployment
       5) Superannuation
    B. Property
       1) Real
       2) Personal
       3) Auto
    C. Liability
       1) Negligence
       2) Intentional torts
       3) Strict liability
    D. Business-related

17. Property, casualty and liability insurance
    A. Individual
       1) Homeowners insurance
       2) Auto insurance
       3) Umbrella liability insurance
    B. Business
       1) Commercial property insurance
       2) Commercial liability insurance
          a) Auto liability
          b) Umbrella liability
          c) Professional liability
          d) Directors and officers liability
          e) Workers' compensation and employers liability

18. Health insurance and health care cost management (individual)
    A. Hospital, surgical, and physicians' expense insurance
    B. Major medical insurance and calculation of benefits
    C. Continuance and portability
    D. Medicare
    E. Taxation of premiums and benefits

19. Disability income insurance (individual)
    A. Definitions of disability
    B. Benefit period

C. Elimination period
D. Benefit amount
E. Provisions
F. Taxation of premiums and benefits

20. Long-term care insurance (individual)
    A. Eligibility
    B. Services covered
    C. Medicare limitations
    D. Benefit period
    E. Elimination period
    F. Benefit amount
    G. Provisions
    H. Taxation of premiums and benefits

21. Life insurance (individual)
    A. Concepts and personal uses
    B. Policy types
    C. Contractual provisions
    D. Dividend options
    E. Nonforfeiture options
    F. Settlement options
    G. Illustrations
    H. Policy replacement
    I. Viatical and life settlements

22. Income taxation of life insurance
    A. Dividends
    B. Withdrawals and loans
    C. Death benefits
    D. Modified endowment contracts (MECs)
    E. Transfer-for-value
    F. §1035 exchanges

23. Business uses of insurance
    A. Buy-sell agreements
    B. Key employee life insurance
    C. Split-dollar life insurance
    D. Business overhead expense insurance

24. Insurance needs analysis
    A. Life insurance
    B. Disability income insurance
    C. Long-term care insurance
    D. Health insurance
    E. Property insurance
    F. Liability insurance

25. Insurance policy and company selection
    A. Purpose of coverage
    B. Duration of coverage
    C. Participating or non-participating
    D. Cost-benefit analysis
    E. Company selection
       1) Industry ratings
       2) Underwriting

2

Exhibit 63: CFP Board's 89 Topics List (page 3 of 8)

26. Annuities
   A. Types
   B. Uses
   C. Taxation

EMPLOYEE BENEFITS PLANNING (8%)

27. Group life insurance
   A. Types and basic provisions
      1) Group term
      2) Group permanent
      3) Dependent coverage
   B. Income tax implications
   C. Employee benefit analysis and application
   D. Conversion analysis
   E. Carve-out plans

28. Group disability insurance
   A. Types and basic provisions
      1) Short-term coverage
      2) Long-term coverage
   B. Definitions of disability
   C. Income tax implications
   D. Employee benefit analysis and application
   E. Integration with other income

29. Group medical insurance
   A. Types and basic provisions
      1) Traditional indemnity
      2) Managed care plans
         a) Preferred provider organization (PPO)
         b) Health maintenance organization (HMO)
         c) Point-of-service (POS)
   B. Income tax implications
   C. Employee benefit analysis and application
   D. COBRA/HIPAA provisions
   E. Continuation
   F. Savings accounts
      1) Health savings account (HSA)
      2) Archer medical savings account (MSA)
      3) Health reimbursement arrangement (HRA)

30. Other employee benefits
   A. §125 cafeteria plans and flexible spending accounts (FSAs)
   B. Fringe benefits
   C. Voluntary employees' beneficiary association (VEBA)
   D. Prepaid legal services
   E. Group long-term care insurance
   F. Dental insurance
   G. Vision insurance

31) Employee stock options
   A. Basic provisions
      1) Company restrictions
      2) Transferability
      3) Exercise price
      4) Vesting
      5) Expiration
      6) Cashless exercise
   B. Incentive stock options (ISOs)
      1) Income tax implications (regular, AMT, basis)
         a) Upon grant
         b) Upon exercise
         c) Upon sale
      2) Holding period requirements
      3) Disqualifying dispositions
      4) Planning opportunities and strategies
   C. Non-qualified stock options (NSOs)
      1) Income tax implications (regular, AMT, basis)
         a) Upon grant
         b) Upon exercise
         c) Upon sale
      2) Gifting opportunities
         a) Unvested/vested
         b) Exercised/unexercised
         c) Gift tax valuation
         d) Payment of gift tax
      3) Planning opportunities and strategies
      4) Employee benefits analysis and application
   D. Planning strategies for employees with both incentive stock options and non-qualified stock options
   E. Election to include in gross income in the year of transfer (§83(b) election)

32. Stock plans
   A. Types and basic provisions
      1) Restricted stock
      2) Phantom stock
      3) Stock appreciation rights (SARs)
      4) Employee stock purchase plan (ESPP)
   B. Income tax implications
   C. Employee benefit analysis and application
   D. Election to include in gross income in the year of transfer (§83(b) election)

33. Non-qualified deferred compensation
   A. Basic provisions and differences from qualified plans
   B. Types of plans and applications
      1) Salary reduction plans
      2) Salary continuation plans
      3) Rabbi trusts
      4) Secular trusts
   C. Income tax implications
      1) Constructive receipt
      2) Substantial risk of forfeiture
      3) Economic benefit doctrine
   D. Funding methods
   E. Strategies

INVESTMENT PLANNING (19%)

34. Characteristics, uses and taxation of investment vehicles
   A. Cash and equivalents
      1) Certificates of deposit
      2) Money market funds
      3) Treasury bills
      4) Commercial paper
      5) Banker's acceptances
      6) Eurodollars
   B. Individual bonds
      1) U.S. Government bonds and agency securities
         a) Treasury notes and bonds
         b) Treasury STRIPS
         c) Treasury inflation-protection securities (TIPS)
         d) Series EE, HH, and I bonds
         e) Mortgage-backed securities
      2) Zero-coupon bonds
      3) Municipal bonds
         a) General obligation
         b) Revenue
      4) Corporate bonds
         a) Mortgage bond
         b) Debenture
         c) Investment grade
         d) High-yield
         e) Convertible
         f) Callable
      5) Foreign bonds
   C. Promissory notes
   D. Individual stocks
      1) Common
      2) Preferred
      3) American depositary receipts (ADRs)
   E. Pooled and managed investments
      1) Exchange-traded funds (ETFs)
      2) Unit investment trusts
      3) Mutual funds
      4) Closed-end investment companies

3

Exhibit 63: CFP Board's 89 Topics List (page 4 of 8)

5) Index securities
6) Hedge funds
7) Limited partnerships
8) Privately managed accounts
9) Separately managed accounts
F. Guaranteed investment contracts (GICs)
G. Real Estate
1) Investor-managed
2) Real estate investment trusts (REITs)
3) Real estate limited partnerships (RELPs)
4) Real estate mortgage investment conduits (REMICs)
H. Alternative investments
1) Derivatives
a) Puts
b) Calls
c) Long-term Equity AnticiPation Securities (LEAPS®)
d) Futures
e) Warrants and rights
2) Tangible assets
a) Collectibles
b) Natural resources
c) Precious metals

35. Types of investment risk
A. Systematic/market/ nondiversifiable
B. Purchasing power
C. Interest rate
D. Unsystematic/nonmarket/ diversifiable
E. Business
F. Financial
G. Liquidity and marketability
H. Reinvestment
I. Political (sovereign)
J. Exchange rate
K. Tax
L. Investment manager

36. Quantitative investment concepts
A. Distribution of returns
1) Normal distribution
2) Lognormal distribution
3) Skewness
4) Kurtosis
B. Correlation coefficient
C. Coefficient of determination (R^2)
D. Coefficient of variation
E. Standard deviation
F. Beta
G. Covariance
H. Semivariance

37. Measures of investment returns
A. Simple vs. compound return

B. Geometric average vs. arithmetic average return
C. Time-weighted vs. dollar-weighted return
D. Real (inflation-adjusted) vs. nominal return
E. Total return
F. Risk-adjusted return
G. Holding period return
H. Internal rate of return (IRR)
I. Yield-to-maturity
J. Yield-to-call
K. Current yield
L. Taxable equivalent yield (TEY)

38. Bond and stock valuation concepts
A. Bond duration and convexity
B. Capitalized earnings
C. Dividend growth models
D. Ratio analysis
1) Price/earnings
2) Price/free cash flow
3) Price/sales
4) Price/earnings ÷ growth (PEG)
E. Book value

39. Investment theory
A. Modern portfolio theory (MPT)
1) Capital market line (CML)
a) Mean-variance optimization
b) Efficient frontier
2) Security market line (SML)
B. Efficient market hypothesis (EMH)
1) Strong form
2) Semi-strong form
3) Weak form
4) Anomalies
C. Behavioral finance

40. Portfolio development and analysis
A. Fundamental analysis
1) Top-down analysis
2) Bottom-up analysis
3) Ratio analysis
a) Liquidity ratios
b) Activity ratios
c) Profitability ratios
d) Debt ratios
B. Technical analysis
1) Charting
2) Sentiment indicators
3) Flow of funds indicators
4) Market structure indicators
C. Investment policy statements
D. Appropriate benchmarks
E. Probability analysis, including Monte Carlo
F. Tax efficiency
1) Turnover
2) Timing of capital gains and losses

3) Wash sale rule
4) Qualified dividends
5) Tax-free income
G. Performance measures
1) Sharpe ratio
2) Treynor ratio
3) Jensen ratio
4) Information ratio

41. Investment strategies
A. Market timing
B. Passive investing (indexing)
C. Buy and hold
D. Portfolio immunization
E. Swaps and collars
F. Formula investing
1) Dollar cost averaging
2) Dividend reinvestment plans (DRIPs)
3) Bond ladders, bullets, and barbells
G. Use of leverage (margin)
H. Short selling
I. Hedging and option strategies

42. Asset allocation and portfolio diversification
A. Strategic asset allocation
1) Application of client lifecycle analysis
2) Client risk tolerance measurement and application
3) Asset class definition and correlation
B. Rebalancing
C. Tactical asset allocation
D. Control of volatility
E. Strategies for dealing with concentrated portfolios

43. Asset pricing models
A. Capital asset pricing model (CAPM)
B. Arbitrage pricing theory (APT)
C. Black-Scholes option valuation model
D. Binomial option pricing

INCOME TAX PLANNING (14%)

44. Income tax law fundamentals
A. Types of authority
1) Primary
2) Secondary
B. Research sources

4

Exhibit 63: CFP Board's 89 Topics List (page 5 of 8)

45. Tax compliance
    A. Filing requirements
    B. Audits
    C. Penalties

46. Income tax fundamentals and calculations
    A. Filing status
    B. Gross income
       1) Inclusions
       2) Exclusions
       3) Imputed income
    C. Adjustments
    D. Standard/Itemized deductions
       1) Types
       2) Limitations
    E. Personal and dependency exemptions
    F. Taxable income
    G. Tax liability
       1) Rate schedule
       2) Kiddie tax
       3) Self-employment tax
    H. Tax credits
    I. Payment of tax
       1) Withholding
       2) Estimated payments

47. Tax accounting
    A. Accounting periods
    B. Accounting methods
       1) Cash receipts and disbursements
       2) Accrual method
       3) Hybrid method
       4) Change in accounting method
    C. Long-term contracts
    D. Installment sales
    E. Inventory valuation and flow methods
    F. Net operating losses

48. Characteristics and income taxation of business entities
    A. Entity types
       1) Sole proprietorship
       2) Partnerships
       3) Limited liability company (LLC)
       4) Corporations
       5) Trust
       6) Association
    B. Taxation at entity and owner level
       1) Formation
       2) Flow through of income and losses
       3) Special taxes
       4) Distributions
       5) Dissolution
       6) Disposition

49. Income taxation of trusts and estates
    A. General issues
       1) Filing requirements
       2) Deadlines
       3) Choice of taxable year
       4) Tax treatment of distributions to beneficiaries
       5) Rate structure
    B. Grantor/Nongrantor trusts
    C. Simple/Complex trusts
    D. Revocable/Irrevocable trusts
    E. Trust income
       1) Trust accounting income
       2) Trust taxable income
       3) Distributable net income (DNI)
    F. Estate income tax

50. Basis
    A. Original basis
    B. Adjusted basis
    C. Amortization and accretion
    D. Basis of property received by gift and in nontaxable transactions
    E. Basis of inherited property (community and non-community property)

51. Depreciation/cost-recovery concepts
    A. Modified Accelerated Cost Recovery System (MACRS)
    B. Expensing policy
    C. §179 deduction
    D. Amortization
    E. Depletion

52. Tax consequences of like-kind exchanges
    A. Reporting requirements
    B. Qualifying transactions
    C. Liabilities
    D. Boot
    E. Related party transactions

53. Tax consequences of the disposition of property
    A. Capital assets (§1221)
    B. Holding period
    C. Sale of residence
    D. Depreciation recapture
    E. Related parties
    F. Wash sales
    G. Bargain sales
    H. Section 1244 stock (small business stock election)
    I. Installment sales
    J. Involuntary conversions

54. Alternative minimum tax (AMT)
    A. Mechanics
    B. Preferences and adjustments
    C. Exclusion items vs. deferral items

D. Credit: creation, usage, and limitations
E. Application to businesses and trusts
F. Planning strategies

55. Tax reduction/management techniques
    A. Tax credits
    B. Accelerated deductions
    C. Deferral of income
    D. Intra-family transfers

56. Passive activity and at-risk rules
    A. Definitions
    B. Computations
    C. Treatment of disallowed losses
    D. Disposition of passive activities
    E. Real estate exceptions

57. Tax implications of special circumstances
    A. Married/widowed
       1) Filing status
       2) Children
       3) Community and non-community property
    B. Divorce
       1) Alimony
       2) Child support
       3) Property division

58. Charitable contributions and deductions
    A. Qualified entities
       1) Public charities
       2) Private charities
    B. Deduction limitations
    C. Carryover periods
    D. Appreciated property
    E. Non-deductible contributions
    F. Appraisals
    G. Substantiation requirements
    H. Charitable contributions by business entities

RETIREMENT PLANNING
(19%)

59. Retirement needs analysis
    A. Assumptions for retirement planning
       1) Inflation
       2) Retirement period and life expectancy
       3) Lifestyle
       4) Total return
    B. Income sources
    C. Financial needs
       1) Living costs

5

CERTIFIED FINANCIAL PLANNER™ | **CFP®**

Exhibit 63: CFP Board's 89 Topics List (page 6 of 8)

2) Charitable and beneficiary gifting objectives
3) Medical costs, including long-term care needs analysis
4) Other (trust and foundation funding, education funding, etc.)
D. Straight-line returns vs. probability analysis
E. Pure annuity vs. capital preservation
F. Alternatives to compensate for projected cash-flow shortfalls

60. Social Security (Old Age, Survivor, and Disability Insurance, OASDI)
A. Paying into the system
B. Eligibility and benefit
1) Retirement
2) Disability
3) Survivor
4) Family limitations
C. How benefits are calculated
D. Working after retirement
E. Taxation of benefits

61. Types of retirement plans
A. Characteristics
1) Qualified plans
2) Non-qualified plans
B. Types and basic provisions of qualified plans
1) Defined contribution
a) Money purchase
b) Target benefit
c) Profit sharing
1) 401(k) plan
2) Safe harbor 401(k) plan
3) Age-based plan
4) Stock bonus plan
5) Employee stock ownership plan (ESOP)
6) New comparability plan
7) Thrift plan
2) Defined benefit
a) Traditional
b) Cash balance
c) 412(i) plan

62. Qualified plan rules and options
A. Nondiscrimination and eligibility requirements
1) Age and service requirements
2) Coverage requirements
3) Minimum participation
4) Highly compensated employee (HCE)
5) Permitted vesting schedules
6) ADP/ACP testing
7) Controlled group

B. Integration with Social Security/disparity limits
1) Defined benefit plans
2) Defined contribution plans
C. Factors affecting contributions or benefits
1) Deduction limit (§404(c))
2) Defined contribution limits
3) Defined benefit limit
4) Annual compensation limit
5) Definition of compensation
6) Multiple plans
7) Special rules for self-employed (non-corporations)
D. Top-heavy plans
1) Definition
2) Key employee
3) Vesting
4) Effects on contributions or benefits
E. Loans from qualified plans

63. Other tax-advantaged retirement plans
A. Types and basic provisions
1) Traditional IRA
2) Roth IRA, including conversion analysis
3) SEP
4) SIMPLE
5) §403(b) plans
6) §457 plans
7) Keogh (HR-10) plans

64. Regulatory considerations
A. Employee Retirement Income Security Act (ERISA)
B. Department of Labor (DOL) regulations
C. Fiduciary liability issues
D. Prohibited transactions
E. Reporting requirements

65. Key factors affecting plan selection for businesses
A. Owner's personal objectives
1) Tax considerations
2) Capital needs at retirement
3) Capital needs at death
B. Business' objectives
1) Tax considerations
2) Administrative cost
3) Cash flow situation and outlook
4) Employee demographics
5) Comparison of defined contribution and defined benefit plan alternatives

66. Investment considerations for retirement plans
A. Suitability

B. Time horizon
C. Diversification
D. Fiduciary considerations
E. Unrelated business taxable income (UBTI)
F. Life insurance
G. Appropriate assets for tax-advantaged vs. taxable accounts

67. Distribution rules, alternatives, and taxation
A. Premature distributions
1) Penalties
2) Exceptions to penalties
3) Substantially equal payments (§72(t))
B. Election of distribution options
1) Lump sum distributions
2) Annuity options
3) Rollover
4) Direct transfer
C. Required minimum distributions
1) Rules
2) Calculations
3) Penalties
D. Beneficiary considerations/ Stretch IRAs
E. Qualified domestic relations order (QDRO)
F. Taxation of distributions
1) Tax management techniques
2) Net unrealized appreciation (NUA)

ESTATE PLANNING (15%)

68. Characteristics and consequences of property titling
A. Community property vs. non-community property
B. Sole ownership
C. Joint tenancy with right of survivorship (JTWROS)
D. Tenancy by the entirety
E. Tenancy in common
F. Trust ownership

69. Methods of property transfer at death
A. Transfers through the probate process
1) Testamentary distribution
2) Intestate succession
3) Advantages and disadvantages of probate
4) Assets subject to probate estate
5) Probate avoidance strategies

6

Exhibit 63: CFP Board's 89 Topics List (page 7 of 8)

6) Ancillary probate administration
B. Transfers by operation of law
C. Transfers through trusts
D. Transfers by contract

70. Estate planning documents
   A. Wills
      1) Legal requirements
      2) Types of wills
      3) Modifying or revoking a will
      4) Avoiding will contests
   B. Powers of Attorney
   C. Trusts
   D. Marital property agreements
   E. Buy-sell agreements

71. Gifting strategies
   A. Inter-vivos gifting

   B. Gift-giving techniques and strategies
   C. Appropriate gift property
   D. Strategies for closely-held business owners
   E. Gifts of present and future interests
   F. Gifts to non-citizen spouses
   G. Tax implications
      1) Income
      2) Gift
      3) Estate
      4) Generation-skipping transfer tax (GSTT)

72. Gift tax compliance and tax calculation
   A. Gift tax filing requirements
   B. Calculation
      1) Annual exclusion
      2) Applicable credit amount
      3) Gift splitting
      4) Prior taxable gifts
      5) Education and medical exclusions
      6) Marital and charitable deductions
      7) Tax liability

73. Incapacity planning
   A. Definition of incapacity
   B. Powers of attorney
      1) For health care decisions
      2) For asset management
      3) Durable feature
      4) Springing power
      5) General or limited powers
   C. Advance medical directives (e.g. living wills)
   D. Guardianship and conservatorship
   E. Revocable living trust
   F. Medicaid planning

G. Special needs trust

74. Estate tax compliance and tax calculation
   A. Estate tax filing requirements
   B. The gross estate
      1) Inclusions
      2) Exclusions
   C. Deductions
   D. Adjusted gross estate
   E. Deductions from the adjusted gross estate
   F. Taxable estate
   G. Adjusted taxable gifts
   H. Tentative tax base
   I. Tentative tax calculation
   J. Credits
      1) Gift tax payable
      2) Applicable credit amount
      3) Prior transfer credit

75. Sources for estate liquidity
   A. Sale of assets
   B. Life insurance
   C. Loan

76. Powers of appointment
   A. Use and purpose
   B. General and special (limited) powers
      1) 5-and-5 power
      2) Crummey powers
      3) Distributions for an ascertainable standard
      4) Lapse of power
   C. Tax implications

77. Types, features, and taxation of trusts
   A. Classification
      1) Simple and complex
      2) Revocable and irrevocable
      3) Inter-vivos and testamentary
   B. Types and basic provisions
      1) Totten trust
      2) Spendthrift trust
      3) Bypass trust
      4) Marital trust
      5) Qualified terminable interest property (QTIP) trust
      6) Pour-over trust
      7) §2503(b) trust
      8) §2503(c) trust
      9) Sprinkling provision
   C. Trust beneficiaries: Income and remainder
   D. Rule against perpetuities
   E. Estate and gift taxation

78. Qualified interest trusts
   A. Grantor retained annuity trusts (GRATs)

B. Grantor retained unitrusts (GRUTs)
C. Qualified personal residence trusts (QPRTs or House-GRITs)
D. Valuation of qualified interests

79. Charitable transfers
   A. Outright gifts
   B. Charitable remainder trusts
      1) Unitrusts (CRUTs)
      2) Annuity trusts (CRATs)
   C. Charitable lead trusts
      1) Unitrusts (CLUTs)
      2) Annuity trusts (CLATs)
   D. Charitable gift annuities
   E. Pooled income funds
   F. Private foundations
   G. Donor advised funds
   H. Estate and gift taxation

80. Use of life insurance in estate planning
   A. Incidents of ownership
   B. Ownership and beneficiary considerations
   C. Irrevocable life insurance trust (ILIT)
   D. Estate and gift taxation

81. Valuation issues
   A. Estate freezes
      1) Corporate and partnership recapitalizations (§2701)
      2) Transfers in trust
   B. Valuation discounts for business interests
      1) Minority discounts
      2) Marketability discounts
      3) Blockage discounts
      4) Key person discounts
   C. Valuation techniques and the federal gross estate

82. Marital deduction
   A. Requirements
   B. Qualifying transfers
   C. Terminable interest rule and exceptions
   D. Qualified domestic trust (QDOT)

83. Deferral and minimization of estate taxes
   A. Exclusion of property from the gross estate
   B. Lifetime gifting strategies
   C. Marital deduction and bypass trust planning
   D. Inter-vivos and testamentary charitable gifts

7

Exhibit 63: CFP Board's 89 Topics List (page 8 of 8)

84. Intra-family and other business transfer techniques
   A. Characteristics
   B. Techniques
      1) Buy-sell agreement
      2) Installment note
      3) Self-canceling installment note (SCIN)
      4) Private annuity
      5) Transfers in trust
      6) Intra-family loan
      7) Bargain sale
      8) Gift or sale leaseback
      9) Intentionally defective grantor trust
      10) Family limited partnership (FLP) or limited liability company (LLC)
   C. Federal income, gift, estate, and generation-skipping transfer tax implications

85) Generation-skipping transfer tax (GSTT)
   A. Identify transfers subject to the GSTT
      1) Direct skips
      2) Taxable distributions
      3) Taxable terminations
   B. Exemptions and exclusions from the GSTT
      1) The GSTT exemption
      2) Qualifying annual exclusion gifts and direct transfers

86. Fiduciaries
   A. Types of fiduciaries
      1) Executor/Personal representative
      2) Trustee
      3) Guardian
   B. Duties of fiduciaries
   C. Breach of fiduciary duties

87. Income in respect of a decedent (IRD)
   A. Assets qualifying as IRD
   B. Calculation for IRD deduction
   C. Income tax treatment

88. Postmortem estate planning techniques
   A. Alternate valuation date
   B. Qualified disclaimer
   C. Deferral of estate tax (§6166)
   D. Corporate stock redemption (§303)
   E. Special use valuation (§2032A)

89. Estate planning for non-traditional relationships
   A. Children of another relationship
   B. Cohabitation
   C. Adoption
   D. Same-sex relationships

ADDENDUM

The following topics are an addendum to the *Topic List for CFP® Certification Examination*. Although individuals taking the CFP® Certification Examination will not be tested directly over these topics, CFP Board registered programs are strongly encouraged to teach them in their curricula) Continuing education (CE) programs and materials that address these topics will be eligible for CFP Board CE credit.

1. Client and planner attitudes, values, biases and behavioral characteristics and the impact on financial planning
   A. Cultural
   B. Family (e.g. biological; non-traditional)
   C. Emotional
   D. Life cycle and age
   E. Client's level of knowledge, experience, and expertise
   F. Risk tolerance
   G. Values-driven planning

2. Principles of communication and counseling
   A. Types of structured communication
      1) Interviewing
      2) Counseling
      3) Advising
   B. Essentials in financial counseling
      1) Establishing structure
      2) Creating rapport
      3) Recognizing resistance
   C. Characteristics of effective counselors
      1) Unconditional positive regard
      2) Accurate empathy
      3) Genuineness and self-awareness
   D. Nonverbal behaviors
      1) Body positions, movements, and gestures
      2) Facial expressions and eye contact
      3) Voice tone and pitch
      4) Interpreting the meaning of nonverbal behaviors
   E. Attending and listening skills
      1) Physical attending
      2) Active listening
      3) Responding during active listening; leading responses
   F. Effective use of questions
      1) Appropriate types of questions
      2) Ineffective and counterproductive questioning techniques

Exhibit 64: 2008 and 2009 Other Tax, Retirement, and Estate Limits

Child Tax Credit

	2008	2009
Maximum Credit	$1,000	$1,000
Refundability	15%	15%
Of Income	$12,050	$12,550

Adoption Credit

Maximum credit is $11,650 (2008)/$12,150 (2009) per eligible child.

Personal Exemption Phaseouts

Filing Status	2008		2009	
Phaseout*	Begin Phaseout	End Phaseout	Begin Phaseout	End Phaseout
Single	$159,950	$282,450	$166,800	$289,300
Married Filing Jointly, Surviving Spouse	$239,950	$362,450	$250,200	$372,700
Head of Household	$199,950	$322,450	$208,500	$331,000
Married Filing Separately	$119,975	$181,225	$125,100	$186,350

*2% for each $2,500 or fraction ($1,250 for married filing separately) above threshhold. For 2008 and 2009, the personal exemption reduction is 1/3 of the calculated amount, limited to $1,167.

Overall Limitation on Itemized Deduction

	2008	2009
Filing Status	AGI Limit	AGI Limit
Married Filing Separately	$79,975	$83,400
All Others	$159,950	$166,800

1. The reduction in itemized deductions is the lesser of 3% of the excess AGI or 80% of the itemized deductions otherwise allowable.

2. Certain itemized deductions are excluded from this reduction.

3. For 2008 and 2009, the reduction is 1/3 of the calculated amount.

Kiddie Tax Threshold

2008	2009
$1,800	$1,900

Unearned income in excess of the threshold is taxed at the parents' rate.

A parent will be able to include a child's income on the parent's return if the child's income is more than $900 (2008)/$950 (2009) and less than $9,000 (2008)/$9,500 (2009).

The exemption amount under Sections 55 and 59(j) for purposes of the alternative minimum tax is the lesser of (1) the sum of such child's earned income for the taxable year, plus $6,400 (2008)/$6,700 (2009), or (2) $33,750 (2008 and 2009).

Earned Income Credit

	Number of Children	Earned Income Amount	Phaseout Threshold (Other/Joint)
2008	None	$5,720	$7,160/$10,160
	1	$8,580	$15,740/$18,740
	2 or more	$12,060	$15,740/$18,740
2009	None	$5,970	$7,470/$10,600
	1	$8,950	$16,420/$19,550
	2 or more	$12,570	$16,420/$19,550

The earned income tax credit is denied under Section 32(i) if the aggregate amount of certain investment income exceeds $2,950 (2008) or $3,100 (2009).

Education Credits

Filing Status	2008 MAGI Phaseout	2009 MAGI Phaseout
Joint/Surviving Spouse	$96,000–116,000	$100,000–120,000
Single	$48,000–58,000	$50,000–60,000

The Hope credit is 100% of the first $1,200 (2008/2009) of qualified higher education expenses plus 50% of the next $1,200 (2008/2009).

Eligible Long-Term Care Premiums

Attained Age Before Year-End	2008	2009
40 or less	$310	$320
More than 40, but not more than 50	$580	$600
More than 50, but not more than 60	$1,150	$1,190
More than 60, but not more than 70	$3,080	$3,180
More than 70	$3,850	$3,980

Archer Medical Savings Accounts

	2008	2009
Self-Only Coverage		
Deductible not less than:	$1,950	$2,000
And not more than:	$2,900	$3,000
Annual out-of-pocket expenses cannot exceed:	$3,850	$4,000
Family Coverage		
Deductible not less than:	$3,850	$4,000
And not more than:	$5,800	$6,000
Annual out-of-pocket expenses cannot exceed:	$7,050	$7,350

Health Savings Accounts

	2008	2009
Self-Only Coverage		
Deductible not less than:	$1,100	$1,150
Annual out-of-pocket expenses do not exceed:	$5,600	$5,800
Family Coverage		
Deductible:	$2,200	$2,300
Annual out-of-pocket expenses do not exceed:	$11,200	$11,600
Maximum:	$5,800	$5,950